MONTRÉAL & QUÉBEC CITY

THIRD EDITION

COLOURGUIDE

Edited by Emma McKay

FORMAC PUBLISHING COMPANY LIMITED

Contents

Maps

For Photo Credits and acknowledgements, see page 208.

CONTENTS

Library and Archives Canada Cataloguing in Publication

Montreal & Quebec City colourguide / edited by Emma Jane McKay. — 3rd ed.

Includes index.
ISBN 0-88780-651-1

1. Montréal (Québec)—Guidebooks. 2. Québec (Québec)—Guidebooks. I. McKay, Emma Jane

FC2947.18.M6535 2005 917.14'28044
C2005-900745-1

Formac Publishing Company Limited
5502 Atlantic Street, Halifax, Nova Scotia
B3H 1G4 • www.formac.ca

Distributed in the United States by:
Casemate
2114 Darby Road, 2nd Floor,
Havertown, PA 19083

Distributed in the United Kingdom by:
Portfolio Book Limited
Unit 5, Perivale Industrial Park
Horsenden Lane South, Greenford, UK
UB6 7RL

Printed and bound in China.

Formac Publishing Company Limited acknowledges the support of the Cultural Affairs Section, Nova Scotia Department of Tourism and Culture. We acknowledge the financial support of the Government of Canada through the Book Publishing Industry Development Program (BPIDP) for our publishing activities.

Montréal Region

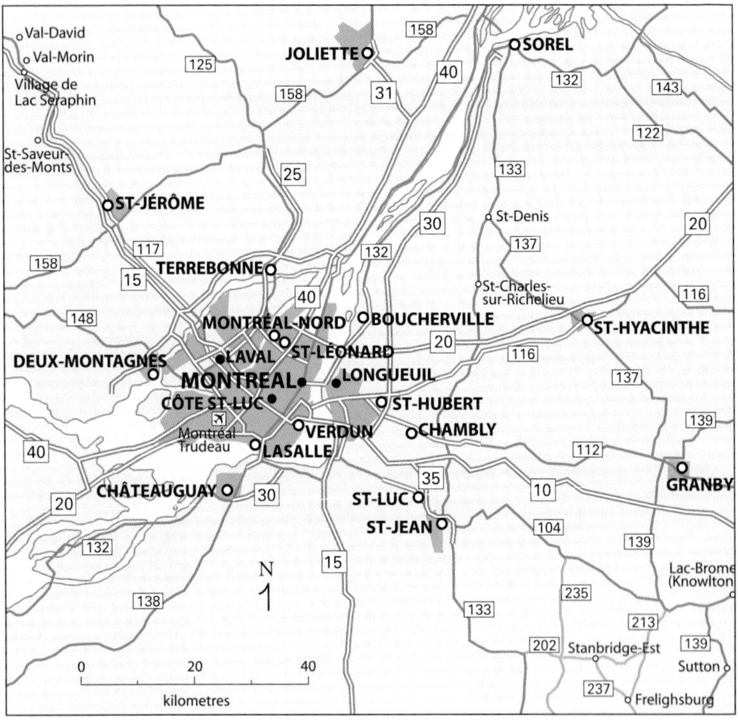

Val-David
Val-Morin
Village de Lac Seraphin
St-Saveur-des-Monts
ST-JÉRÔME
JOLIETTE
SOREL
TERREBONNE
MONTRÉAL-NORD
BOUCHERVILLE
ST-HYACINTHE
DEUX-MONTAGNES
LAVAL
ST-LÉONARD
MONTREAL
LONGUEUIL
CÔTE ST-LUC
ST-HUBERT
Montréal Trudeau
VERDUN
CHAMBLY
LASALLE
GRANBY
CHÂTEAUGUAY
ST-LUC
ST-JEAN
St-Denis
St-Charles-sur-Richelieu
Lac-Brome (Knowlton)
Stanbridge-Est
Sutton
Frelighsburg
N
0 20 40
kilometres

Québec City Region

Lac Saint-Joseph
Lac Saint-Charles
L'Ange-Gardien
Saint-Pierre
Île d'Orléans
Lac Saint-Charles
Charlesbourg
Fossambault-sur-le-Lac
Loretteville
Sainte-Pétronelle
Chenal des Grandes Volliers
Saint-Catherine-de-la-Jacques-Cartier
Québec
Lévis
Sainte Foy
Sillery
Saint Romuald
Cap Rouge
Saint-Augustine-de-Desmaures
euville
St. Lawrence River
Charmy
Bernières-Saint-Nicolas
Saint-Antoine-de-Tilly
0 5 10 15
kilometres

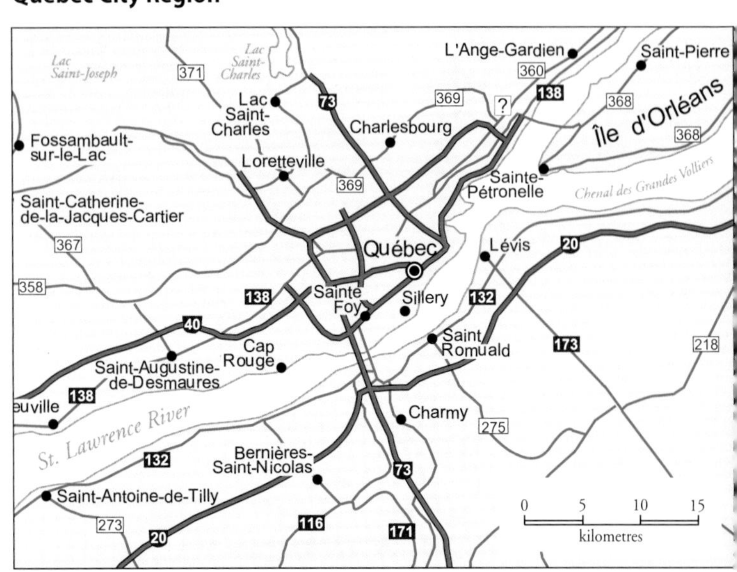

Québec City Hotels

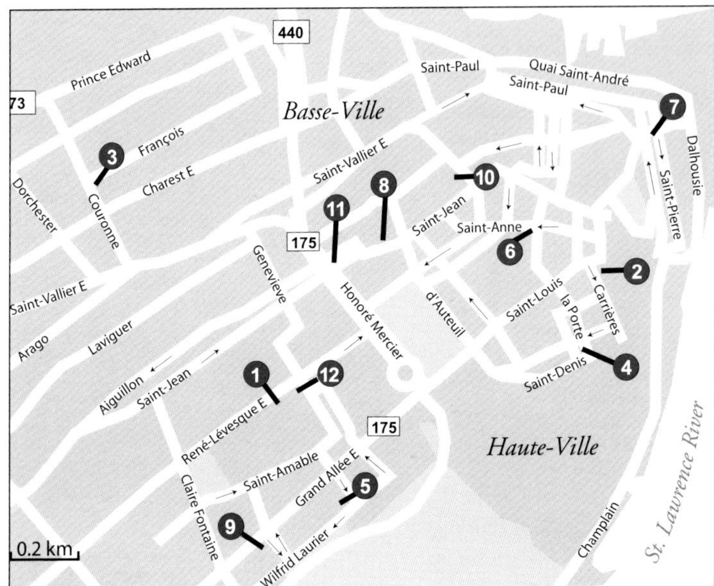

1 Delta Québec
2 Fairmont Château Frontenac
3 Holiday Inn Select Québec City-Downtown
4 Hôtel Château Bellevue
5 Hôtel Château Laurier
6 Hôtel Clarendon
7 Hôtel Dominion 1912
8 Hôtel du Capitole
9 Hôtel Loews Le Concorde
10 Hôtel Manoir Victoria
11 Hôtel Palace Royale
12 Québec Hilton

Locator Map

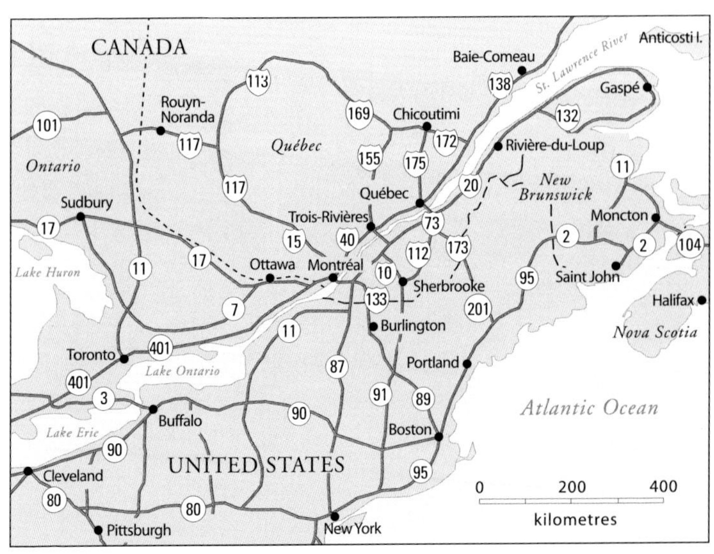

Neighborhoods of Montréal

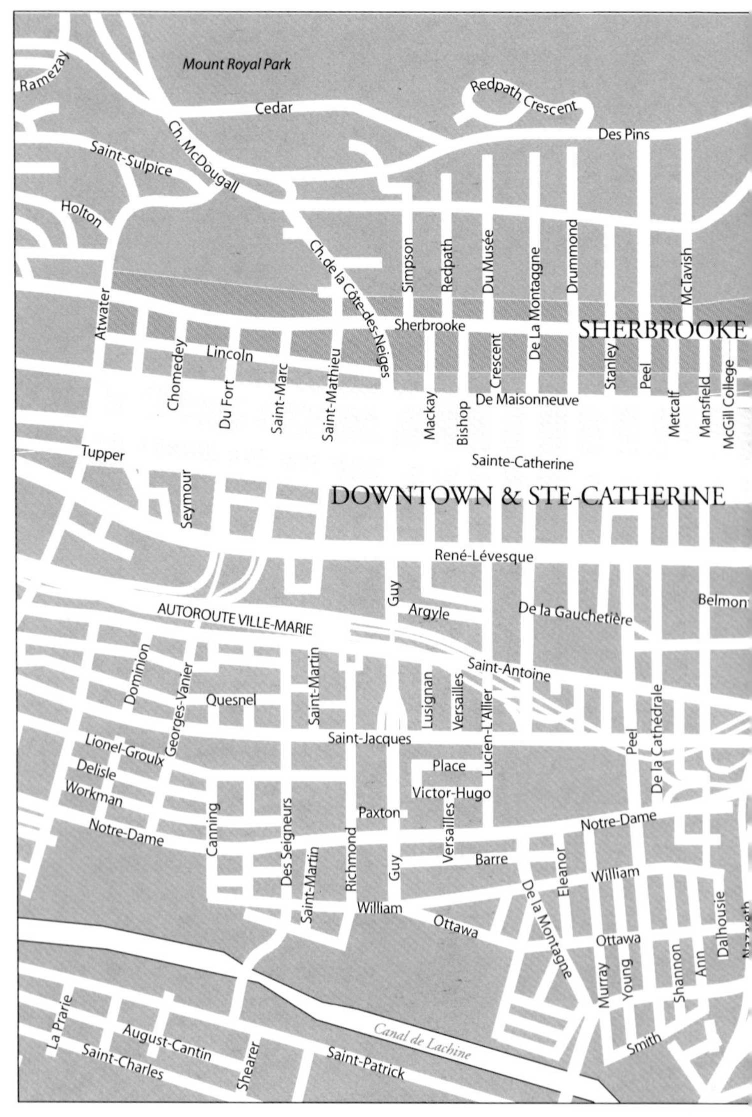

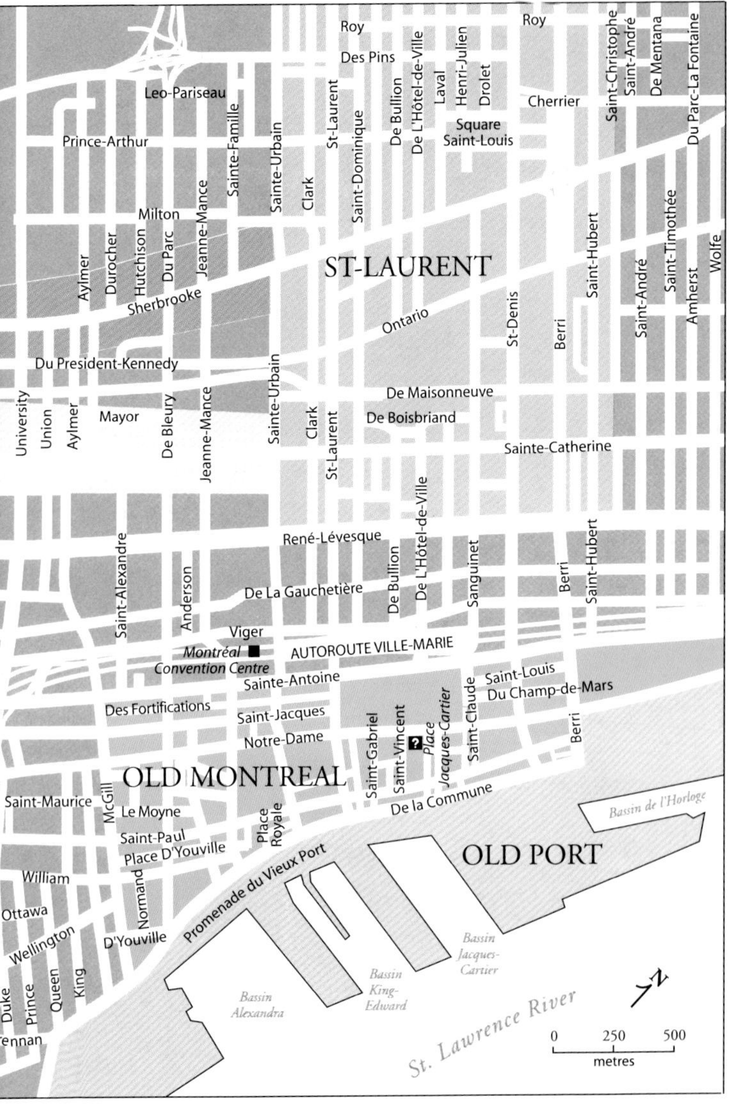

Roy
Des Pins
Roy
Leo-Pariseau
Prince-Arthur
Milton
Cherrier
Square Saint-Louis
Sainte-Famille
Sainte-Urbain
Clark
St-Laurent
Saint-Dominique
De Bullion
De L'Hôtel-de-Ville
Laval
Henri-Julien
Drolet
Saint-Christophe
Saint-André
De Mentana
Du Parc-La Fontaine
Aylmer
Durocher
Hutchison
Du Parc
Jeanne-Mance
Sherbrooke
ST-LAURENT
Ontario
St-Denis
Berri
Saint-Hubert
Saint-André
Saint-Timothée
Amherst
Wolfe
Du President-Kennedy
University
Union
Aylmer
Mayor
De Bleury
Jeanne-Mance
Sainte-Urbain
Clark
St-Laurent
De Maisonneuve
De Boisbriand
Sainte-Catherine
René-Lévesque
Saint-Alexandre
Anderson
De La Gauchetière
De Bullion
De L'Hôtel-de-Ville
Sanguinet
Berri
Saint-Hubert
Viger
Montréal Convention Centre
AUTOROUTE VILLE-MARIE
Sainte-Antoine
Saint-Louis
Du Champ-de-Mars
Des Fortifications
Saint-Jacques
Notre-Dame
Saint-Gabriel
Saint-Vincent
Place Jacques-Cartier
Saint-Claude
Berri
OLD MONTREAL
Saint-Maurice
McGill
Le Moyne
Saint-Paul
Place D'Youville
Place Royale
De la Commune
Bassin de l'Horloge
OLD PORT
Promenade du Vieux Port
William
Ottawa
Wellington
Normand
D'Youville
Duke
Prince
Queen
King
Brennan
Bassin Alexandra
Bassin King-Edward
Bassin Jacques-Cartier
St. Lawrence River
N
0
250
500
metres

Montréal Hotels

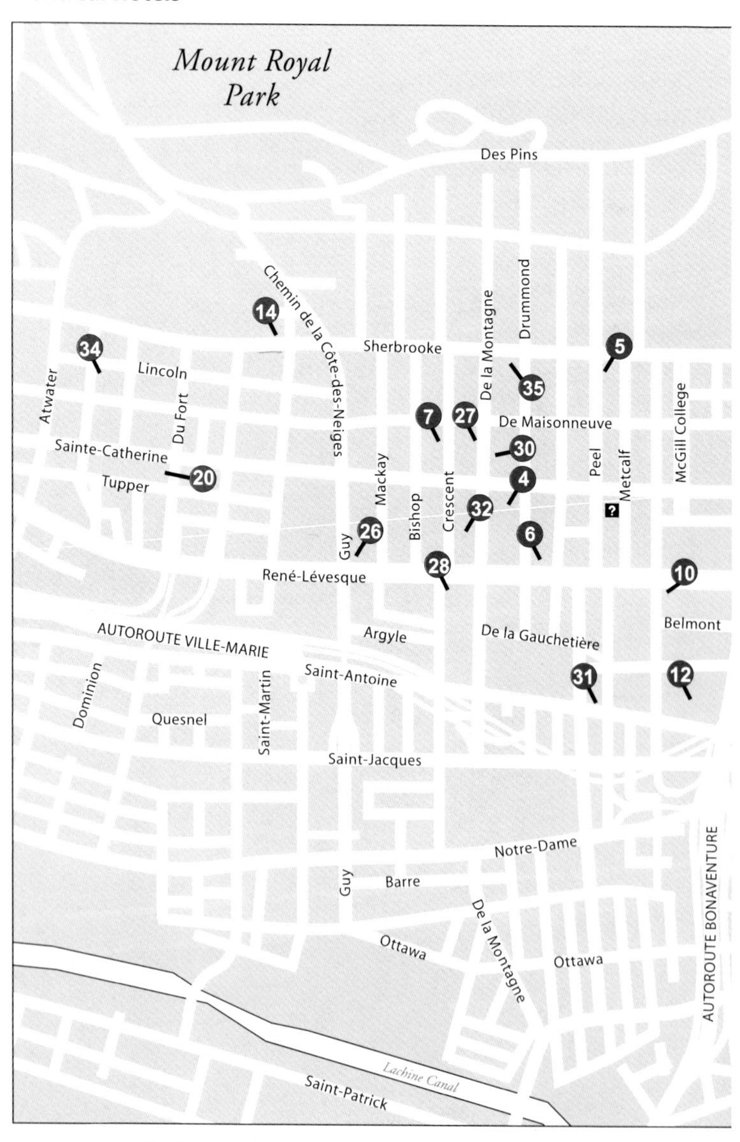

1 Appartements Touristiques du Centre-Ville
2 Auberge de la Fontaine
3 Auberge le Jardin d'Antoine
4 Best Western Europa Centre-Ville
5 Best Western Ville-Marie Hôtel
6 Le Centre Sheraton
7 Château Royal Suites
8 Day's Inn Montréal Centre-Ville
9 Delta Centre-Ville
10 Fairmont The Queen Elizabeth
11 Four Points Sheraton Centre-Ville
12 Hilton Montréal Bonaventure
13 Holiday Inn Montréal-Midtown
14 Hôtel Château Versailles
15 Hôtel Courtyard Marriott Montréal
16 Hôtel de la Couronne
17 Hôtel Delta Montréal

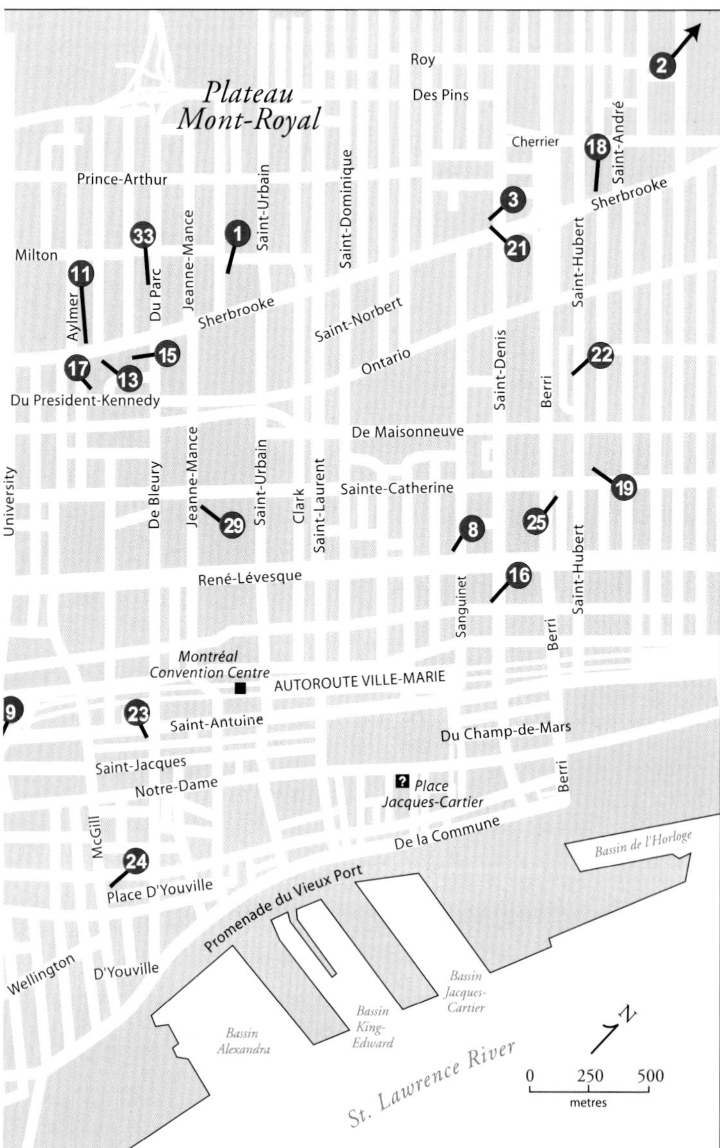

18 Hôtel de Paris
19 Hôtel des Gouverneurs Place Dupis
20 Hôtel du Fort
21 Hôtel du Manoir Saint-Denis
22 Hôtel Dynastie
23 Hôtel Inter-Continental Montreal
24 Hôtel Le St-Paul
25 Hôtel Lord Berri
26 Hôtel Maritime Plaza
27 Hôtel de la Montagne
28 Hôtel Montreal Crescent
29 Hyatt Regency Montreal
30 Loews Hôtel Vogue
31 Marriott Château Champlina
32 Novotel Montreal Centre
33 Quality Hotel (Journey's End)
34 Residence Inn by Marriott
35 Ritz-Carlton Kempinks

Welcome to Montréal and Québec City!

From cobblestone streets to neon-lit strips, there are endless possibilities to explore in the province of Québec's two largest cities. This guide has been written to help you get the most out of your stay in and around Montréal and the provincial capital, Québec City.

The introductory chapter provides an overview of each city as well as a historical introduction to the province of Québec. The maps in the preliminary section of the book provide a general view of each city and its major road arteries, while more detailed downtown and specific area maps give key locations such as hotels. In addition, a neighbourhoods map for Montréal shows the districts covered by separate chapters later in the book. When using the maps take note, both cities have an east-west axis. A streetname with O. indicates 'ouest' — French for west. For example, in Montreal, Ste-Catherine O. is west of St-Laurent Blvd and Ste-Catherine E. is east of it.

The guide is divided by city and then, within these sections, into the best each city has to offer and its distinct areas. The chapters "Montréal's Best" and "Québec City's Best" are thematic, covering topics such as museums, architecture and heritage, shopping and excursions; the chapters under "Montréal by Area" and "Québec City by Area" are divided into well-recognized streets or neighbourhoods that define how most people experience each city.

The final section of the guide contains select listings, with practical information on everything you'll want to do or find in either Montréal or Québec City: accommodations, dining, night life, museums and galleries, attractions, festivals and events, shopping and galleries — along with special travel services and tips.

This book is an independent guide. Its editor and its contributors have made their recommendations and suggestions based solely on what they believe to be the best, most interesting and most appealing sites and attractions. No payments or contributions of any kind are solicited or accepted by the creators or the publishers of this guide.

In a city as lively as Montréal — and even in a solid bastion of francophone culture such as Québec City — things change quickly. The safest thing to do with information you're relying on in this book is to confirm it with a brief phone call. If your experience doesn't match what you read here — or if you think we've missed one of

either city's best features — please let us know. Write us at the address on the Contents page (page 3).

This book is the work of a team of talented writers, editors and photographers. You can read about the people associated with this guide below.

JAMES BASSIL is a Montréal-based writer and editor.

PHIL CARPENTER is a freelance photojournalist working out of Montréal. His photos have appeared in the *National Post* and the Montréal *Gazette*.

SOVITA CHANDER is a historical researcher and freelance writer. Her Québec City home affords her much grist for both avocations.

PATRICK DONOVAN is a heritage conservationist, history lecturer, writer, world-traveller and musician. He recently moved back to his native Québec City.

BRAM EISENTHAL is an award-winning travel writer and a film unit publicist with more than 60 credits on movies and TV series. He lives in the Montréal suburb of Côte St-Luc.

SEAN FARRELL is a Montréal journalist specializing in sports and travel.

PIERRE HOME-DOUGLAS is a Montréal writer and editor who contributes travel stories and opinion pieces to newspapers and magazines.

THÉODORE LAGLOIRE is a professional photographer working out of Québec City.

EMMA McKAY is a writer, editor and book packager who grew up in Vancouver. Since graduating from McGill, she's found it impossible to leave Montréal.

JIM McRAE is a partner in a Montréal communications firm who freelances as a journalist and book editor to local newspapers and trade magazines.

ANASTASIA MICHAILIDIS is a television journalist who grew up in Montréal's Greek community.

SARAH MORGAN is a Montréal-born television

producer and writer.

SARAH LOUISE MUSGRAVE is a Montréal food critic and the author of *Resto à Go-Go* (ECW Press), a guide to budget eating in the city. She writes a weekly restaurant column for the *Gazette* and contributes regularly to other publications.

LORRAINE O'DONNELL is a Québec City–based historian with a long-standing interest in shopping. Her doctoral dissertation, currently underway, looks at the history of women at the Eaton's department store.

MONIQUE POLAK teaches English literature at Marianopolis College in Montréal. She has published two novels for children: *Flip Turn* (James Lorimer and Co.) and *No More Pranks* (Orca Books). In her spare time, she cultivates a widely varied career as a freelance journalist and dines out as often as possible.

MARY ANN SIMPKINS is a travel writer who contributed to the *Ottawa Colourguide*. After living in Québec City for six years, she's now back to enjoying life in Ottawa.

Formerly Canada's most sought-after late-morning to mid-afternoon life consultant, PAUL J. SPENCE now concentrates his efforts exclusively on nightlife. He lives in Montréal.

When not teaching children with intellectual disabilities, SARAH WATERS explores the nooks and crannies of her home city.

PAUL WATERS works as a travel journalist for the city's English daily, the *Montréal Gazette*.

MATTHEW WOODLEY is the Arts Editor at the *Montreal Mirror*, the city's premier English cultural weekly.

Introducing Montréal and Québec City

Christ Church Cathedral

Steeped in nearly 400 years of history, Québec City and Montréal are Canada's two most storied cities. These two urban sisters — capital and metropolis — grew up 200 kilometres apart on the banks of the mighty St. Lawrence River. The hefty river sustained these strategic posts, aiding the flow of commerce, the spread of religious ideals and offering substantial defensive advantages. Together, Québec City and Montréal formed the heart of New France, an enormous empire that at one point extended from Hudson's Bay in the north to Florida in the south.

Rue St-Denis

In the 15th century, these

QUÉBEC CITY

territories were part of an early democracy: the Five Nations, a longstanding union of native tribes that expanded to become the Six Nations in the 18th century. When Jacques Cartier first arrived at what is now Québec City, then called Donacona, friendly Iroquois chief Stadacona spoke to him of a shiny stone upriver. Thinking it was gold (it later proved to be quartz), Cartier set sail and soon reached the village of Hochelaga on what is now the Island of Montréal. Following the natives to the top of the local mountain, he planted the first cross atop Mont Royal.

PETIT CHAMPLAIN

Québec City's name comes from an Algonquin word meaning "where the river narrows," and this narrowing caught the attention of Samuel de Champlain when he sailed upriver in 1608. The site could be defended against Dutch and English rivals with just a few cannons. At the foot of the great cliff that is now crowned by the towers and turrets of the Château Frontenac Hotel, the city was born. Champlain never managed to attract quite as many settlers as he'd dreamed of; French farmers had found reasonable prosperity back home. But fur traders and merchants gravitated to the new city, and it became quite wealthy — wealthy enough that the English wouldn't forget about it. And wealthy enough for merchants to build fine stone homes and churches on the banks of the St. Lawrence.

Eventually, Québec City's governors, military and clergy abandoned the cramped quarters along the river in Basse Ville for the lofty heights atop Cap Diamant, considering them easier to defend. The elevation didn't offer any advantage, however, when General James Wolfe's army surprised the French in 1759 by scaling the cliffs and taking the city.

Montréal's beginnings were also stimulated by the flow

PLACE D'ARMES IN QUÉBEC CITY

of commerce, but religion steered the new community even more than it had Québec City. In 1639, Jerome LeRoyer, a French tax collector, established a settlement on the Island of Montréal. When Paul de Chomedey, Sieur de Maisonneuve, landed on the island in May 1642, he and his followers dreamed of converting the natives and creating a new Catholic society in the wilderness. As Cartier had done years earlier, Chomedey planted a cross at the summit of Mont Royal, a symbol of his faith that endures (albeit not in its original incarnation) to this day.

Chomedey's missionary ambitions didn't amount to much, however, perhaps because he tried to construct his utopia at Place Royale, where the St. Lawrence and Ottawa rivers meet, and commercial incentives soon eclipsed spiritual intentions. Even the name of the settlement — Ville-Marie, in honour of Christ's mother — survives only as the name of an expressway and a skyscraper.

The French regime ended in 1763 with the Seven Years' War, and the Treaty of Paris transferred New France to Britain. English and Scottish settlers, hungry for commercial conquest, spilled into the new territories, and both cities thrived. In 1775, American troops attempted, and failed, to capture Québec City, testament to its growing strength. But Montréal was the main beneficiary of the region's new-found wealth. By 1821, Montréal was Canada's transportation centre, and by the mid-19th century, millionaire barons with Scottish names, Protestant values and grand mansions on the slopes of Mont Royal controlled 70 percent of the wealth in Canada.

Layer upon layer of history has settled over these two cities to create a culture that is anything but dull. Commerce and conquest, linguistic and cultural tensions, religious fervour and conflict, prosperity and poverty, have created two cities that manage to retain their individual character despite the ever-encroaching influences of North American melting-pot globalization.

SUN LIFE BUILDING

Both cities are rich in culture and entertainment. On any given evening, crowds gather in a host of galleries and performance venues — spaces often as creative as the works they house — to toast the art scene's latest debuts and seasoned greats. And there is much to celebrate. The two cities boast the finest French theatres in North America, and Montréal's symphony orchestra is one of the best on the continent. The circus arts, rooted in the busking scenes of both cities, have undergone a renaissance in recent years, and the arrival of La Tohu, a "circus city" complex that houses training and performance spaces for Cirque du Soleil and the National Circus School, cements Montréal's title as capital of the circus arts. Equally exciting are the choreographic leaps of Montréal's renowned dance companies, namely Les Ballets Jazz de Montréal, Les Grands Ballets Canadiens and La La La Human Steps.

It's not all turtlenecks and horn-rimmed glasses here, either. Both Montréal and Québec City have superb restaurants, lively nightclubs and endlessly enticing shops. French Canada, because of its long linguistic separation, has developed its own vast pop culture (movies, rock stars, soap operas, folk singers) that is virtually unknown outside of Québec, spawning the likes of Céline Dion.

MONTRÉAL AT NIGHT

Montréal is the metropolis — a jumble of cultures

where seldom a day goes by without a reason to celebrate something. From the days of Prohibition, when the city was a mecca for sin-seeking Americans, to Expo '67, when the whole world came to town, Montréal's reputation for good times is long established and still growing. These days, the gay village is one of the largest in North America, and the city hosts some of the hottest circuit parties around. In the summer, rarely a week goes by without a street or two being closed off to cars for one or another of the city's many festivals, and crowds battle heat waves at the Sunday "Tam-Tams" (spontaneous gatherings of drummers) at the foot of the Sir George-Etienne Cartier monument on Mont Royal. In the winter, not even an ice storm will stop locals

SUNSET OVER MONTRÉAL

from heading out for a pint of microbrew.

The two cities are very different. It's very possible to live in Montréal without speaking a word of French, although your experience will be richer if you do. Québec City, on the other hand, is more solidly French, and as the capital, it's the center of government. It is staid and assured, without Montréal's insomniac edge. Both cities, however, have far too much joie de vivre to let seven months of icy weather get in the way. Montréal's winter festival celebrates gourmet dining and classical concerts; Québec City's focuses on traditional parades, ice palaces and canoe races across the half-frozen St. Lawrence. And both cities are magnificently illuminated when the snow is deep and the nights are long.

The following chapters offer plenty of ideas for how best to explore each city, whether your aim is to sip sundowners on a terrasse, go antiquing on a Sunday, sample the finest market cuisine, enjoy experimental theatre, explore digital and technological arts or dance until daybreak. But how best to travel between the two? A boat would be the ultimate option — romantic, adventurous and historically appropriate. But for most, it's fairly impractical. That leaves road and rail.

The main highway between Québec City and Montréal is the Autoroute Jean-Lesage — or Highway 20. It's about a three-hour drive. The scenery along the main north shore road — Highway 40 — is much more pleasing and the history far more interesting. If you get bored with the four lanes, you can always get off and follow the old route along the river.

Trois-Rivières is worth stopping for. The city may seem dingy and industrial to those who sweep through on the highway, but it's actually older than Montréal, and there are some 17th- and 18th-century gems along the historic section that skirts the river. Just across the Mauricie River in Cap-de-la-Madeleine is a major Marian shrine, Notre-Dame-du-Cap, where the pope stopped to say Mass on his visit to Canada in 2002.

Train service between the two cities is frequent and efficient. The train follows essentially the same route as that truck-bearing Highway 20, so the scenery on the trip isn't particularly breathtaking. You might as well sleep, and arrive well rested.

Whether you're lacing up your winter boots or slathering on sunscreen, enjoy your adventures in Montréal and Québec City.

Montréal's
Best

Montréal's Top Attractions

Paul Waters

View of downtown from Mont Royal

Montréal is a vibrant city with so much happening that it might seem like you'll never manage to take it all in. But there's no harm in trying. The best way to begin a thorough tour of the city and its many attractions is with a bird's-eye view from the top of the mountain from which the city gets its name, Mont Royal.

It's really nothing more than a big hill, but the 232-metre-high mountain, or *montagne,* looms large in the minds of Montréalers. The cross visible on the summit and illuminated at night commemorates an important event in the city's early history.

In 1642, the year the colony of Ville-Marie was founded, the settlement was threatened by flood waters. Colony founder Paul de Chomedey, Sieur de Maisonneuve, prayed for the town's salvation. When the floods receded, Maisonneuve thanked God by carrying a wooden cross up the mountain, where it was erected in 1643. The metal cross seen today dates from 1924.

The mountain has two lookouts with spectacular views of the city. The Mont Royal lookout and its beautiful chalet offer a panoramic view of downtown, the St. Lawrence River and the south shore. The lookout on the Voie Camillien-Houde presents an equally stunning view of the eastern part of the city. This view is dominated by the mighty Stade Olympique (Olympic Stadium) and the Pont Jacques-Cartier (Jacques Cartier Bridge). You can follow paths from either lookout to the summit of the mountain, where you can see the cross.

The mountain is worth visiting not only for its spectacular views, but also for the wonderful Parc du Mont-Royal. This green oasis was designed in 1876 by Frederick Law Olmsted, who also designed Central Park in New York City.

Olmsted's plan was to keep the whole 101 hectares (250 acres) as untouched as possible. Along with the lookouts, he laced the meadows and hardwood forests with a series of footpaths. Others spoiled this dream by adding an artificial pond (Lac aux Castors, or Beaver Lake) and the Voie Camillien-Houde, a winding thoroughfare that cuts across the park from east to west. Still, this park is Montréal's favourite, and easiest, escape from the stone and concrete canyons of the city.

Basilique Notre-Dame

From the chalet, look out towards the waterfront to spot the landmarks of Old Montréal, especially its top attraction, Basilique Notre-Dame. It is probably the most celebrated church in Canada. Funerals for former prime minister Pierre Trudeau and Montréal Canadiens hockey great Maurice Richard were held there. Famed chanteuse Céline Dion was married there and her son was baptized there. It was the venue for one of Luciano Pavarotti's most famous appearances, a Christmas concert that has been endlessly recycled by the Public Broadcasting System in the United States. The basilica's vast blue ceiling, sprinkled with thousands of gold-leaf stars, graces postcards, posters, calendars and placemats.

All this fame sits well on the old place. It's a magnificent building that could accommodate almost every Catholic in the city when it opened in 1829. It was, oddly enough, designed by an American Protestant, James O'Donnell, who was so pleased with his work that he converted to Catholicism and was eventually buried in the crypt. The pulpit and high altar were designed by Victor Bourgeau, and O'Donnell's vaulted stone cave was filled with dozens of paintings, pine and walnut carvings, ornate panelling, fanciful pillars and stained-glass windows from Limoges. The reredos features a larger-than-life-sized depiction of the crucifixion surrounded by four life-sized scenes of sacrifice from the Old Testament — all carved in wood by local artisans. The pulpit, with its curving staircase, and the baptistery, with murals by Ozias Leduc, are works of art. Hearing the Casavant organ in this jewel box is a delight to the senses. Behind the main altar is the Chapelle du Sacré-Coeur, the most popular wedding chapel in Montréal. In 1978 much of its Spanish-style Gothic revival interior was destroyed in a deliberately set fire. Architects rescued what they could and added a modern roof with a huge skylight as well as a Plexiglas altar designed by Charles Daudelin, with an enormous bronze sculpture rising above it. Although not to everyone's taste, somehow it all blends in. Daily tours are offered in English and French, and in the evenings, a multimedia sound-and-light show illuminates the founding of Montréal and the creation of this architectural masterpiece.

Top: Old Montréal
Above: Musée d'Archéologie Pointe-à-Callière

Notre-Dame is located in the heart of the old city. Old Montréal, or Vieux-Montréal, was a rundown area until the late 1960s, when Montréal finally woke up to its treasures along the waterfront. Now, its narrow cobblestone streets are packed in summer and still well populated in winter, with visitors admiring the fine examples of 18th- and 19th-century architecture that line its sidewalks. Old Montréal is also home to some of the city's most popular museums: the Musée d'Archéologie Pointe-à-Callière and the Centre d'Histoire de Montréal (see Museums), and an art gallery dedicated to the work of Marc-Aurèle Fortin (see Galleries). All this borders the Old Port, or Vieux-Port — a strip of wharves, grassy expanses and once-dilapidated warehouses on the St. Lawrence River — which has evolved into one of the city's

Sailing past the casino

Casino de Montréal

most popular parks. (See Old Montréal and Old Port.)

From the Old Port you can spot the Casino de Montréal. The casino is a success story with more than 15,000 visitors a day, and it tinkles with the sounds of 3,000 slot machines and offers 120 tables for baccarat, blackjack, roulette and other games. It also has two Keno lounges, Royal Ascot electronic racetracks, four restaurants, four bars, a cabaret-style dinner theatre and (just in case you should run short of cash) lots of automatic bank machines. Lest you should be misled into thinking this is Las Vegas North, there are some rules: no jeans, no running shoes and no drinking alcohol on the gaming floors (one vice at a time, please). Some of the restaurants are buffet style, familiar to Nevada gamblers, but one of them, Nuances, is very posh indeed, and it offers great views of the Montréal skyline. From the Jean-Drapeau Métro station, a city bus (#167) will take you right to the casino door, or you can inquire at any tourist information centre about the seasonal free shuttle service.

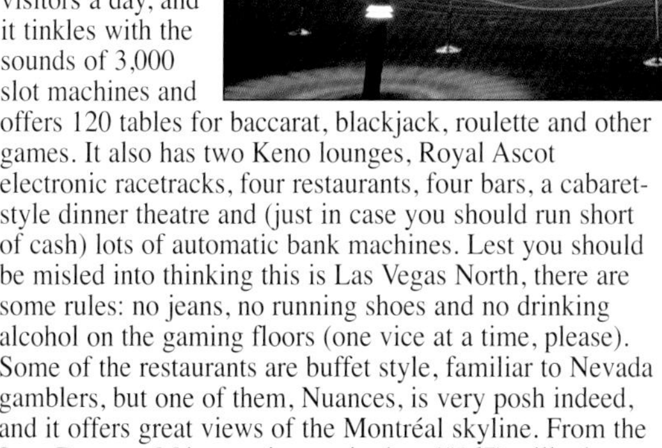

The casino is on Île Notre-Dame, which is part of Parc des Îles. The park was the home of Expo '67, the World's Fair that trumpeted Montréal's arrival as a modern metropolis and the party capital of Canada. In fact, the casino opened in the futuristic glass-and-aluminum building that was the French pavilion during Expo '67. When that space got too crowded, the government agency running the casino took over the adjoining Québec pavilion. (First, though, it tinted the cubic building an alluring and appropriate shade of gold.) Île Notre-Dame didn't exist before Expo. The artificial island rests on a solid foundation of stone rubble excavated for the construction of the Métro system. The park has since been renamed Parc Jean-Drapeau in honour of the late, larger-than-life mayor who brought Expo '67 to Montréal and followed up with the 1976 Olympics. In summer, shuttle boats carry passengers from the Quai Jacques-Cartier across the St. Lawrence River to the park. (Less romantic and more practical visitors can take the Métro instead.)

At least one other Expo building (atop Île Ste-Hélène, another artificial island constructed for the fair) is still in use. Buckminster Fuller's gigantic geodesic dome (originally the United States pavilion) houses the Biosphère, an interactive exhibit

Old soldiers at the Stewart Museum

La Ronde Amusement Park

about the Great Lakes–St. Lawrence water system (see Nature & Natural History). One of the most successful reminders of Expo's glory days is La Ronde amusement park. The Expo symbol — stick figures (or chicken feet, depending on how you look at it) — still decorates the park's 45-metre-high Ferris wheel. La Ronde has a couple of giant roller coasters that rival the best in the world. It was purchased by the American corporation Six Flags Inc. a few years ago, and each season the company adds more new and exciting family-oriented attractions to the park.

Within the sound of the roller-coaster screams is a completely different attraction: the Musée Stewart au Fort de l'Ile Sainte-Hélène (see Museums). The fort was built to fend off an American attack that never came, and it is now used as a drilling ground for the Olde 78th Fraser Highlanders and the Compagnie Franche de la Marine, so sometimes the sound of muskets drowns out the shrieks from La Ronde.

Beyond the rides and museum, the park has enough to keep even the most casual visitor content for a day or two. It has the city's only natural beach, with a cleverly disguised filtration system to keep the water clean; a rowing basin; a vast floral display called Floralies; and a couple of hundred acres of trees and walkways. Grand Prix drivers compete here every summer in one of only two North American Formula One auto races, and pyrotechnicians from a dozen countries spend summer weekends trying to outdo each other during the Montréal International Fireworks Competition, Le Mondial SAQ, which has been a key part of summer in Montréal for the past 20 years.

Stade Olympique

Japanese garden

If you make a little trek east on the Métro to the Viau station, you'll be able to take a peek at one of the great white elephants of all time: the Stade Olympique. English-speaking Montréalers call the place the Big Owe, describing both its shape and the state of Montréal's finances after it was built. Mayor Jean Drapeau hired French architect Roger Taillibert to design the building for the 1976 Olympics. It was supposed to be the prince of stadiums and a monument to sport, and it is indeed a dramatic structure, rising like a great white mirage out of the low-lying architecture of Montréal's east end. But it never functioned very well as a sports stadium, and it makes most of its money from trade shows and mega-concerts. Céline Dion and the Rolling Stones do a better job of filling its vast interior than baseball or football ever did. In fact, Montréal lost its baseball team, the Expos, in 2003, largely due to the fact that few ever came to see them play at the Stadium. So why go look? Well, there are at least four reasons. First, the stadium's spectacular. It looks like a giant clamshell, and while the collapsible fabric roof never worked and was replaced by an equally disastrous permanent one, the interior does have a bright and airy feel. Second, the 17-storey-high leaning tower, which was intended to hold up the collapsible roof, features a funicular, a neat tram that climbs its shaft to a great viewing platform overlooking Montréal. Third, the Olympic swimming pools under the tower are open to the public. Finally, the stadium is right next door to at least two very successful attractions.

The Biodôme is housed in the velodrome built for the Olympic track-cycling races and

Long house in First Nations Garden

EXAMINING AT THE INSECTARIUM

was designed to look a bit like a 1970s-style cyclist's helmet. But the building has been gutted and transformed into an indoor outdoors (see Nature & Natural History). It re-creates four habitats — a rain forest, a Laurentian forest, a polar landscape and the St. Lawrence marine ecosystem — complete with all the requisite plants and animals. For those who prefer their plants in a more natural setting, the Jardin Botanique de Montréal is right across the street from the Biodôme. It is one of the largest botanical gardens in the world, with over 20,000 different plant species in 185 acres of gardens, including Japanese, Chinese and First Nations gardens. Also on site are 10 greenhouses and a bug-shaped Insectarium that's full of live and dead insects (see Nature & Natural History).

Back on the northern side of Mont Royal is another of the city's top attractions, the Oratoire Saint-Joseph du Mont-Royal. Its interior is drab when compared with the spectacular Basilique Notre-Dame, but what this huge church lacks in opulence it makes up for in size and setting. Thousands of pilgrims visit it every year; many still climb the outside stairs on their knees, seeking favours and cures from both St. Joseph and Blessed Frère André Bessette, the humble Christian brother who was responsible for the building of the oratory. Successful supplicants have left behind hundreds of canes and crutches that are now used to decorate the walls of the votive chapel. The building actually houses two churches: the nondescript little crypt church on the ground floor and the immense but sombre oratory church beneath the copper dome. The latter is the home church of the Petits Chanteurs du Mont-Royal, the finest boys' choir in the city. Surrounded by gardens and trees, the complex also includes a museum dedicated to Frère André, a cafeteria, a souvenir shop and a hostel for pilgrims.

Finally, what Montréal guidebook is complete without a mention of the famed Underground City? It is a vast, nearly 32-kilometre (20-mile) network of underground corridors linking 60 commercial buildings, shopping centres, cinemas, hotels and 10 Métro stops. More than 500,000 people use this network each day, but that number rises considerably on cold winter days. The Underground City doesn't really offer much to see apart from lots of shopping malls and some interesting art in the Métro stations, but the concept never fails to fascinate visitors.

HERITAGE & ARCHITECTURE

JIM MCRAE

HÔTEL DE VILLE

Montréal is a city of many gifts. It brims with cultural diversity, flourishes with art and fashion and serves up fine dining and entertainment in banquet-like proportions. And all this is celebrated in an urban setting decorated with some of the richest architecture on the continent. Since its founding in 1642, Montréal has grown from a frontier settlement of New France to a cosmopolitan city in the new millennium. Along the way, pioneer settlers, Victorian industrialists and international masters of the classical school have added their flourishes to the city's architectural heritage.

FRAGMENTS OF 17TH- AND 18TH-CENTURY NEW FRANCE

While it is commonly believed that Old Montréal is full of buildings that date from the French regime, there are only a handful of gems from that epoch still standing (not including L'Église de la Visitation de la Bienheureuse Vierge Marie, which is located in the north end of the city). These structures are, however, historical jewels, some over three centuries old.

The Séminaire de Saint-Sulpice, built in 1685, is one such gem. Located beside Basilique Notre-Dame, it is the oldest building in Montréal, constructed to house Sulpician priests. The seminary features several medieval characteristics: cradle-vaults in the foundation, corner towers with staircases and building practices common to

artisan tradesmen of the period. The low storeys and small windows are signatures of French Regime architecture. The central door is engraved with the date 1740, the year when the portico was added to the seminary.

Several blocks to the southwest, the Grey Nuns' general hospital at Rue St-Pierre and Place d'Youville was built in 1693 as the second hospital in the city. Its name honours the congregation of the Sisters of Charity, also known as the Grey Nuns, founded by Marguerite d'Youville around 1750. The hospital was destroyed by fire in 1765 and the walls that were left undamaged were used in the rebuilding. It was later partially demolished to be replaced by an imposing greystone warehouse.

CHATEAU DE RAMEZAY

Roughly a kilometre's walk from the old hospital, the Château de Ramezay on Rue Notre-Dame E. stands as a well-preserved monument of the French Regime. The residence was constructed for the governor of Montréal, Claude de Ramezay, and work on it began in 1705. The Château is a blend of urban row house and detached rural home, a trend in Montréal-area dwellings of that time. It was converted into a museum in 1895. There is some debate about whether the Maison du Calvet, on the northeast corner of Bonsecours and St-Paul, actually dates back to 1725. Early city maps show a building in the location, but it's not certain that this was the original house. Other reports indicate that the fieldstone structure with a steeply sloping roof was built in 1770, a decade after the city was taken over by the British. Regardless, it is a fine example of 18th-century architecture. The house is named after Pierre du Calvet, a Frenchman and republican partisan during the American Revolution who became a resident of Montréal. It now houses a charming little inn and one of the city's fine French restaurants.

MAISON DU CALVET

VICTORIAN INFLUENCE, 1837–1914

Victorian architecture is an influence, not a single style. And in Montréal, rich Scottish and British industrialists would wield considerable influence over the city's

buildings for seven decades — well past the reign of Queen Victoria. The nouveau riche of this New World borrowed from classical traditions, putting their own elaborate stamps on the business addresses where they plotted their economic conquests. Some say that Basilique Notre-Dame, although constructed prior to the reign of the famed British monarch, heralded the era of Victorian architecture in Montréal. Built in 1829, Notre-Dame is the neo-Gothic creation of Irish-American architect James O'Donnell. He used decorative components of the Gothic style to produce a monument resembling the celebrated cathedrals of Europe: a majestic façade, elaborate portico and soaring bell towers. A Protestant by birth, O'Donnell converted to Catholicism before his death in 1830 and is buried beside the altar in his famous creation.

BASILIQUE NOTRE-DAME

BANQUE DE MONTRÉAL

Opposite Notre-Dame at Place d'Armes is the Banque de Montréal building, perhaps the richest example of Victorian architecture in the city. It was designed by Englishman John Wells and dates to 1847. Although a major expansion at the turn of the century left only the façade as part of the original construction, it alone is considered a magnificent architectural achievement. Its detailed and expert stonework, often compared with that of the Bank of the United States in Philadelphia, evoked the power of Montréal's commercial elite. A short distance to the southeast, William Footner's Marché Bonsecours on Rue St-Paul is an example of the level of extravagance associated with the Victorians. Costing a staggering $70,000 when completed in 1842, Bonsecours Market features cast-iron Doric columns in its portico, while an imposing dome rises above its roof line. Located on the harbour, thc three-storey-high, 152-metre-long building was a beacon for

MARCHÉ BONSECOURS

RAVENSCRAG

the era, sending a message of the city's commercial success to those arriving by river. Bonsecours once served as parliament and town hall. Today, cultural events and exhibitions are frequently held here. Montréal's current city hall, or Hôtel de Ville, is also a Victorian structure. Designed by architect H. Maurice Perrault, it is an example of the French Second Empire style. Built between 1872 and 1878, it fell to fire in 1922. The remaining walls were used in its reconstruction and a tall mansard roof was introduced. Elaborately decorated and massive in size, the building sits across from Château de Ramezay. Juxtaposed, the two illustrate the difference between the simple lines of the French regime and the ornamentation of the Victorian era.

THE SQUARE MILE

While the mercantile elite of the Victorian era were branding their edifices with labels of commercial success, they were also building domestic monuments to themselves in an area known as the Square Mile, later dubbed the Golden Square Mile. This neighbourhood was bordered by Rue Sherbrooke to the south, the slope of Mont Royal to the north, Chemin de la Côte-des-Neiges to the west and Rue de Bleury to the east. Its residents controlled 70 percent of Canada's wealth at the turn of the 20th century. These magnates owned some of the most extravagant private homes ever constructed on the continent.

Unfortunately, many of these urban palaces were razed in the late 1960s and early 1970s during a time of careless city planning. The few examples that remain do, however, offer a glimpse of the lifestyle of Canada's early business barons. Principal among these estates is Ravenscrag (now the Allan Pavilion Memorial Institute of the Hôpital Royal Victoria on Avenue des Pins), home to Sir Hugh Allan, railway baron and the richest of Montréal's elite. The sprawling house features a mixture of architectural styles but borrows mostly from the Italian Renaissance. From its location on the southern flank of Mont Royal, it represented the pinnacle of personal success for the rest of the growing metropolis to see.

While not as ostentatious as Allan's mountainside monument, Trafalgar House, located on Avenue Trafalgar on Mont Royal's southwest side, is a fine example of a wealthy Victorian domicile. Built in 1848, it was designed by John George Howard, an English draftsman and engineer who had immigrated to Toronto. He incorporated Gothic and Tudor features into the design of the house. Its red-brick façade and stone-framed windows and doors display considerable craftsmanship and contribute to an overall look of solidity. The former Engineers' Club (now empty after a popular hockey player's restaurant closed) is another example of an opulent Victorian residence. Located

at Place du Frère André (formerly Beaver Hall Square), just north of Boulevard René-Lévesque, the mansion was completed around 1860. It is said to be designed by William T. Thomas, one of the most accomplished architects of the period, and the mastermind behind Église St- George, the Anglican church at Square Dorchester. The residence has the flavour of an Italian Renaissance mansion.

ÉGLISE ST-GEORGE

RESIDENTIAL ARCHITECTURE

If the homes of the Victorian era's elite were an expression of the individual through elaborate decoration and outward displays of wealth, the row houses of the working class of Montréal were the opposite: nondescript structures designed to huddle the masses close to the industries that kept the Square Mile golden.

Multifamily vertical housing, one or two flats above a main-floor flat, first appeared in Montréal between 1850 and 1860 in Pointe St-Charles. These buildings were erected to house Irish immigrants who worked either on the construction of the Pont Victoria (Victoria Bridge) or in the yards and shops of the Chemin de Fer du Grand Tronc (Grand Trunk Railway). Streets such as Sébastopol, Charon and Le Ber are lined with these dwellings. Recently, Montréal architect Michael Fish renovated 12 of these structures on Sébastopol that were originally homes for Grand Trunk Railway employees. The condos he refitted are the oldest extant multiple dwellings in Montréal. Wooden frame in construction, they are finished with red brick and extend right to the sidewalk, with no balcony. Each structure has twin doors that share a common landing, one leading to the main floor, the other to an inside staircase that accesses the second level. The roof is flat, mansard or has a steep, sloping side with dormers

VERTICAL HOUSING

looking out onto the street. Any decoration on the façade usually occurs at the roof line, incorporating the dormers and simple cornices.

Although the working-class homes closer to the city centre exhibit more architectural flair than those in the Pointe, they are still models of simplicity. Apart from some examples of upscale, stone-faced British-style row houses on Avenue Laval and Carré St-Louis, they are, typically, like those on nearby Rue Hutchison: two storeys high with greystone façades and picturesque architectural motifs; this style became common throughout the city. Grey limestone quarried on the island of Montréal is also a common façade in the solidly built apartment blocks on St-Hubert and St-Denis between Ste-Catherine and Sherbrooke.

FLAT-ROOFED HOMES

In the more densely populated areas of Verdun, Rosemont and Plateau Mont-Royal, the row houses feature two or three levels of flats finished in brick. These flat-roofed homes have porches, balconies and outside staircases in front and back. This type of dwelling became typical housing for the city's working class, and, because it is more prevalent than any other building type in the city, it represents a de facto Montréal architectural style. These buildings were erected to house the 400,000 people who moved to the city between 1891 and 1921.

When duplexes and triplexes were springing up all over the city to handle the influx of rural migrants and immigrants, builders began to standardize their techniques and to use prefabricated building materials, such as the outside staircase. Montréal's distinctive outside staircases were seen as a space- and cost-saving feature: having the stairs on the outside meant more living space inside and required less fuel to heat an area that would only be used for entering and exiting the unit. Curved versions are used where homes have little frontage. The drawbacks are that the stairs can be slippery in winter (many people affix outdoor carpeting to combat this problem) and they tend to block sunlight from reaching the ground-level flat.

DISTINCTIVE OUTSIDE STAIRCASES

CHURCH ARCHITECTURE

Mark Twain once said that you couldn't throw a brick in Montréal without breaking a church window. And although there is no hard evidence to prove that the American literary icon ever put his theory to the test during his visit in 1881, several important churches dominated the core of the city at the time, their spires and domes competing for

BASILIQUE ST-PATRICK

space on the skyline. Notre-Dame, located at Place d'Armes, was principal among these historic houses of worship, its chapel having been part of the main fort in 1642; the present building dates from 1829. Basilique St-Patrick on Boulevard René-Lévesque, completed in 1847, also punctuated the landscape, as did Cathédrale Christ Church, built in 1859, near Carré Phillips. The Cathédrale Marie-Reine-du-Monde (originally named St-Jacques) is a scaled-down version of St. Peter's Basilica in Rome, and was the project of Montréal's second archbishop, Ignace Bourquet. It was in the heart of the Anglo-Protestant district and was over halfway built by 1881, when Twain visited Montréal. While many of the churches mentioned were a stone's throw from the Windsor Hotel, where he made his quip, further afield stood the only church that dated back to the French regime. Located at Sault-au-Récollet, west of Papineau on Boulevard Gouin, Église de la Visitation was begun in 1749 and was ready for Mass by 1751. Charles Guilbault, a parishioner, supplied the rough masonry of the main building, which also features classical arched windows. In the early 1850s, the prolific Montréal architect John Ostell added a new front in a severe English neo-Baroque style. The interior is equally rewarding, as master sculptors such as Philippe Liébert, Louis-Amable Quévillon and David Fleury-David lent their skills to various aspects of the church over time. The tabernacle of the main altar was completed in 1792, the altars between 1802 and 1806 and the vault and much of the present interior between 1816 and 1831.

CHRIST CHURCH CATHEDRAL AT STE-CATHERINE AND UNIVERSITY

SKYSCRAPERS THEN AND NOW

Although church steeples and bell towers defined Montréal's skyline from its earliest days, the city's first office towers began to challenge them near the end of the 19th century, when elevators and the use of iron and steel framing allowed architects to push buildings higher than the standard of five or six storeys.

Oddly enough, the city's first "skyscraper," or *gratte-ciel,* featured neither of these innovations. Still, the New York Life Insurance Co. building at Place d'Armes, completed in 1888, was the city's first 8-storey office building. Although

Notre-Dame's 66-metre-high twin spires still rose above any other structure in the city, taller buildings were soon to follow. Basilique Notre-Dame relinquished its height title when the Banque Royal Bank, reaching 23 storeys, was completed in 1928. Located on Rue St-Jacques, not far from the renowned church, the bank's exquisite ground floor was a symbol of Montréal's mercantile elite. Another example of the increasing wealth of the city was the Sun Life building on the east side of Square Dorchester. Built in three stages between 1914 and 1931, it resembled a wedding cake and was the largest building in the British Empire when completed. Its steel framing is wrapped in Stanstead granite, and Corinthian columns line its ground floor.

BNP and Laurentian Bank

The era of the modern-day Montréal skyscraper began in the early 1960s and involved the efforts of several world-renowned architects. Place Ville-Marie, an I.M. Pei creation, was conceived in the late 1950s but not fully completed until 1966; the tower dates from 1962. Its cruciform design makes it one of the most recognizable structures in Montréal.

Slightly to the east at Square Victoria, Luigi Moretti and Pier L. Nervi put their finishing touches on La Tour de la Bourse in 1964. It was the first earthquake-proof building ever constructed and, at 47 storeys, was the tallest concrete structure in the world at the time. In the main lobby, a 13-metre-tall stalactite comprising 3,000 pieces of Murano glass welcomes visitors. Slightly to the west of the city core, the black-metal and tinted-glass office towers of Westmount Square, unveiled in 1965, are considered masterpieces of Ludwig Mies van der Rohe, the former director of the Bauhaus School.

1000 Rue de la Gauchetière, Marie-Reine-du-Monde, Sun Life

In recent years, other significant towers have staked their claim in the celebrated skyline. The quiet elegance of the 205-metre-high 1000 Rue de la Gauchetière is one example, the 47 storeys of glass and granite at 1250 Boulevard René-Lévesque is another. The former has a glass-domed exhibition hall featuring a year-round skating rink, the latter a 25-metre-high interior garden.

The glass and steel of the downtown skyscrapers may punctuate Montréal's modern skyline, but in no way do they supersede the structures that are cast in their shadows. The city has been under construction for over 350 years and its architecture is rich and diverse. It reflects the influences of its founding fathers and incorporates the styles, and often the personal tastes, of those who followed. Just as few cities in North America can match Montréal's history, few can match, in age and diversity, its architectural heritage.

Museums

Sarah Morgan

Artifacts on display at the Musée McCord

It would be hard to find a North American metropolis with more history than Montréal. The city's roots reach back to the middle of the 17th century, and it's virtually impossible to dig up a sewer or repair a street without turning up some artifact from Montréal's past. There was a time in the 1950s and 1960s when history was viewed as something you knocked down or pushed aside to make room for another skyscraper or freeway. But Montréalers have learned to revere — even revel in — their rich heritage. You can see that pride in the cobbled streets of Old Montréal, the Victorian row houses of the McGill

KAHNAWAKE MOHAWKS IN 1869

INSET: IROQUOIS BEADWORK

University ghetto and the comfortable Second Empire homes built by the francophone elite in the Quartier Latin. You can also see it in the city's museums, where every effort is made to bring the past to life and render it vivid and relevant for modern visitors. Some museums are tiny. The Banque de Montréal, for example, has squeezed a modest but interesting little display on early banking practices into one room on the ground floor of its head office at Place d'Armes. Some focus on the contributions of one person; others, like the Musée McCord and the Musée d'Archéologie Pointe-à-Caillère, take a much broader view.

THE BROAD VIEW

The broad view is probably a good way to start any exploration of the city's history, and it would be hard to find any museum broader than the Musée McCord d'Histoire Canadienne, just across Rue Sherbrooke from the McGill University campus. The heart of its collection is a glorious hodgepodge of artifacts collected by a lawyer named David Ross McCord (1844–1930). He was an inveterate pack rat with a passion for anything that had to do with life in Canada — books, photographs, jewellery, furniture, clothing, guns, old documents, paintings, toys, porcelain. And he gave all this to McGill University so it could open a museum of social history. Some of the best exhibits are the collections of First Nations and Inuit artifacts. These items aren't limited to the ubiquitous west coast and Arctic art but include tools and weapons and intricately decorated clothing. The museum also has one of the best photographic archives in Canada, with more than 70,000 pictures. Some of the most interesting images come from the studio of William Notman, a photographic pioneer who captured life in Victorian Montréal. Notman's work includes a lot of exterior pictures: families tobogganing, soldiers marching and members (several hundred of them) of the posh Montréal Amateur Athletic Association posing in snowshoe regalia on the slopes of Mont Royal. The remarkable thing about these pictures is that all the figures were photographed individually in a studio and then painstakingly

MUSÉE D'ARCHÉOLOGIE POINTE-À-CAILLÈRE

assembled onto the exterior background.

The Musée d'Archéologie Pointe-à-Caillère, in the middle of Old Montréal, probes a little deeper — literally — into the city's history. It's housed in a startlingly modern building on the waterfront that looks rather like a concrete ship. It's quite a tall building, but the guts of the museum are in the basement, where archaeologists have dug their way through several layers of settlement down to the remnants of the city's earliest days. You can wend your way down to the banks of a long-filled-in river where early settlers used to trade with the local First Nations bands, visit the oldest Catholic cemetery on the island and examine the foundations of an 18th-century waterfront tavern. A tunnel connects the museum to the Vieille Douane (Old Customs House) at Place Royale, a fine old building with a huge gift shop.

BEDROOM, CHÂTEAU RAMEZAY

The Musée du Château Ramezay on Rue Notre-Dame E. is one of the few reminders the city has of the French regime. This mansion was built in 1702 by Claude de Ramezay, Montréal's 11th governor, and its interior reflects the grace and tastes of the early-18th-century elite. The most magnificent room is the Nantes Salon, which is decorated with intricately carved panelling by the French architect Germain Boffrand. The uniforms, documents and furniture on the main floor reflect the life of New France's ruling classes, while several rooms in the cellars depict the more ordinary doings of humbler colonists. But the museum's collection is fairly eclectic. One of its most prized possessions, for example, is a bright red automobile that was produced at the turn of the 20th century by the De Dion–Bouton company.

At first, the exhibits in the Centre d'Histoire de Montréal, a 19th-century firehouse, seem to cover much the same ground as those at the Château Ramezay and the Musée d'Archéologie Pointe-à-Caillère. That's a misleading impression, however, as the focus here is fixed firmly on everyday life. Some of the most effective parts of

CENTRE D'HISTOIRE DE MONTRÉAL

the museum are the exhibits on city life in the 1930s and 1940s. You can sit in a period living room and listen to a play-by-play of a Canadiens hockey game or step into a phone booth and eavesdrop while a young factory worker tries to make a date with the shop clerk he adores.

A TALE OF TWO WOMEN

One of the unique things about Montréal history is the large and acclaimed part that women have played in it. Two women in particular were absolutely vital to the city's development: Jeanne Mance, who co-founded the original settlement of Ville-Marie with Paul de Chomedey, Sieur de Maisonneuve, and Marguerite Bourgeoys, the colony's first schoolteacher and now a canonized saint. Both women were feisty, devout and determined; they left behind concrete reminders of their presence: Jeanne Mance's Hôtel-Dieu de Montréal hospital still serves the city's sick, and the religious order that Marguerite Bourgeoys founded still runs schools and colleges across Canada. Several museums offer insights into the lives of these remarkable and indomitable women.

Maison Saint-Gabriel on Place Dublin is an isolated little fragment of New France lost among the apartment buildings of working-class Pointe St-Charles. It was a farm when the formidable Marguerite Bourgeoys bought it in 1668 as a residence for the religious order she had founded in 1655. The house, rebuilt in 1698 after a fire, is a fine example of 17th-century architecture, with thick stone walls and a steeply pitched roof built on an intricate frame of heavy timber.

Marguerite Bourgeoys and her tireless sisters worked the farm and ran a school on the property for First Nations and colonial children. They also housed and trained the filles du roi (the king's daughters), orphaned young women sent to New France by Louis XIV to be the wives and mothers of his new colony. The house's chapel, kitchen, dormitory and drawing rooms are full of artifacts from 17th, 18th and 19th centuries, including a writing desk the saint actually used. There's a smaller museum dedicated to Marguerite Bourgeoys and her mission in North America attached to the chapel of Notre-Dame-de-Bon-Secours in Old Montréal. It too is worth a visit.

Musée des Hospitalières is located near the McGill University campus on Avenue des Pins O. Jeanne Mance was as pious as her friend Marguerite Bourgeoys and even more important to the establishment of a colony on the island of Montréal. But she never joined or founded a religious order, so she left behind no band of sisters to promulgate her memory. She did, however, bring the Religieuses Hospitalières de Saint-Joseph to Montréal in

the mid-1600s to run Hôtel-Dieu, the hospital she'd founded. And while the sisters no longer run the hospital, they still maintain this small but charming museum that relects Jeanne Mance's zealous spirit. Books, documents and artifacts from the early days are on display, and there is a sometimes-chilling exhibit on the history of medicine and nursing.

Great Personalities

Montréal's history is filled with colourful characters — strongman Louis Cyr, hockey player Maurice (Rocket) Richard, artist Marc-Aurèle Fortin and Mayor Camillien Houde, who spent time in an internment camp for his opposition to conscription during World War II. Every one of them would be worthy of a museum, but only a few have permanent exhibitions in their honour.

Maison Sir George-Étienne Cartier, exterior and interior

The Maison Sir George-Étienne Cartier historic site on Rue Notre-Dame E. is the most elaborate museum dedicated to a single individual. George-Étienne Cartier (1814–73) was largely responsible for persuading French Canada to join the new Canadian confederation in 1867, arguing that a federal system would give French Canadians the powers necessary to protect their language, religion and culture. The national historic site comprises two adjoining greystone houses the Cartier family owned on the eastern edge of Old Montréal. One is dedicated to Cartier's career as a lawyer, politician and railway builder. An exhibit within gives visitors the opportunity to sit at a round table with plaster models of the Fathers of Confederation and listen in either French or English to a very good summary of the founding of Canada. The second house, on the other side of a covered carriageway, focuses on the Cartiers' domestic life and the functioning of an upper-middle-class family in the mid-19th century. Visitors wander through formal rooms full of fussy, overstuffed furniture, listening to snatches of conversation from "servants" gossiping about the lives of their master and mistress.

The Musée du Bienheureux Frère André, tucked away in the Oratoire Saint-Joseph du Mont-Royal, is a little museum dedicated to the diminutive man who started the whole project — Brother André Bessette. Models, photographs and documents chronicle his early life, and a shrine containing his embalmed heart is testimony to the reverence in which he is still held. The office where Frère André worked, the room where he slept and the hospital

Oratoire Saint-Joseph de Mont Royal

room where he died have been reconstructed and preserved. Not a bad monument for a man who was born into abject poverty and never held a job more important than that of porter in a classical college.

Le Monde de Maurice (Rocket) Richard isn't really a museum at all, just a room tucked way in the Aréna Maurice-Richard. One of the most exciting hockey players who ever lived probably deserves much more, but the exhibits do reverently trace the great man's life and career.

La Compagnie Franche de la Marine

Marc-Aurèle Fortin is the only Québec artist with his own museum, the Musée Marc-Aurèle Fortin. And he deserves it. The man virtually invented Québec landscape painting. He also pioneered the painting of images on a black background — a technique that has been abused by schlock merchants ever since. No one, however, has painted grander trees than Fortin.

Military Adventures

The Old Fort on Île Ste-Hélène was built in 1825 to protect Montréal from an American attack that never came. Its red stone walls enclose a grassy parade square that is used today by members of the Olde 78th Fraser Highlanders and the Compagnie Franche de la Marine, re-creations of two 18th-century military formations that fought each other over the future of New France. The fort also houses the Musée Stewart, a small but excellent historical museum with an interesting collection of 17th- and 18th-century maps, firearms and navigational instruments. Its costumed guides give an accurate, unsentimental and yet quite humorous account of the first encounters between Europeans and Native North Americans.

At play in the Old Fort

Trade and Commerce

North façade from entrance gate, CCA

A cyclist can coast comfortably into Montréal's industrial past by following the bike path along the Canal de Lachine from the Old Port to Lac St-Louis. The canal, built to enable shipping to avoid the treacherous Rapides de Lachine, was supplanted by the St. Lawrence Seaway in the 1950s and has become a kind of long, thin and very popular park. Near the end of the trail in the lakeside suburb of Lachine is the Canal de Lachine Centre d'Interprétation, which houses an interesting display on the building and operation of the canal. Further along the Lachine waterfront is an old stone warehouse with a cumbersome name: Lieu Historique National du Commerce-de-la-Fourrure-à-Lachine (Fur Trade in Lachine National Historic Site). Constructed in 1802 as a trading depot, today the building offers displays on the trade that created Montréal's wealth. Because of its position west of the trade-blocking rapids, Lachine became a prosperous town. One of its oldest houses, built in 1670 by merchants Jacques Le Ber and Charles LeMoyne, is now the Musée de Lachine, with historical exhibits and an art gallery.

Stones and Laughter

Not all city museums are dedicated to Montréal's history. There are art museums (see Galleries), museums that focus on nature (see Nature & Natural History) and some museums that are just difficult to categorize.

The Centre Canadien d'Architecture (CCA) is a place for serious scholars. Its library has more than 165,000 volumes on various aspects of architecture, and the centre's collection of plans, drawings, models and photographs is the most important of its kind in the world. It also has six well-lit exhibition rooms for rotating exhibits that range from the academic to the whimsical. Recent shows have focused on dollhouses, miniature villages and American lawn culture. All this is housed in an austere, modern building that embraces a grand old mansion built in 1874 for the family of the president of the Canadian Pacific Railway, Sir Thomas Shaughnessy. The house is open to visitors and has a remarkable art nouveau

Bookstore at the CCA

Shaughnessy House Tea Room at the CCA

conservatory with an intricately decorated ceiling. The CCA's most playful exhibit, however, is outside — the architecture designed by artist Melvin Charney. It's stuck in an unlikely spot, between two highway ramps across busy Boulevard René-Lévesque and separated from the museum itself, but its whimsical bits and pieces of architecture perched in unlikely places is a delight.

Musée Juste Pour Rire

The Musée Juste Pour Rire opened in 1993 as an outgrowth of the city's Just for Laughs Comedy Festival, and it seems appropriate somehow that one of the world's few museums dedicated to laughter is housed in an old brewery. The museum uses film clips and old movie sets to explore the history of comedy.

Galleries

Matthew Woodley

Art abounds in Montréal, from works by classical masters to experiences by cutting-edge contemporary artists and everything in between. With all there is to see, even if you're planning on indulging in just a few art spaces, it's a good idea to pick up a Montréal Museums Pass. The $39 package gives three days of access to 30 of the city's art, archaeology and science hot spots. As an added bonus, the pass also permits access to public transport, including the Métro, an arty landmark in its own right, as each of its 65 colourful stations bears the mark of a different architect.

Top: Jean-Noël Desmarais and Benaiah Gibb pavilions (also below). Middle: Ceramic display at the Musée des Beaux-Arts.

An essential stop in the city is the Musée des Beaux-Arts de Montréal, the oldest fine arts museum in Canada, with a permanent collection of over 30,000 works and an ever-impressive series of special exhibitions. The museum is housed in two principal buildings across the street from one another on Sherbrooke O.: the Benaiah Gibb Pavilion and the newer Jean-Noël Desmarais Pavilion. Designed by architect Moshe Safdie, the Desmarais building integrates the façade of an early 20th-century apartment block with a variety of modern materials, from glass to steel, creating a balance between the area's Gothic churches, Victorian houses and the downtown buildings with which they share the cityscape.

One wing of the Desmarais Pavilion houses many of the museum's special exhibitions. Over the years, these shows have included borrowed masterpieces from the Guggenheim in New York and the Hermitage in St. Petersberg and have encompassed themes focusing on such movements as the French avant-garde and the 1960s. The museum also exhibits works by such celebrated artists as Lichtenstein, Colville, Magritte, Picasso, Riopelle and Monet.

L'ÉTANG AUX ANTILLES BY JAMES WILSON MORRICE AT THE MUSÉE DES BEAUX-ARTS DE MONTRÉAL

The museum's Canadian section highlights the history and cultural diversity of the country with an eclectic selection of First Nations, colonial and modern works. Traditional carvings from pre-colonial cultures share the space with works that trace the course of European immigration through paintings, sculpture and furniture. Distinctive landscapes by the Group of Seven hang alongside pivotal works by Paul-Émile Borduas, who, along with a group of like-minded artists, spawned the controversial 1940s Automatisme movement and subsequent anti-establishment manifesto, the *Refus Global*. Works by distinguished Montréal artist Betty Goodwin, whose striking use of the figure as symbol of the human condition, are another highlight.

The museum's European collection spans eras in art from the Middle Ages to present times. There, you can take in 14th-century religious paintings and artifacts, and an extensive collection of Baroque art, featuring French, Italian and Dutch works by masters such as Rembrandt, Emmanuel de Witte and Peter Bruegel the Younger. Nineteenth-century works in the collection have been largely donated by wealthy Montréal families, with a leaning towards the French-realist Barbizon School, including Tissot's famed *October*. Impressionist and post-Impressionist paintings include works by Renoir, Monet and Cézanne, while a sampling of 20th-century works are on display from artists such as Picasso, Matisse and Dali.

The year 2001 marked the opening of the Liliane and David M. Stewart Pavilion, bringing some 700 objects spanning six centuries to the museum's decorative art collection. This acquisition adds to a display of objects donated by several major connoisseurs that includes English porcelain, antique glass and a collection of 3,000 antique Japanese incense boxes, the largest such assembly in the world. Among the pieces in the Mediterranean archaeology collection are Greek and Roman sculptures, as well as woods that have been discovered in the anaerobic sands of Egypt and Luristan bronzes from the 6th to the 4th century B.C. The museum also features a massive art library, the oldest in Canada, with a collection of over 200,000 books, auction catalogues, artist files, slides and CD-ROMs. A reference service is offered to the public on Wednesday afternoons.

Just a few Métro stops from the Museé des Beaux-Arts is the Musée d'Art Contemporain de Montréal, located on the city's main commercial artery, Rue Ste-Catherine. The museum is Montréal's central contemporary art site, which, since 1993, has stood next to Place des Arts, the central performing arts complex and home to the Orchestre Symphonique de Montréal and Les Grands Ballets Canadiens.

The fundamental component of the museum is its vast permanent collection. Some 6,000 works make up the collection, produced by 1,500 artists, 80 percent of whom are still living. An ongoing

JEUNE FILLE AU CHAPEAU BY PIERRE AUGUSTE RENOIR AT THE MUSÉE DES BEAUX-ARTS DE MONTRÉAL

ANCIENT EGYPTIAN CAT

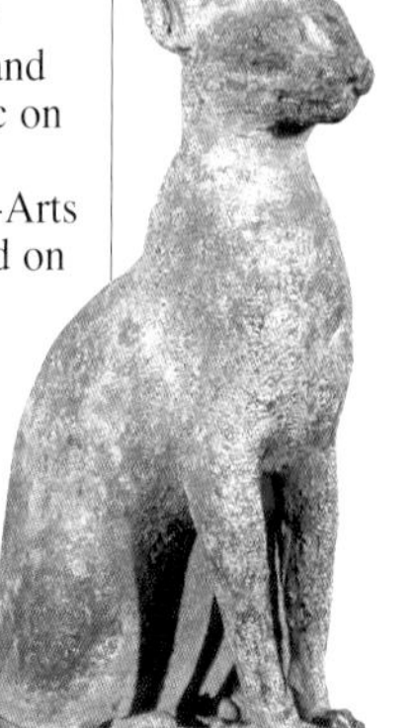

MUSÉE D'ART CONTEMPORAIN DE MONTRÉAL, EXTERIOR (ABOVE) AND INTERIOR (BELOW)

acquisition of works and related research reflecting ever-changing trends in expression keeps the museum on a progressive edge. This approach stems from the Contemporary Arts Society of Montréal. Founded by John Lyman in 1939, the organization fuelled a newfound interest in contemporary art. Since then, the museum has obtained works by major artists such as Picasso, Lichtenstein and Warhol. Given that the museum's principal goal is to conserve and promote Québec art, more than half of its collection originates *chez nous*, including the largest assembly of paintings by Paul-Émile Borduas in the world.

The Salle Beverly Webster Rolph in the lower level of the museum presents art that branches beyond the visual, including modern dance performances, theatre and conferences with established artists. In many senses, these activities define the museum's character, where alongside traditional media, it's not uncommon to find digital creations and interactive installations. A decidedly un-digital experience can be had by stepping out for a breath of fresh air in the sculpture garden, which is accessible through the temporary exhibition area.

The Centre Canadien d'Architecture (CCA), located on Rue Baile, is a prominent landmark on Montréal's Golden Square Mile. The name refers to a district bounded by four streets that held roughly 70 percent of Canada's wealth at the turn of the 20th century and formed roughly a square mile. The CCA is housed in the 125-year-old Maison Shaughnessy, one of the few old Montréal mansions open to the public, and in a modern building that was integrated into the house in 1989. Since then, the structure has won numerous international design awards. Inside the CCA, a collection of works dating from the Renaissance to the present focuses on the art of architecture throughout the world, with a keen eye on the future. Incorporating drawings, models, plans, prints, artifacts and conceptual studies, the CCA exposes the roots of design and presents plenty of fodder for the imagination.

The collection at the Musée Marc-Aurèle Fortin, located on Rue St-Pierre, is solely devoted to the artist of the same name. Fortin is one of Québec's most celebrated painters, recognized for his poetic depiction of the

province's landscapes through its dynamic four seasons and for the glimpse he offers into provincial rural life in the 1900s. His works have a distinctive mosaic quality, with rich colours capturing village scenes and majestic trees, often set against black backgrounds reflecting the mezzotint style he adopted after a stay in Europe in 1935. Before painting his subjects, Fortin would prime the canvas or wood panel in black paint, then would sketch in grey and paint from the tube, adding a characteristic intensity to his hues. The two-storey gallery is housed in a 19th-century building, with exposed brick walls, which add a homey feel to Fortin's work. Though the gallery is solely dedicated to the work of this one artist, it hosts a few temporary exhibitions every year.

Sculpture installations by Pierre Granche, Musée d'Art Contemporain de Montréal

Though it's somewhat off the beaten track, the Liane and Danny Taran Gallery at the Centre des Arts Saidye Bronfman on Chemin de la Côte-Ste-Catherine is a short walk from the Côte-Ste-Catherine Métro station and well worth the trip. The gallery has emerged as one of Montréal's finest in presenting innovative works from both emerging and established artists from places local to international. The Saidye, as it is commonly known, serves its mandate in presenting provocative, often playful, work in all media. Contemporary artists showcased over the years have included Betty Goodwin, Jochen Gerz, Susan Rothenberg and John Scott. Complementing the major exhibitions, the gallery presents conferences, screenings, lectures and other special events.

Inuit art on display at Musée des Beaux-Arts

The Leonard and Bina Ellen Gallery is Concordia University's main art venue, located in the school's urban-integrated campus in the downtown core on Boulevard de Maisonneuve O. The gallery is dedicated to presenting creations by students and graduates of Concordia's innovative fine arts department, one of the most acclaimed in Canada, showcasing a rotating sample throughout the year alongside its permanent collection of over 2,000 works.

Two large buildings on Rue Ste-Catherine O., a mere five-minute walk west from the Musée d'Art Contemporain, house an eclectic array of smaller galleries that can be sampled in an afternoon (please note, though, that many of them close during the summer months). The Belgo Building has emerged from a rundown refuge for struggling local artists to one of the city's most important art spaces, with bright, airy lofts branching off long hallways on several levels. Optica Gallery has a consistent line-up of provocative contemporary exhibitions, while Galerie René Blouin is home to several renowned artists, including Betty Goodwin. Galerie 303, curated by playful local artists the Group of n, is also a good spot to find a fun show. Next door you can find La Centrale, one of Canada's oldest artist-run galleries and the only one dedicated to the diffusion of women's art. Nearby, Dare-Dare Gallery offers exhibitions that poke fun at some aspects of contemporary culture with a political, yet often humorous, bent.

In contrast to the galleries in these two more worked-in buildings, Galerie de Bellefeuille, on Avenue Greene, just inside the borough of Westmount, is an excellent place to see realistic figurative paintings as well as sculptures and limited-edition prints, in an elegant setting. Then there's Gallery VOX's recently opened space on Boulevard St-Laurent, mixed in with the lingering clubs of the former red-light district and the theatres and performances in an area that the city of Montréal is actively converting into an arts district. VOX, which has retained the mirrored ceilings of the former tenants, is responsible for the large biannual Mois de la Photo festival and home to some of the best contemporary photo exhibitions in town. Up the street, Zeke's Gallery curates its exhibitions on the grounds that they must be an artist's first solo show, resulting in a hit-or-miss rotation, yet one that's often worth the risk.

Back in the Old Port, Quartier Éphémère in the Darling Foundry, located on Rue Ottawa, supports up-and-coming artists by providing them with space in old abandoned buildings, including its own: a bright and serene warehouse that opened in 2002. Old Montréal is full of such spaces, as well as many commercial galleries that cater to all areas of interest and taste. With such choice, wonderful art experiences are bound to be had just strolling about the cobblestone streets, peeking through windows and leaving your discoveries to fate.

PHOTOGRAPHY ON DISPLAY ALONG AVENUE MCGILL-COLLEGE

NATURE & NATURAL HISTORY

ANASTASIA MICHAILIDIS

ST. LAWRENCE MARINE ECOSYSTEM IN THE BIODÔME

There are the obvious ways to slip away from the bright lights and hard excitement of the big city. You can hike up Mont Royal, for example, or take the Métro to Île Ste-Hélène for a picnic. But there are other, more exotic ways to get a taste of the wild in Montréal. One of the best is the Biodôme.

BIODÔME

From the outside, Montréal's most popular natural-science museum resembles a bicycle helmet. This isn't as odd as it sounds. It was originally built as a stadium for the 1976 Olympic Games track-cycling races. Its transformation into an ecological museum that re-creates four different ecosystems found in the Americas is remarkable. The animals and most of the plants are real, but their habitat — the cliffs, caves, rocks and even some of the enormous trees — is made of concrete. The rocks conceal most of the water and heating systems that keep the ecosystems functioning, and the enormous concrete trees emit warm, moist air to maintain the proper humidity.

BIODÔME

The Biodôme attracts a million visitors a year,

Tropical Forest and Laurentian beaver in the Biodôme

many of them winter-weary Montréalers who are drawn to the museum's tropical forest, where the temperature never dips below 25 degrees Celsius and the air is heavy with the scent of vegetation. Dozens of animals creep, crawl and scurry amid all that vegetation, most of them quite freely, but the more ferocious (the anaconda, piranha and poison-arrow frogs) are safely behind glass. Many of the residents of the tropical forest belong to endangered species, including the hyacinth macaw, the world's largest species of parrot, and the golden lion tamarin, a cute little primate that is now scarce in its native Brazil. Through its involvement in the global Species Survival Plan, the Biodôme breeds endangered animals in captivity with the ultimate goal of reintroducing them into the wild.

Spring comes slightly earlier in the Biodôme's Laurentian forest than it does in its natural counterpart north of Montréal. But, like the real thing, this exhibit changes with the seasons. Plants become dormant towards the end of the summer, the leaves on the live hardwood trees turn red and yellow and fall in the autumn, and leaves and blossoms reappear and the cycle begins anew in the spring. Among the inhabitants of this ecosystem are dozens of species of fish, along with reptiles, birds and mammals such as beavers, porcupines and lynx.

The main feature of the St. Lawrence marine ecosystem is a glass-walled tank holding 2.5 million litres of sea water produced by the Biodôme itself. As you stroll by, you can spot 20 different species of fish, including cod, halibut and salmon. Eventually, the pathway leads to a saltwater marsh and past a rocky shore basin filled with starfish, sea anemones and crabs.

St. Lawrence Marine Ecosystem in the Biodôme

The subpolar regions of the Arctic and Antarctica are both represented at the Biodôme's polar ecosystem. You'll find puffins at the subarctic exhibit, while the subantarctic exhibit features those ever-lovable penguins. Don't worry about getting cold; you can watch the antics of the birds from a glassed-in corridor that protects you from these frosty climates.

Another recommended stop is the Naturalia Discovery Room. Find it by following the green frog tracks. This is an exploration and discovery room where touching is encouraged. You can inspect a whale bone, stroke an otter pelt or examine a feather under a microscope. The nature guides on duty organize special games and demonstrations for children.

You can enjoy the Biodôme's ecosystems at your own pace. An easy-to-follow pathway leads you through the different environments. Information panels are posted along the way, and nature guides are on patrol to answer your questions. And if travelling from the humid heat of the tropical forest to the cool air of the Laurentian forest makes you hungry, there's a restaurant on site. There's also a souvenir shop where you'll find neat stuff like bat houses and bug-catching kits.

Polar World penguins at the Biodôme

Reception garden at Jardin Botanique

Jardin Botanique de Montréal

If you visit the Jardin Botanique de Montréal during the summer, you're likely to come across at least one wedding party posing for photographs in one of the 30 outdoor gardens. There are many stunning locations within the botanical garden's 185 acres. One of the most popular is the refined Japanese garden. Here, every plant and rock has

been carefully placed to create a meditative atmosphere. An elegant pavilion at the entrance houses a tea room where the Japanese tea ritual is often enacted. The Jardin Botanique de Montréal is also the site of the largest Chinese garden outside of Asia, as well as a pond garden, an alpine garden and a superb rose garden filled with the perfume of 10,000 bushes. But the newest attraction is a singular achievement. The First Nations garden, inaugurated in 2001, is inspired by Amerindian and Inuit cultures. It highlights native use of plants and trees, from growing corn, squash and beans, to gathering berries and medicinal plants, to building homes and canoes. A pavilion houses a permanent exhibition that includes a slide show on contemporary native lifestyles and a gift shop selling native art and handicrafts.

If you want ideas for your own perennial garden, this is the place to come. And if you've wondered what cooking herbs and medicinal plants look like before they're dried and stuffed into a jar, there's a collection of healthy, live

Above: Chinese garden at the Jardin Botanique de Montréal
Below: The magic of lanterns in the Chinese garden every fall

specimens. There's also a garden of plants to avoid. No matter how good a diagram may be, it's much easier to identify poison ivy in the wild if you've already seen the live plant.

Construction of the Jardin began in the early years of the Great Depression, funded partly by federal and provincial make-work project grants. Directed and inspired by its founder, Frère Marie-Victorin, it has grown to become one of the world's leading horticultural centres. There are 21,000 species on display. A sightseeing train can help you cover the grounds quickly, or you can stroll at your own pace along one of the many nature trails.

Each fall, from early September through till the end of October, the Chinese garden stays open until 9 P.M. to host La Magie des Lanternes, or the Magic of Lanterns. Thousands of silk lanterns handcrafted in Shanghai twinkle as night falls, transforming the garden into an illuminated sanctuary. It is a truly spectacular sight to behold.

When snow covers the outdoor gardens in the winter, the trails are taken over by cross-country skiers, but if you'd rather pretend you're in the desert or the tropics, you can amble through 10 connected greenhouses and admire the orchids, cacti and banana plants. The main greenhouse stages special annual events, such as a pumpkin-decorating contest at Halloween and Christmas and Easter shows.

In the Chlorophyll Room children learn about plant life, and for adults there are horticultural clinics throughout the year. One of the most popular clinics is the mushroom-identification session, which takes place in the fall.

ABOVE: WIGWAM FRAME
BELOW: FIRST NATION DISPLAYS

INSECTARIUM

Montréal's Insectarium started with one man's personal fascination with bugs. For many years Georges Brossard travelled the world collecting insects of every size, shape and colour. He identified and mounted thousands of specimens, but his spectacular collection was hidden like a

buried treasure in his basement. Fortunately, he managed to persuade the city of Montréal to build a museum to house it, and now anyone can see and learn about the creatures that some people have described as our rivals for control of the Earth.

Even if you've spent most of your life thinking that insects are repulsive, your loathing will turn to intrigue when you see their amazing variety. There are insects that look like green leaves, dry leaves, sticks or thorns, and insects that reflect every colour of the rainbow. The colours and patterns on the wings of the butterflies and moths are stunningly beautiful. Many varieties of beetles have such brilliant metallic bodies that people make jewellery out of them, and you'll be astonished at how big some of them get.

ABOVE AND BELOW: INSECTARIUM EXTERIOR AND EXHIBITS

Not all the insects are dead and mounted. The Insectarium has several live exhibits. Stroll through a room where butterflies fly freely from flower to flower, watch bees come and go through a glass-cased hive to the Jardin Botanique outside, or observe ants at work in a wall-length ant farm.

From time to time the Insectarium becomes a restaurant of sorts, serving up delectable dishes such as biscuits made of ground-up beetles and chocolate-covered grasshoppers. Believe it or not, this event attracts 20,000 insect gourmets.

Yes, people do try the samples and although most prefer their insect tidbits in a disguised form, many happily crunch right into a cricket or gobble up a mouthful of larvae. This event is organized only occasionally, but if you are really tempted to have a taste you can buy a cookbook specializing in insect cuisine at the Insectarium's boutique. With recipes in hand, you'll be ready to cook up a feast anytime, any place....

BIOSPHÈRE

Did you know that less than 1 percent of all the water on Earth is fresh and available for use by living organisms? And did you know that the water formed 3.8 billion years ago is the same water that exists today and will exist in the future? The water that made up a tear in Cleopatra's eye could be part of that apple you are about to bite into.

Everything you could possibly want to know about water you can learn at the Biosphère, an interactive museum dedicated to our most precious resource. The Biosphère is on Île Ste-Hélène, in the St. Lawrence River. The location is fitting because the St. Lawrence is one of the great rivers of the world, flowing out of the Great Lakes, which themselves make up one-fifth of the world's supply of fresh water. The Biosphère's exhibition halls are designed to entertain and educate. Discovery Hall focuses on how essential water is on earth. Most of the fascinating facts about water are stored in interactive terminals. They are easy to operate, with touch-screen technology, but it's a slow process because you have to wait for the screens to reload. A giant globe and large-scale models are more interesting for younger children.

INTERACTIVE EXHIBITS AT THE BIOSPHÈRE

FINDING OUT HOW WATER WORKS AT THE BIOSPHÉRE

The Water Delights exhibit lets you experience water as a source of pleasure and a medium for recreation. Take a virtual trip down a ski hill, squirt at targets with a water pistol and compose your own water music. Finally, treat your feet to a refreshing dip in a pool of water. There are stacks of pastel towels available for drying off.

As a member of the EcoWatch Network for conservation, the Biosphère encourages environmental awareness through education. Its EcoAction Hall is a reference centre with access to computer databases and a library with more than 2,000 books, documents and videos about water. By the time you have completed your tour you will understand the cyclical nature of water: water evaporates into the sky, falls back to earth, penetrates plants and animals, flows through streams, is piped in and out of our homes, and returns to the water cycle. When it comes into contact with pollutants it picks them up and carries them along. Because we all share the water that is on this planet, the way each of us uses it affects the people who will come into contact with it down the line, and because that line draws a circle, the people affected along the circle could be ourselves.

The Biosphère is worth a visit for the simple admiration of the sphere itself. Buckminster Fuller's enormous geodesic dome was built for the United States pavilion at Expo '67. A fire destroyed its acrylic skin in 1976 but left the impressive skeleton that surrounds the museum. The Visions Hall at the very top of the Biosphère and the outdoor observation deck provide a magnificent view of Montréal and the St. Lawrence River.

BIOSPHÈRE

SHOPPING

EMMA MCKAY

FAUBOURG MERCHANT DISPLAYING TIBETAN TEXTILES

Montréal is one of North America's premier shopping destinations. From next year's trends to turn-of-the-century treasures, this uniquely cosmopolitan city is sure to assuage every retail craving. One of the great things about shopping in this city is that the main retail streets are all relatively close to one another. Even so, shoppers — especially those on foot — might want to set aside more than just one day to see it all. Many spend a whole day in Old Montréal alone, which is filled with art galleries and antique shops as well as the ubiquitous souvenir shops filled with cheap trinkets made in faraway places. But chances are that the perfect souvenir is waiting elsewhere in the city.

There may be a memento hiding in Antique Alley on Rue Notre-Dame O. Two long stretches between Avenue Atwater and Rue Guy boast a string of stores that stock antiques and collectibles to fit all budgets and suitcases. Or perhaps a treasure lies nestled in the Golden Square Mile downtown, where the bankers and railway barons who built Montréal in the 19th and early 20th centuries lived. This is still a tony district, and the shops along Rue Sherbrooke are some of the city's finest. Those who live for designer labels will want to peruse Rue Peel, being sure to stop in at the Cours Mont-Royal mall. The same crowd that frequents these boutiques also patronizes nearby Avenue Greene in Westmount, which features more exclusive establishments. The wares on Sherbrooke and Greene are complemented by offerings uptown on Avenue Laurier. The stretch between Boulevard St-Laurent and

THE BAY

Chemin de la Côte-Ste-Catherine is home to many unique and generally upscale shops.

To sample the city's latest styles, St-Laurent and St-Denis are the streets to visit. Nestled among the nightclubs and restos are a bevy of mod-ish shops vying to spot trends first. Hard-core bargain hunters should trek out to the Rue Chabanel area at the northern end of St-Laurent. It's home to the city's garment district, and showrooms in the factory buildings are filled with men's and women's fashions at wholesale prices.

SIMONS

Remember that most stores are open from 10 A.M. to 6 P.M. on Monday through Wednesday, 10 A.M. to 9 P.M. on Thursday and Friday, 10 A.M. to 5 P.M. on Saturday, and noon to 5 P.M. on Sunday. If you're a foreign visitor, remember to save your receipts because you can claim a refund on the 7 percent Goods and Services Tax when you leave the country. The GST is levied on just about all goods except basic groceries.

CLOTHING

Montréal is known for its jaw-dropping style, and as you begin to get a feel for the city, chances are that you'll be driven to refresh your own wardrobe to better blend in with the locals. From thrift-shop threads to designer digs, it's all here.

Rue St-Denis boasts many specialty shops like the Boutique Médiévale Excalibor, which stocks an array of one-of-a-kind period dresses (and outfits many a medieval bride) as well as an arresting collection of decorative swords, knives and jewellery. Another interesting niche for seafaring folk to explore is Depart en Mer, which stocks the kind of clothing needed for sailing trips, as well as unique gifts and decorations for diehard mariners.

Those who love vintage clothes but don't want to rummage around in dusty bins for them will want to check

FRIPERIE ST-LAURENT

out some of Montréal's famous friperies. Requin Chagrin on St-Denis is one such place, as is Montréal Fripe on Avenue du Mont-Royal and Friperie St-Laurent on St-Laurent at Avenue Duluth. Eva B., on St-Laurent below Sherbrooke, carries a mélange of vintage clothes, creations by local designers and an assortment of shoes and accessories. Natural-fabric fanatics might want to visit Je L'ai, a boutique filled with all things hemp, including clothing, located on Duluth, not far from St-Laurent.

FIDEL

Fidel is a Montréal-based label that has become increasingly popular in recent years. From trendy T-shirts to quasi-couture, the St-Denis boutique outfits its patrons in youthful style. Bedo is another clothing line that originated here. Its collection ranges from basics to fun and funkier pieces, and overall, it's quite reasonably priced. There are about six Bedo shops in Montréal, including one on St-Denis, another on Ste-Catherine and an outlet at the corner of St-Laurent and St-Joseph, at which there are some great deals to be had.

The tried-and-true chains, such as Mexx, Gap, Roots and Le Château, can be found on St-Denis close to Rue Rachel as well as on Ste-Catherine in the downtown core.

The stretch of St-Laurent between Sherbrooke and Avenue des Pins might be considered the center of style in Montréal. In these few blocks is a range of boutiques to suit eclectic tastes. Soho Mtl is worth a look for its selection of shoes and fashionable clothing for men and

Shopping on Ste-Catherine

women. Space FB is a local institution, filled with hot tracksuits and simple but flattering T-shirts in brilliant colours and soft, clingy fabrics. Those who like basics with a twist, or sweats that are equally at home in the gym and on the city streets, will find this the ultimate destination. For breathtaking and utterly unique style, U&I can't be beat. West of St-Laurent on Rue Prince Arthur, a few higher-end boutiques have opened their doors in recent years. One of these, IMA, carries designs by David Bitton, best known for his more widely accessible Buffalo clothing line, which specializes in denim.

It's worthwhile to save some time for Ste-Catherine. The street is home to most of the city's malls and some of its seediest strip clubs, and shop windows are filled with colour year-round. The street has enjoyed a revitalization of sorts in recent years, evident in the abundance of new boutiques and buildings that stretch from Rue University westward to Atwater. One such new development is the Caban store on the corner of Ste-Catherine and Avenue McGill-College. It carries all the "essentials" for modern life, from martini glasses to patio furniture to bathrobes to denim.

There are elegant staples for both men and women at InWear/Matinique. A little further down the road, BCBG carries that special something to spruce up every wardrobe, be it evening wear or office attire. Olam, with locations on both St-Denis and Ste-Catherine, is filled with vibrant pieces that will take clients from the beach to the bar and beyond.

And fashion-forward shoppers can't forget to accessorize. For lovely soft leather bags in unexpected colours, visit Rudsak. The shop also carries leather jackets, belts and other wearable treasures for both men and women.

When it comes to style, Montréal is always a step ahead. It's a given that it's home to the hippest of chains: Urban Outfitters, a massive shop filled with all kinds of novel and funky paraphernalia for living. But digging a little deeper reveals shops unique to Montréal, filled with the work of local designers and fresh gear that can't be found elsewhere. Young hip-hop heads flock to shops such as City Styles and Off the Hook, both of which overlook Ste-Catherine from second-floor vantage points. Those in the know will also visit FLY, which carries a wide selection of urban attire from established labels as well as up-and-coming Montréal-based designers.

Shoes

If stylish Montréalers can agree on one point, it's that shoes are the most important

part of any outfit. Whether it's Cinderella slippers or pavement pounders, there's no shortage of selection in this town. The typical chains, such as Aldo, Transit, Simard, Brown's and Footlocker, are well represented, with shops along St-Denis and Ste-Catherine. But there is an increasing number of smaller specialty shops that carry footwear the rest of the world isn't wearing yet.

You might want some sensible shoes for walking around town. Try Sena, at the corner of Rachel and St-Denis, for brands such as Ecco, Birkenstock and Rockport. Or you might just want to get a comfortable pair of running shoes at Boutique Courir on St-Denis, which carries all kinds of clothing and gear for running and other outdoor activities. For sneakers that put the "fun" in "functional," check out La Godasse, with locations on St-Denis and St-Laurent. They've got all the latest models, as well as simpler old-school styles from brands such as New Balance and Saucony in a rainbow of colours that can be hard to find anywhere else.

Top: UN Iceland boots
Above Left: Boutique Courir
Above right: Mona Moore shoes

For dressier shoes, try UN Iceland on Ste-Catherine or, if money is no object, stop in at Mona Moore on Sherbrooke. The window displays never fail to entice, and it's easy to dream if you don't check the price.

Jewellery

There's much that glitters in Montréal — it all depends on what you're looking for. Start at Birks, a Montréal institution. Many an engagement ring and anniversary gift has been purchased here. Birks deals in fine jewellery and also has a wonderful selection of silverware and china.

A short distance further east on Ste-Catherine, there are a number of small but excellent jewellers that deal primarily in gold but sell a wide selection of other trinkets. For something a little more specialized, visit AmberLux in the Promenades de la Cathédrale. Here the jewellery comes in all shapes and sizes but only one colour: amber.

For something a little more low-key, stroll through Carré Phillips, nestled in the shadow of the Birks building. Weather permitting, it's filled with artisans and entrepreneurs selling a range of items, from handmade, one-of-a-kind treasures to imported costume jewellery.

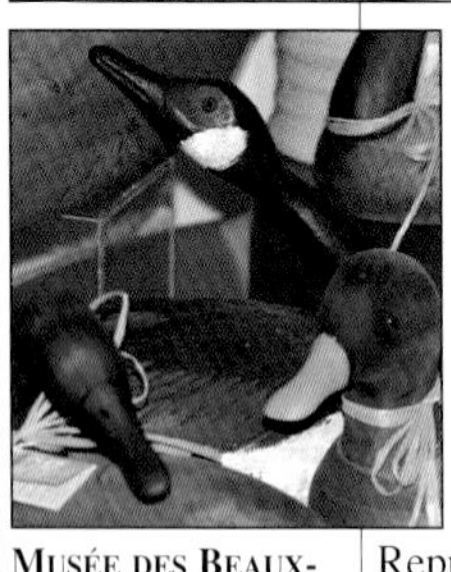

Musée des Beaux-Arts

Galerie Walter Klinkhoff

Art

Art is in the eye of the beholder, so it's hard to recommend any one gallery in Montréal. Shoppers who are willing to do a little exploring will certainly find one to suit their tastes. The two best areas for this quest are Rue St-Paul in Old Montréal and Rue Sherbrooke O. downtown, between Rue de la Montagne and Rue Guy. Both are lined with numerous galleries that are wonderful places to browse. Many galleries feature the canvasses and prints of established artists from Canada and abroad. Representative of the spectrum are Galerie Laroches and Galerie Parchemine in Old Montréal and Galerie Walter Klinkhoff on Sherbrooke.

Galerie de Chariot, at Place Jacques-Cartier, bills itself as the largest collection of Inuit art in Canada, with an exquisite collection of soapstone and whalebone carvings from the country's northern communities. Take a look at what this gallery has to offer before buying a cheap imitation in a souvenir shop.

In the summer months artists display their wares at the corner of McGill-College and Ste-Catherine and on parts of St-Paul in Old Montréal. There are reasonably priced watercolours and sketches of the city to take home as souvenirs.

The Musée des Beaux-Arts de Montréal has a fantastic gift shop. The selection is always changing to reflect the exhibits on display at the museum and includes posters, reproductions, art books and much more.

Antiques

Excursions along Antique Alley on Rue Notre-Dame O. are always good for surprises. This strip is bliss for collectors of curios and artifacts from bygone eras. "Antiquing" is a popular Sunday afternoon pastime for Montréalers, so it may be wise to visit in the middle of the week to avoid the crowds. Noteworthy shops in the alley include Antiques Hubert, Spazio and Grand Central.

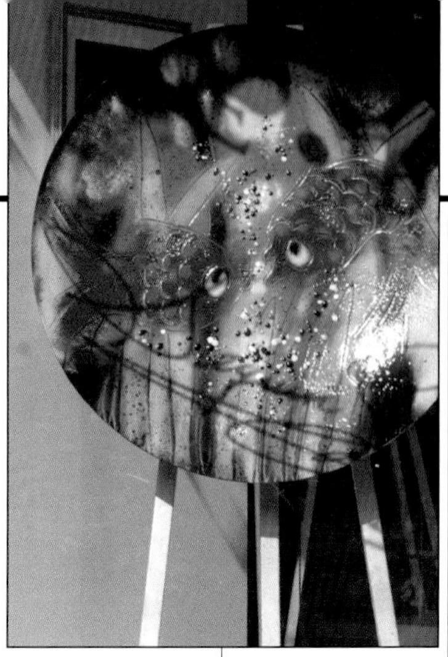

Gallery on Sherbrooke

Le Village des Antiquaries concentrates several dealers under one roof. Some deal in old jewellery, others in furniture, still others in vintage clothing. There's something for everyone at this location.

Milord sells elegant European furniture, mirrors and the like. Shifting gears, the Salvation Army's giant thrift store is like a year-round garage sale. Located at the eastern end of Antique Alley, it offers browsers a chance to prove that one person's castaway is indeed another's antique. A smattering of other antique stores can be found around town, notably in Old Montréal and on Avenue Greene in the borough of Westmount.

Collectibles

Collectors who can't go another day without that particular baseball card or memorial buffs who'd get a thrill from buying a hockey stick autographed by Jean Béliveau will find a few shops in Montréal to feed their obsessions.

Gift Shop at the Musée des Beaux-Arts

Sports collectors won't want to miss Antiques Lucie Favreau on Rue Notre-Dame O., which specializes in sports memorabilia. Even those who aren't buying will enjoy taking a look at the amazing items in stock. It's like visiting a sports hall of fame.

A few steps away is Retroville, a paradise for lovers of all things vintage. For sale are old magazines, toys, neon signs, Coca-Cola collectibles and much, much more. Pause Retro is a similar sort of nostalgia store on Rue St-Denis, with an emphasis on sports cards.

Books

Montréal is a bibliophile's paradise. Amazingly, quite a few independent bookstores have survived — and even thrive — in this city. The western part of Ste-Catherine

VORTEX BOOKS

has developed into a tidy little book district with a number of small used-book shops. Notable are Vortex, which carries literary works, and Argo, which boasts a number of art books. It's easy to lose track of the time while browsing through the selection of books and music at Cheap Thrills, located just southwest of McGill University. In the McGill ghetto, a few blocks east of the main campus, visit The Word, a tiny shop that carries used textbooks at the beginning of each semester but stocks a wide selection of other works too.

For new books, try Paragraphe, at the corner of McGill-College and Sherbrooke; it has an excellent selection of literature. And there's no shortage of specialty stores. The Double Hook in Westmount (named for the modernist novel by Canadian writer Sheila Watson) stocks books exclusively by Canadian authors, many of whom don't get wide distribution in chain stores. Ulysses travel bookstore stocks guidebooks and maps for just about every place on the planet. Bibliophile on Chemin Queen Mary specializes in Judaica, and the Diocesan Book Room in the Promenades de la Cathédrale mall specializes in Christian books. Ethnic Origins, across from the Lionel-Groulx Métro station, specializes in books from the African and African-American diaspora.

The biggest bookstore in the city is Chapters' flagship store for Montréal on Rue Ste-Catherine O. It has four floors of books and a comfortable, library-like atmosphere that encourages readers to linger. The in-house Starbucks coffee shop makes it even more attractive. The store sells books on just about every topic imaginable. Indigo Books in the Place Montréal Trust stocks a wide variety of books and sells a range of delightful objects for the home in addition to cards, stationery and other paper items.

FURNITURE AT ATMOSPHÈRE

HOUSEWARES

There's no place like home — and with the range of housewares available in Montréal, home bodies can create an abode like no other. In the past couple of years, a mini furniture district has come into being along Boulevard St-Laurent, just south of Avenue du Mont-Royal. The shops display goods straight from the latest home décor magazines, as well as vintage gems and all the basics needed to outfit a stylish home. There's also an assortment of shops that cater to domestic needs, from bathrooms to patios, along Rue St-Denis. Morphée carries stylish furniture, but if there's no room in your suitcase for a sofa, no problem — it's got a great selection of smaller accessories too. The pieces at Atmosphère bridge the gap between furniture and art. The shop is worth a look, even if redecoration isn't in your immediate plans. A little further down St-Denis, Côté Sud has lots of enticing items for the home, from novel gifts to must-have classics.

FURNITURE AT ATMOSPHÈRE

The welcoming blue-and-yellow prints in the window of Senteurs de Provence will catch your eye — if the delicate scents wafting out the door don't grab you first. This is the place for stocking up on all things Provence: tablecloths, ceramics, soaps, even bolts of fabric.

Along Ste-Catherine, Caban has eye-catching and mouth-watering goods for the house and home. It's brimming with stylish gifts to take home for friends and family — or for yourself! To give your surroundings a slightly younger, funky feel, browse through Urban Outfitters, also on Ste-Catherine. From shower curtains to lampshades, this is the place for fun items that shoppers elsewhere might

TOP: CHINATOWN GATES
ABOVE: SHOPPING IN CHINATOWN

otherwise spend months hunting down.

Stroll through Chinatown, on the northern border of Old Montréal, to look for tableware from teapots to rice cookers, plates to chopsticks. A number of shops sell exquisite items at unbelievable prices. It's worth taking a good look around.

ELECTRONICS

For gadgets galore, Boulevard St-Laurent between Avenue du Président-Kennedy and Rue Sherbrooke is the place to visit. This strip is home to numerous stores dealing in discount electronics that include items such as TVs and DVD players. These are generally grey-market items, semi-legally imported from the United States or other countries. Great deals can be had for those who know what they're buying, but ask about warranties, and be prepared to haggle.

Those who prefer to read prices on tags will like nearby Audiotronic or Dumoulin La Place. Both offer a similar range of consumer electronics at decent prices, and both also stock camera equipment. Audiotronic has another shop on Ste-Catherine near the behemoth Future Shop, a Canadian chain that sells relatively low-priced computer equipment, home electronics, CDs and DVDs.

RECORDS

Montréal may march to the beat of a different drum, but music lovers can find just about any rhythm they desire in the city's multiple music stores. The biggest and loudest is HMV's main store on the corner of Peel and Ste-Catherine. There are three floors of selections to choose from, with the main floor now dominated by racks of reasonably priced DVDs.

One of HMV's closest competitors is Archambault, with two locations further east along Ste-Catherine: one in the Les Ailes de la Mode complex, and the other at the corner of Rue Berri. Besides CDs, Archambault locations carry a large collection of sheet music and songbooks.

Montréal's cultural mosaic is well represented in the musical selection available at smaller record shops, several of which also stock a wide range of used vinyl. Check out Pop Shop on St-Laurent for CDs and vinyl that reflect Montréal's cosmopolitan character, or visit Primitive on St-Denis, which also has a terrific selection of CDs and vinyl.

OINK OINK

CAMERAS

Camera buffs will want to visit Simon Cameras. It's an old-fashioned camera store that looks as if it hasn't changed since Kodak introduced its first Brownie. They have all the latest camera technology as well as an excellent selection of used equipment.

Another great source for camera equipment is Image Point, on Ste-Catherine. Visitors who need to have something fixed or just more film can stop by Place Victoria Cameras near Old Montréal — it carries all the essentials and the service can't be beat.

GAMES & TOYS

This city boasts a fantastic array of toys for children of all ages. Stop by Le Valet d'Cœur on St-Denis for its awesome selection of games as well as its collection of gadgets and playthings to stimulate creative exploration. And it's not just for kids — in stock are board games for grown-up get-togethers, Tarot cards and novel knick-knacks sure to amuse and delight. Further down St-Denis is FrancJeu, full of art supplies, toys and games for children. Stop by the shop to pick up a copy of the calendar of free Saturday-morning workshops — kids can take their projects home with them.

A refreshing alternative to the world of mass-produced plastic toys can be found on Avenue Duluth, at a charming little shop called La Grande Ourse. The beautiful handmade wooden toys here are designed to engage young minds and to endure the test of time. And on Avenue Greene in Westmount, Oink Oink has a great selection of top-quality toys.

ODDS & ENDS

Many of the shops that make shopping in Montréal such a unique experience don't fit into any conventional categories — all the more reason to visit them. One such shop is Kamikaze

Curiosités on St-Denis, which purveys fanciful socks and accessories. Shoppers entering this place may notice a faint odor reminiscent of a smoky nightclub. Indeed, they're not mistaken. By night, the racks are pushed aside, and this space is converted into a bar!

MÉLANGE MAGIQUE

Further up on St-Denis is Rubans, Boutons, a store that sells only buttons and ribbons. These items aren't on your shopping list? No matter — the overwhelming selection is a wonder to browse, and few shoppers leave empty-handed.

Those who fold for fancy paper products will want to visit L'Essence du Papier. This charming St-Denis boutique has a lovely selection of stationeries and cards. Another paper store to visit is the Japanese Paper Store on Avenue St-Viateur, which sells delightful handmade paper products and offers a number of workshops on making paper, kites, lanterns and other imaginative creations.

Montréal's Dix Mille Villages, one of a growing chain of fair-trade café-shops in the U.S. and Canada offering products made by artisans in developing countries, allows its customers the satisfaction of knowing that their purchase will make a positive impact on real people's lives. It's a great place to find gifts or to stop and enjoy a cup of coffee before resuming the trek down St-Denis.

For frequent travellers, Jet-Setter on Avenue Laurier has every sort of travel gadget anyone could possibly need, along with more traditional items such as suitcases, backpacks and outdoor wear. Another shop for travellers is Tilley Endurables, also on Laurier. Tilley sells sensible travel clothing but is best known for its hats, which inspire a cult-like devotion among wearers.

Maybe it's the French influence, but more than a few shops in Montréal carry toys for adults. One of these, La Capoterie on St-Denis, specializes in condoms. This isn't a sex shop with gag gifts but rather a place for playful couples to have fun shopping for contraceptives.

Another shop to visit is Mélange Magique, which offers something for every New Age need. And no matter what the time of year, it's always holiday time at Noël Éternel, a shop that only sells Christmas goodies.

Finally, what visit to Montréal would be complete without a trip to the home of its hockey heroes, the Canadiens? The Bell Centre souvenir shop should be on the itinerary of any sports fan. It has jerseys, books, photos and many other items that are tough to find elsewhere.

FESTIVALS & EVENTS

BRAM EISENTHAL

Montréal has its problems, economic and political, but no city in North America is better at throwing a party. It's a tradition that goes back at least as far as Expo '67, the world's fair that marked Canada's 100th birthday, and it continues to the present day. Every summer is filled with festivals, from late June until Labour Day.

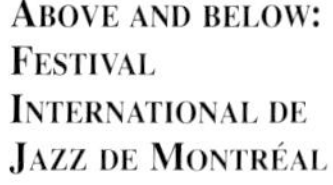

ABOVE AND BELOW: FESTIVAL INTERNATIONAL DE JAZZ DE MONTRÉAL

The granddaddy of all these celebrations is the Festival des Films du Monde, or World Film Festival (WFF), founded by Serge Losique in 1977. This celluloid showcase presents a plethora of films from more than 60 countries. It's the only competitive festival in North America recognized by the International Federation of Film Producers Association; winning films in competition receive the prestigious Grand Prix of the Americas and other prizes. Held the final week of August through Labour Day, the WFF screens some 400 films (250 features and 150 shorts) plus a dozen or so outdoor ones. The city is rapidly becoming one of the main film-production locales in North America. In recent years stars such as Marlon Brando, Richard Gere, Denzel Washington, Bette Midler, Ben Kingsley, Charlie Sheen, Mira Sorvino, Ewan McGregor, Aidan Quinn and Québec's own

Donald Sutherland have come to the city to work and to play. During the film festival you can usually increase your odds of spotting a star by hanging around Boulevard St-Laurent after the show.

Outdoor festival sites have serious clout — the streets around the Place des Arts complex are closed to vehicle traffic for much of the summer as one celebration flows after another. The first major event of the festival season is the Festival International de Jazz de Montréal, which fills the first two weeks of July with concerts and jam sessions. This is one of the premier jazz fests around, attracting performers such as Manhattan Transfer, Chick Corea, Count Basie, Dave Van Ronk, France's Orchestre National de Barbes and Canada's hottest singer-pianist, Diana Krall. Virtually every big-name jazz entertainer and band has appeared here since the festival's debut — including many legends. In addition to ticketed events, there are more than 300 free outdoor concerts, some attracting as many as 100,000 people.

Top: Performance at Festival International de Jazz

Above: Just for Laughs Comedy Festival

The Just for Laughs Comedy Festival hasn't been around as long as the other two. It began as a humble two-night French-language show that attracted little attention, and it laboured for the first couple of years in the shadow of the jazz festival. But its founders — Gilbert Rozon and Andy Nulman — have turned it into the most important festival of its kind in the world. Just for Laughs fills two weeks in July with more than 1,300 shows and performances, indoors and out. Many of the performers are household names — people like Jerry Seinfeld, Tim Allen, Roseanne Barr, Michael Richards, Drew Carey, John Candy, Rowan (Mr. Bean) Atkinson, Sandra Bernhard, Sinbad, Mary Tyler Moore, Marcel Marceau and the late George Burns — but this is also where many new comics get their first real recognition. Comedians like Mike McDonald and Bowser and Blue, for example, make a point of appearing as often as they can. It's wise to book early if you're thinking of attending, especially the French and English Gala performances and the most popular events.

Almost 40,000 people seeking a mid-June event whose motto is "no artistic direction, no minimum standards and no limits" attended 2003's Festival St-Ambroise Fringe de Montréal (Montréal Fringe Festival), a theatrical celebration of differences and, often, lunacy, as some of the more unusual acts you have ever encountered play the city's venues. Acts range from comedy to dance, drama and musical performances.

MONTRÉAL INTERNATIONAL FIREWORKS COMPETITION

While these three festivals attract most summer tourists to Montréal, there are a slew of smaller events year-round that add to the charm and excitement of this city that never sleeps, where joie de vivre brings people back year after year. Festival des Nuits d'Afrique in mid-July is a celebration of African and Creole film, dance and music.

The event that opens the summer season is arguably the most beautiful to gaze at: the Mondial SAQ, or the Montréal International Fireworks Competition. Incendiary masters from around the world light up the night skies over Montréal every weekend between June 12 and July 28, with some midweek displays thrown in. These spectacles have become so popular that the best viewpoint, the Pont Jacques-Cartier (Jacques Cartier Bridge), is often clogged with spectators and closed to traffic from 10 P.M. to midnight. Prizes are awarded to the winning entries.

If hot-air ballooning is your passion, investigate the Festival des Montgolfières, held at nearby St-Jean-sur-Richelieu (half an hour south by car, over the Pont Champlain). Enthusiasts from around the world assemble to share some hot air, fly their contraptions and fill the skies with yet more beauty for all to behold. You can take a ride in a balloon for a fee, weather permitting. This festival is held at the middle of August.

For something a little more traditional, try the Festival de la Gibelotte in Sorel, a 90-minute drive downriver from Montréal. Gibelotte is a robust stew made with barbotte, a fatty, flaky species of catfish that lives in the waters around the Îles de Sorel. Every August, the cooks of the town make gallons of the stuff and serve it up with bread and locally brewed beer in one of the finest and most cheerful street festivals in the province. Beer lovers can also attend Montréal's Mondial de la Bière, a five-day outdoor extravaganza that attracts some 25,000 brew fans. It's held in early- to mid-June at the Quai Jacques-Cartier in the Old Port and provides an opportunity to sample beer from breweries such as McAuslan's (St. Ambroise) and Les Brasseurs du Nord (the Boréale line). The Ontario-based Sleeman Brewing and Malting Company has been making sudsy waves in the field and is well represented at this gathering.

LES FRANCOFOLIES DE MONTRÉAL

The Holocaust Education Series, held mid-October to mid-November, is much more than that. Free activities held citywide include lectures by world-class speakers, panel discussions, films and a variety of exhibitions. The series culminates with the moving commemoration of Kristalnacht, or the Night of Broken Glass, the shattering events of November 9-10, 1939, considered to be the turning point for the Jews of Europe. Wednesday nights till 9 P.M. during the month, admission to the new Montréal Holocaust Museum is free of charge.

TOUR DE L'ÎLE DE MONTRÉAL

The Présence Autochtone, or First People's Festival (2005 marks the 15th festival), is a 12-day exploration of film, dance, crafts, music and workshops that ends with events on Mont Royal to mark the summer solstice on National Aboriginal Day, June 21. Some 50,000 people attend.

Outdoor urban events proliferate during the summer. Two of the best are the Tour de l'Île de Montréal and Les Francofolies de Montréal. The first is the world's largest gathering of cyclists, attracting some 40,000 riders for a 66-kilometre route through the city in early June. The tour generally marks the end of the Féria du Vélo de Montréal (Montréal Bike Fest), which includes a children's tour and a night tour held the preceding week. Les Francofolies are equally impressive, bringing some 1,000 musicians into the open at Place des Arts. Rock, pop, hip-hop, jazz, funk and Latin music are just some of the rhythms you'll hear in late July and early August — *en français,* of course.

Finally, back to film festivals. You just can't escape them. Some of the others held throughout the year include the Montréal International Festival of Cinema and New Media, previously held during the summer but now moved to the fall to avoid scheduling clashes with the major competition. This festival features unusual films as well as interesting venues — virtually every place but movie theatres. A New York version of this event has been held as well. Cinemania celebrates French films with English subtitles. Maidy Teitelbaum, the wife of an entrepreneur who owns a large chain of lingerie stores, loved French films and wanted to share that joy with other English-speaking movie fans, so she and a tiny staff cobbled this festival together on a shoestring budget. It has become quite respectable after several years and is worth a visit if you're in Montréal in November. Teitelbaum is showing more and more premières, often with the stars and directors in attendance. The venue is the Musée des Beaux-Arts de Montréal.

The Jewish Film Festival is a small event that showcases the best of international filmmaking. Movies presented by creator-president Susan Alper feature viewpoints representative of Jewish culture, with topics such as the Holocaust, Israel and modern Jewish issues. The festival runs in March, coinciding with a similarly named but unrelated event in Toronto.

Finally, one of my personal favourites is FanTasia, The International Festival of Fantastic Cinema. It started in 1996 primarily as a vehicle for Asian action and fantasy films and rapidly became a celebration of international horror, sci-fi and fantasy, a lot like France's now-defunct Avoriaz Festival used to be. Screenings, in the classic old Imperial Theatre, are generally sold out. Many premières feature the directors. This month-long festival begins in the middle of July, which should add to your sweet dilemma: How many festivals can I possibly attend? Just ask yourself how much fun you want to have, and act accordingly. In Montréal, fun is strictly de rigeur. Bonne chance, mes amis.

Dining

Monique Polak

Terrace diners in Old Montréal

Montréal is a great city for food. It could be the French influence or the long, cold winters, but Montréalers love to eat. Nothing stops us from indulging our gourmet tastes. Not ice storms, not even politics. You'll notice that life here revolves around eating. We spend an inordinate amount of time shopping for food — picking out just the right shallots, going from one specialty shop to the next in pursuit of cheese, baguettes, coffee and wine. We also talk endlessly about food, and of course we love to go out to eat. What distinguishes dining out in Montréal from dining out in other major cities is that there's so much good food. It's everywhere. And you don't have to pay a fortune to sample it. Though the city has its share of pricey restaurants, there are plenty of inexpensive alternatives. Historically, Montréal has been known for its French cuisine. Today there are still plenty of French restaurants, though many of them have been influenced by the latest trends in Thai and California cooking. The many immigrants to Montréal have also brought their own unique flavours to the city. Just follow your nose to find delicious Greek, Italian, Chinese, Indian, Vietnamese and Caribbean food.

Part of the joy of visiting Montréal is discovering some of these places. One thing is certain: you'll be back for more.

Breakfast at Beauty's

Brunch

Sunday brunch is a Montréal tradition. And in summer, when the weather's good, every day is Sunday.

Expect a line that heads out the front door and

onto nearby Rue St-Urbain if you turn up at Beauty's later than 10 A.M. on a weekend. Located at the foot of Mont Royal on Avenue du Mont-Royal O., Beauty's has been a hit with Montréalers since it opened in 1942. The restaurant is named after its original owner, Hymie Skolnick, whose nickname was Beauty. Today, Skolnick's son, who is also named Hymie, runs the place. Everything here is sold à la carte, so expect to pay extra for your freshly squeezed orange juice. The most popular item on the menu is the Beauty's Special, a bagel sandwich filled with cream cheese, lox, tomato and onion. If you're too hungry to survive the line, it'll take you less than five minutes to walk to Pizza des Pîns on Avenue du Parc. The food is similar and just as good, but you won't be able to say you had breakfast at Beauty's.

Chez Cora Déjeuners

Though sophisticated Montréal diners disapprove of food chains, one that specializes in breakfasts has been drawing crowds. With more than a dozen locations on the island of Montréal, Chez Cora Déjeuners offers a variety of hearty breakfasts, most of them served with an artful — and abundant — arrangement of fresh fruit. Downtown, there's a Chez Cora on Rue Stanley. Everything sounds so good on the colourful menu that it'll be difficult to choose, but you might try the French toast made with zucchini bread.

Café Santropol

Or you can go for something completely different: dim sum breakfast. "Dim sum means 'touch your heart,'" says Chuck Kwan, owner of Maison Kam Fung, one of the most popular dim sum spots in town. "In Hong Kong, people eat dim sum for breakfast, lunch and even for a snack." Consider it a good sign that most of the diners here are Chinese. Located on the mezzanine level of a small shopping mall, this huge restaurant overlooks Chinatown. Dim sum is available here seven days a week from 7 A.M. until 3 P.M. Waiters go by with stainless-steel carts carrying a variety of exotic delicacies. You wave them over to get what you want. Each item costs between $2 and $5.50, but beware — with so much temptation, the bill climbs quickly. The steamed shrimp or pork dumplings and the deep-fried crab balls are delicious. For dessert, try the sesame seed balls or the mango pudding — or both.

If you prefer to sleep in a little longer, Café Santropol on St-Urbain opens at noon. In summer, try to get a spot in the garden, an urban paradise complete with small pond, chimes and birdfeeders. The specialty here is huge, healthy sandwiches made with thick slabs of pumpernickel bread. The Midnight Express is filled with cream cheese and peanut butter, the Killer Tomato with cream cheese and sun-dried tomatoes. The combinations might sound odd, but they taste delicious.

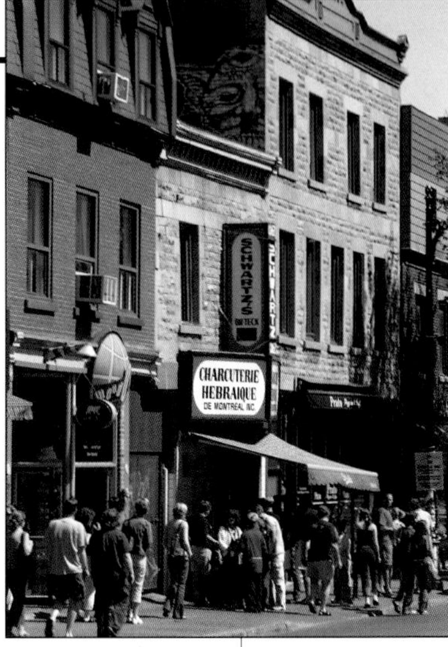

SCHWARTZ'S

ARAHOVA SOUVLAKI

QUICK EATS

At some Montréal landmarks you can order take-out as well as eat on the premises. But though the service is fast, this ain't fast food. Forget your diet and order your smoked meat medium when you go to Schwartz's delicatessen on Boulevard St-Laurent. Built in 1930, this old-fashioned deli has long, plain tables at which customers literally rub elbows. To pass for a local, order a cherry Coke and pickles on the side. Arahova Souvlaki is probably Montréal's best-known souvlaki joint. The original Arahova, located on Avenue St-Viateur O. in Montréal's Mile-End district, has been around since 1972. Two others have opened in recent years, one in the heart of downtown on bustling Rue Crescent. A combo plate with a souvlaki pita, salad and fries goes for $9.95. What makes Arahova souvlaki so good? "The secret is our tzatziki sauce. It's yogurt-based, with garlic, cucumber and salt," says Nector Koutroumanis, whose father began the business. Drive slowly on Avenue Victoria in the Côte-des-Neiges district or you might just miss the Caribbean Curry House. The décor is pretty humdrum, but the Caribbean food here is out of this world. Try the roti — curried meat and potatoes served in a chapati, or Indian flatbread. If you're feeling brave, go for the jerk chicken. You'll need a rum-based calypso punch — or two — to wash it down. Luckily, a calypso punch here costs only $2.95 — and it's the best-tasting one this side of Jamaica. A slightly different twist on roti can be found at the Jardin du Cari on St-Viateur. Here, the home-style Guyanese food made to order and hot sauce is to die for.

For a taste of Jerusalem, head to Pizza Pita for the finest falafel in town. Located on Boulevard Décarie, this kosher restaurant is equally popular with hip Montréal vegetarians and Orthodox Jews. The falafel sandwiches are made fresh daily with chickpeas, garlic, coriander and spices. They're served on pita bread with tahini, a sauce made from ground sesame seeds. Charisa, a hot sauce, is optional. Other specialties here include homemade soups, vegetarian pizza, shawarma sandwiches and spicy french fries. Say hello to Chaim and Zvi Spiegelman, the friendly brothers who own the restaurant.

Restaurant Daou

Family Fare

It's a bit of a trek, but Restaurant Daou on Rue Faillon in Montréal's northeast is worth it. This family-owned Lebanese restaurant has been around since 1975. The atmosphere is informal, with long tables set close together. Begin with the fattouch salad — morsels of cucumber, parsley, tomato, onion and toasted pita in a dressing of olive oil and lemon. Proceed directly to the marinated breast of chicken. Shadia Daou, one of the four sisters who run the restaurant, won't divulge the secret spices used in the marinade. "But the chicken marinates for a couple of days," she says. If you have a craving for Indian food, try La Maison du Curry (not to be confused with the previously mentioned Caribbean Curry House). Located downtown on Rue Bishop in what might be described as a hole in the wall, this restaurant serves food that is authentic and spicy. Try the onion bhaji or samosas — phyllo triangles stuffed with vegetables and meat — as an appetizer. The butter shrimp and butter chicken are the most popular main dishes. Be sure to order them spicy. Served with aromatic basmati rice, the shrimp and chicken will transport you directly to India. The nan bread here is also first class. Wash the whole thing down with a British beer.

Another good bet for lovers of Indian food is Ganges Restaurant on Rue Sherbrooke O. in Notre-Dame-de-Grâce, a leafy neighbourhood in the city's west end. "We use lean meat, no MSG, no peanut oil and no artificial anything," says Mohammed Haque, who opened the restaurant in 1994. Regulars swear by the butter chicken, the shai rezala — a sweet-and-sour beef dish — and the shrimp tikka masala, charcoal-broiled shrimps served in a ginger-garlic sauce. Also on the Indian theme, the lunch buffet at Bombay Palace on Rue Ste-Catherine O. is great for better-than-average favourites.

For a market dining experience that's fun for the whole family, indulge at the Marché Mövenpick Restaurant at Place Ville-Marie downtown. Diners wander from station to station with the ability to choose from countless freshly prepared items — everything from pastas to grilled meats to huge salads to fruits and desserts. It's a great place for satisfying the diverse palates of all family members.

BYOB

BYOBs, or bring-your-own-bottle establishments, abound in Montréal. They help keep dinner prices down, making fine dining accessible to the budget-conscious. And because Québec liquor stores carry an excellent selection of French wines (some from lesser-known regions such the Loire Valley and Languedoc), you can treat yourself to a nice bottle of wine. Consider it a good investment.

Bring a bottle of Chianti to La Trattoria on Chemin Upper Lachine in the Notre-Dame-de-Grâce district, or NDG for short. With its brick walls and checkered tablecloths, this restaurant could easily be in Italy. Choose from 15 kinds of pizza, including one made with fresh tomato sauce, Italian sausage and mozzarella cheese. Pasta dishes are equally authentic. Owner Frank Gallo mans the kitchen; his partner, the charming Angelo Di Stavolo, works the room.

TRATTORIA INTERIOR

One BYOB that everyone keeps raving about is La Colombe on Avenue Duluth. Because it only seats 36 people, you'll need to phone ahead for a reservation, especially on a weekend. The specialty at this elegant yet cozy restaurant is French cuisine. Chef Moustafa Rougaibi's menu changes weekly. The $34 table d'hôte includes soup, appetizer, main dish, dessert and coffee. The venison, the veal chops and the ostrich are highly recommended. Leave room for the fondant au chocolat, a chocolate cake served with a dark chocolate sauce.

Restaurant Le P'tit Plateau on Rue Marie-Anne E. near St-Denis is another popular BYOB. Here, too, you'll need to reserve at least a week in advance for a weekend rendezvous. The table d'hôte that includes soup or salad, main course and coffee, tea or tisane is available for $25 to $29. The restaurant is owned by Alain Loivel, a young Bordeaux-born chef and his wife, Geneviève Desnoyers. Loivel's specialties include confit de canard, jarret d'agneau confit and cassoulet Toulousain. Doesn't everything sound delicious en français? Loivel's duck is cooked in its own fat in the traditional style of southwestern France; his lamb is cooked in its own juices and is served with spring vegetables; and his cassoulet — another French classic — is made with white kidney beans, pork and sausage and is topped with duck confit. "Here, we promise you wonderful food and a friendly ambience," says Desnoyers. But in case you can't get a reservation, consider ordering in your dinner: all of the food on the menu is available for take-out.

FOUR-STAR DINING

If you have money to burn (or are in the mood to splurge) there are plenty of four-star restaurants in Montréal just waiting for you.

Toqué! has been attracting a lot of attention since it first opened in the mid-1990s. It recently moved from Rue St-

TOQUÉ!

Denis to a new location at Place Jean-Paul-Riopelle in Old Montréal. Chef Normand Laprise is known for his innovative market cuisine. His menu changes constantly and relies heavily on local produce. The word *toqué* is Québécois slang and means "stubborn" — but in a good way. According to Laprise's business partner, Christine Lamarche, that's exactly how the couple feels about food: "The emphasis here is on food. Almost all of the vegetables we use are organic." Delicacies include roast saddle of lamb, served with Chioggia beets and cauliflower purée, king oyster mushrooms and turnip cabbage sprouts. There's also roasted wild striped bass, served with homemade raspberry vinegar and sabayon, day-lily buds and yellow-foot mushrooms. For dessert, Lamarche recommends the chocolate cookie with pure Caraïbes ice milk.

Another vedette on Montréal's four-star dining scene is Restaurant Cube. This restaurant on Rue McGill, at the edge of Old Montréal, is where well-heeled Montréalers go to see and be seen. Though it's located inside a building that's nearly a century old — now called Hôtel le Saint-Paul — everything about Restaurant Cube is sleek and modern. The walls are off-white, the tables are solid walnut and the napkin rings are made of blown glass. "This is an urban restaurant — and for me, the cube is a metaphor for that. Besides, the word *cube* translates well into French and English," says Hubert Marsolais, the restaurant's co-owner.

Marsolais's partner is prize-winning local chef Claude Pelletier. Pelletier's specialties include a foie gras appetizer, served with a green-apple purée, green-apple chips and a fried green-apple doughnut. If you like fish, indulge in the salmon confit. It comes with a fennel and green-apple sauce as well as fennel pollen. Don't pass up the American brownies, served with vanilla ice cream and hot caramel sauce. Expect dinner for two to cost $150 before wine, taxes and tip.

LES CAPRICES DE NICOLAS

Another four-star favourite is Les Caprices de Nicolas, located downtown on Rue Drummond. There are three dining rooms from which to choose; each is decorated with paintings by well-known contemporary Québec artists. The garden room, a covered atrium with a fountain, is particularly delightful. One room is a private salon. Here, too, the menu is constantly changing, but signature dishes include Le Caviar — a potato crêpe appetizer made with caviar, fresh salmon and lemon sauce — as well as the foie gras. For your main dish, consider the rack of Québec lamb, served with its braised shoulder and sweetbreads. The lamb is accompanied by artichoke purée and a Béarnaise sauce with tarragon. "The flavour of lamb sweetbreads is completely different from

the more commonly known veal sweetbreads. The taste of lamb sweetbreads is hard to describe, but for a lamb lover, it's the ultimate," says the restaurant's owner, Dan Medalsy. A dessert that will make you think you've died and gone to heaven is the dish of seven scoops of homemade ice cream and sherbet. Dinner for two will set you back some $120 before wine, taxes and tip.

BRUNOISE

One of the most recent arrivals on the city's fine-dining scene is Brunoise, on Rue St-André near Parc Lafontaine. This elegant and intimate restaurant seats only 50 people, and because it's attracting so much attention, you may need to phone several weeks in advance for a reservation — especially on a weekend. Brunoise is owned by two young chefs, Zach Suhl and Michel Ross. Their goal, says Suhl, is to offer an upscale dining experience at a reasonable price: "We're trying to get away from the elitism attached to high-end restaurants. We think good food should be available to everyone."

The table d'hôte, which changes seasonally, ranges in price from $27 to $37. Favourites include the salmon, served with a shellfish vinaigrette, crusted potatoes and braised shallot cake, as well as the skate wing, served with braised squid. If you're dining as a couple, order one dessert each and share. Try the cheese plate — a lovely way to prolong your meal — and the panacotta with basil syrup and fresh passion-fruit pulp.

On the more established side, Montréalers have been coming to Chez La Mère Michel on Rue Guy for over 30 years. Specialties of the house include barquette Alsacienne and lobster served out of the shell with a garlic-flower sauce. The fish (try the Arctic char) is brought in fresh each day. Caribou and bison appear as seasonal dishes. The wine list is large and reasonably priced; dinner for two will you see you adding $100 or so to the cost of your bottle.

MILOS

Where do Paul Newman and Bette Midler hang out when they visit Montréal? At Milos Restaurant, an upscale version of the traditional Greek *psarotaverna* located just north of Mont Royal on Avenue du Parc. There's no better fish restaurant in town. Start with an appetizer of crab cakes — they're served with a light mustard sauce. Grilled octopus is another specialty, but most customers order fish by the pound. They choose it themselves from what looks like an open market at the back of the dining room. Imported from as far away as Tunisia and Greece, your fish is grilled whole and is then deboned before being served up on a platter. Dinner for two starts at about $100 before wine, taxes and tip. Don't forget to

check out the bathrooms downstairs — they're the swankiest in all of Montréal.

The stretch of Boulevard St-Laurent between Rue Sherbrooke and Avenue des Pins could well be known as restaurant row. Restaurant Globe is a favourite with local gourmands. Chef and co-owner David McMillan is known for his innovative cuisine, all of it made with seasonal, organic produce. This is a large place, with room for some 120 diners. Seven sumptuous banquettes, complete with red leather cushions, are especially popular. If you haven't made a reservation, you might end up eating at the huge walnut bar — not a bad way to spend an evening, actually, particularly if you want to meet Montréal's beautiful people. Though all the food here is first rate, the appetizers are especially good. Some regulars come here just to graze; they order up a slew of appetizers and skip the main course altogether. Favourite starters are the fresh organic beet salad; the oysters that arrive fresh daily from Prince Edward Island and New Brunswick; and the hot goat cheese served with Yukon potatoes and oven-roasted tomatoes. Popular main-course items here are the honey-roasted salmon and the roasted grain-fed chicken. The salmon is served with carrots and lentils that have been cooked in red wine. The chicken is served with mashed potatoes and a gravy made from hen broth. Try McMillan's chocolate torte for dessert — it's served hot with espresso ice cream. Expect dinner for two, before wine, taxes and tip, to cost about $100.

THE BEAVER CLUB

Located off the main lobby of the Hôtel Le Reine-Élizabeth, The Beaver Club is a Montréal dining institution. First opened in 1958, the restaurant has its roots in the 18th-century fur trade. The walls are done in brick and oak panelling; there's an open rotisserie by the restaurant's back wall. Specialties include roast prime rib of beef and chateaubriand. Jacket and tie are required for men. Dinner for two runs about $100 before wine, taxes and tip.

Lastly, if you feel like a short excursion, Au Tournant de la Rivière is a just reward for those who can find it, on Rue Salaberry in Carignan. (Take Autoroute Décarie south to Highway 10 East, turn west at Exit 22 and then immediately take the right turn for Sherbrooke, then make a left on Boulevard Brunelle — the restaurant is at Brunelle and Salaberry in a converted barn behind a farmhouse.) The atmosphere is luxurious and the service first rate. Chef Jacques Robert gives conventional dishes the kind of treatment that makes them exceptional, but they can be prohibitively priced. If you decide to splurge, go all the way with the crème brûlée with maple syrup before you wend your way back to the city.

RESTAURANT GLOBE

Night Life

Paul Spence

Winnie's and Thursday's on Rue Crescent

Montréal's nightlife begins far before night falls. Suppertime is a very European eight-ish here, and by then, most residents have already been socializing over food and drink for some time during the daily *cinq-à-sept*. What's a *cinq-à-sept*, you ask? Why, it's a brilliant doubling of happy hour, and it literally translates to "five-to-seven." At Edgar Hypertaverne on Avenue du Mont-Royal, for example, one can enjoy a pint of fantastic local brew while nibbling on a platter of wonderful cheeses from all over the world!

A great place to start an evening on the town is the heart of the club scene for Montréal's English-speaking crowd. Between Rue Ste-Catherine O. and Boulevard René-Lévesque are the well-known party streets of Peel, de la Montagne, Crescent, Bishop and MacKay. The imposing old stone buildings now house dance bars, discos and pubs and cater to both visitors and locals alike, so long as they have a taste for enthusiastic crowds and the smell of strong perfumes.

Rue Crescent is the epicentre of downtown nightlife, where many of Montréal's most established bars sling suds and grub every night of the week. Thursday's is a good choice for relaxation in an old-style pub environment with a Montréal classic — bagels with cream cheese and lox.

In 1967, Sir Winston Churchill Pub opened its doors on Crescent, and in almost forty years it has lost none of its charm. Nothing goes with a cigar like a luxurious leather seat! Crescent is also home to Vocalz, a popular karaoke bar where both amateur and professional singers belt out

the classics. There's also the Hard Rock Café and Hurley's Irish Pub.

Still in the neighbourhood but a little more laid-back and offering a genuine pub atmosphere are McKibbon's and O'Reagan's, both on Rue Bishop. Imported beers, wood panelling and live Celtic music lend a rustic feeling to these popular joints.

Don't want to miss a moment of the "big" game (be it soccer, baseball, hockey or cricket)? The Dominion Pub on Metcalf is the place to be. This friendly neighbourhood pub offers a big-screen TV and a host of tasty dishes such as roast-beef sandwiches, burgers, steaks and pizzas. The adventurous spirit might be inclined to try the house specialty: pig knuckles with sauerkraut!

NEWTOWN, JACQUES VILLENEUVE'S BAR ON CRESCENT

Just yonder down the road aways on Rue MacKay is Upstairs Jazz Bar and Grill, a spot for great jazz and classy eats every night. There's generally a cover charge, but it's well worth it for the atmosphere and food. For more great music, head up to the House of Jazz (formerly known as Biddles) on Rue Aylmer for a classic trio: jazz, booze and ribs.

Even if the sleazy side of life normally doesn't appeal, the walk east towards St-Laurent by way of Ste-Catherine is pretty safe and the seemingly endless strip of garish lights and unabashedly revealing posters that promise unspeakable pleasures are amusing. Have a giggle at the names: Pussy Corp, Club Super Contact, Cabaret Sex Appeal and Club Super Sexe being just a taste.

If walking is impossible (those enjoying Montréal's nightlife are often impeded by "club foot," a.k.a. high heels), hop in a cab and direct the driver to the corner of St-Laurent and Sherbrooke, where, for a significant stretch, St-Laurent welcomes the beautiful and the chic. Hip restaurants like Shed Café and Sofia compete for clientele who like to keep an eye on their shiny sports cars from tables by the window.

FIDDLERS AT McKIBBIN'S IRISH PUB

Further up there are classic watering holes such as Bifteck, Frappé and the newer Le Pistol, which cater to the university crowd. For great live music and no pretension, stop by Barfly, which features live bands almost every night and hosts excellent open country jams on Sundays.

There's something to be said for theme bars that manage to stay open longer than a front door during a Winnipeg winter. The Go Go Lounge opened its trippy multicoloured doors in the late 1990s and has been spinning classic 1960s and 1970s music for sweaty kids of almost all ages ever since. For more dancing, the Blue Dog and Blizzarts offer a host of musical styles (electronica, reggae, old school, etc.).

Another area that buzzes at night is St-Laurent's sister street to the east, the noticeably more francophone St-Denis. It's home to some of Montréal's best patios, including the massive backyard party found nightly at Le Saint-Sulpice (just below Rue Ontario), the great live venue L'Escogriffe and Le Monkey (two storeys of fun). Quai des Brûmes offers live music from all genres.

Though historically quiet after dinnertime, Old Montréal is making a bit of a comeback on the nightlife scene. The owners of Holder have brought their winning formula for a successful French bistro to the corner of Rue St-Paul and Rue McGill, and next door, Bistro Boris has great food as well as a patio that's always hopping on the weekend.

O'REGANS BAR

Tending bar on Crescent

Rue Ste-Catherine runs all the way from its residential anglophone origins in the west to the more francophone east, extending deep into the gay village. For drag shows and wild theme nights, the Cabaret Mado is a must, while just down the street is the giant Bourbon complex, housing such favourite gay hangouts and discos as Le Drugstore, Club Mississippi, La Track and Bar Cajun.

Some of the city's best after-hours clubs are also in the area. Stereo, Le Parking, Aria and Millennium all keep the party going until 10 a.m. and feature some of the world's best DJs on a regular basis.

But not everyone wants to keep on going after the bar closes. Many just want something to soak up the booze, and Montréal is anything but short of late-night eateries. For 24-hour casse-croûte (burgers, fries and poutine) in the Plateau Mont-Royal neighbourhood, there's Rapido on Avenue du Mont-Royal and Chez Claudette on Rue Laurier (try the famous Michigan Burger). And if a poutine is judged by the size of its curds, don't miss Frites Dorée, where uniformed grease jockeys right out of a 1950s steakhouse serve up the best poutine in Montréal until 4 a.m.

Downtown Montréal ny night

Montréal by Area

Old Montréal

Sean Farrell

Viger
AUTOROUTE VILLE-MARIE
Square Victoria
Saint-Antoine
Old Montréal
Saint-Louis
Gosford
Du Champ-de-Mars
Des Fortifications
Saint-Jacques
Notre-Dame
McGill
Saint-Pierre
Saint-François-Xavier
Saint-Laurent
Saint-Jean-Baptiste
Saint Gabriel
Saint-Vincent
Place Jacques-Cartier
Saint-Claude
Bonsecours
Berri
Le Moyne
Place Royale
Saint-Sulpice
De la Commune
Bassin de l'Horloge
Saint-Paul
Place D'Youville
Promenade du Vieux Port
Bassin Bonsecours
Pavillon Jacques-Cartier
Parc du Bassin Bonsecours
Quai de l'Horloge
William
Normand
Old Port
Bassin Jacques-Cartier
D'Youville
Bassin King-Edward
Jacques-Cartier Pier
Gare Maritime Iberville
King-Edward Pier
King
Bassin Alexandra
Alexandra Pier
N
Parc des Écluses
Point du Moulin à Vent
St. Lawrence River
0 250 500 750 1000
metres

18th Century Market

Montréal's first settlers had dreams of establishing a new civilization founded on Christian principles when they straggled ashore in 1642. They christened their collection of rude dwellings Ville-Marie in honour of Christ's mother and set out to convert the Indians. The name's all that's left of that old settlement, but there's still plenty of history in Vieux-Montréal, or Old Montréal, the little chunk of land that stretches along the waterfront from Rue McGill in the west to Rue St-Denis in the east. This was the heart of the city's commercial and political life for most of the 19th century. Today it thrives in its new role as the city's centre of tourism. You can, if you wish, rattle along the cobbled streets in a horse-drawn calèche or rumble along them on a tour bus, but there's really no need. The district's easy to get to by Métro — get off at the Square-Victoria, Place d'Armes or Champ-de-Mars station — and small

enough to be explored on foot. So put on a comfortable pair of walking shoes and step out. Most of the history you'll see is 19th century, but there's a generous scattering of 18th-century gems, and some of the buildings rest on 17th-century foundations.

PLACE JACQUES-CARTIER

Place Jacques-Cartier, near the Champ-de-Mars Métro station, is a good place to start for two reasons: first, there's a tourist office on the northwest corner of the square where you can pick up a copy of a booklet that outlines a self-guided walking tour; second, Place Jacques-Cartier is one of the prettiest and liveliest squares in the whole city. It stretches from Rue de la Commune on the riverfront north to Rue Notre-Dame, and its whole length is lined with restaurants and snack bars with terraces that open onto the square. In summer, jugglers, fire-eaters and musicians amuse the crowds and the whole area is bright with flowers. The column at the north end of the square bears a statue not of Jacques Cartier, as you might expect, but of Admiral Horatio Nelson. It was erected in 1809 to celebrate Nelson's victory over the French fleet at Trafalgar.

French seafaring does get its due at Place Vauquelin, on the other side of Notre-Dame. This little square and its fountain are named for the French admiral who defended Louisbourg. Just beyond Place Vauquelin, a flight of stone steps leads down to Champ-de-Mars, a handsome green space that used to be a parking lot and, before that, a

HÔTEL DE VILLE

parade ground. It's now used occasionally for public gatherings. Archaeologists have also excavated the foundations of the walls that used to surround the old city.

Captains of commerce fled Old Montréal long ago, but the district is still the heart of civic and legal activity. The extravagant Second Empire building on the east side of Place Vauquelin, for example, is city hall, and the balcony above the main door is where Charles de Gaulle made his infamous "Vive le Québec libre!" speech in 1967. If you look west along Notre-Dame you will see three courthouses — two on the north side of the street and one on the south side. They are the old courthouse, the old new courthouse and the new new courthouse. Only the last is still active as the Palais de Justice, and you should have no trouble picking it out: it's the big modern slab that doesn't belong.

Far handsomer is the Château Ramezay, right across from city hall. It was built in 1705 as a residence for the city's governor and looks a little like a Norman castle. It houses a museum with an extensive collection of art, furniture and documents dating from the 18th and 19th centuries. A five-minute stroll east along Notre-Dame to Rue Berri brings you to two grand old buildings that used to be train stations. The Dalhousie station on the southeast corner of Berri and Notre-Dame linked Montréal to Vancouver, while the Viger station on St-Antoine at Berri served points to the east. Walk south on Berri, stopping to visit the lovingly restored home of Sir George-Étienne Cartier, the man who led Québec into Confederation in 1867. When you get to Rue St-Paul, turn right and walk west to the Notre-Dame-de-Bon-Secours chapel at the foot of Rue Bonsecours. The huge statue of the Virgin Mary on the roof faces the river with its arms outstretched in welcome. Sailors regularly visited this little church to give thanks for a safe crossing. The beautifully restored interior is decorated with lamps in the form of model boats, which were left as gifts by grateful mariners.

CHÂTEAU DE RAMEZAY

Across St-Paul at the corner of Bonsecours is one of the finest examples of 18th-century architecture in Montréal: the greystone Maison du Calvet, built in 1725. Pierre du Calvet was a merchant and ardent admirer of the American Revolution, and Benjamin Franklin was a regular visitor. The long, low building with the tin-roofed dome next to the chapel is the Marché Bonsecours. The market has had a number of incarnations over the years, serving at various times as a concert hall and even as city hall. The Marché Bonsecours had new life breathed into it when it was restored to its original purpose as a marketplace for the city's 350th anniversary celebration in 1992. The market's sidewalk café offers an opportunity to take a break — once you've made it through the bustle of people dallying through the lovely boutiques and exhibitions housed inside.

Notre-Dame-de-Bon-Secours Chapel

A short stroll west and you're back at the southern end of Place Jacques-Cartier. Walk another 50 metres or so and turn right on Rue St-Vincent, a narrow lane jammed with artists and artisans peddling their wares. When you get back to St-Paul, take a careful look at the buildings on the south side of the street. Merchants once coveted these places. They could take in their goods directly from the docks along Rue de la Commune behind their shops and sell them to the customers they received on the fashionable St-Paul side.

Waterfront Rue de la Commune, from Berri to the Canal de Lachine, connects Old Montréal with the Old Port. Many of the buildings on de la Commune still display the names of the businesses once housed there with what is left of old signs painted on the brick or stone walls. A few blocks to the west along de la Commune sits Pointe-à-Callière, the site where Paul de Chomedey, sieur de Maisonneuve, and his brave followers landed in 1642. The triangular building with the lookout tower is an archaeological museum built over an excavation of the site. Visitors can actually wander among the various layers of development, from the 17th century to the Victorian age. The museum is linked underground with the Vieille Douane (Old Customs House), which boasts one of the finest museum gift shops in the city.

Waterfront Rue de la Commune

POINTE-À-CALLIÈRE

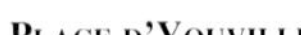

PLACE D'YOUVILLE

The Centre d'Histoire de Montréal, just a few blocks away in the heart of Place d'Youville, is worth seeking out for a better appreciation of the city's past. Renovated and housed in a beautifully restored fire station, the museum displays objects and models from its collection of over 1,500 artifacts. The ground-floor exhibit takes you through five episodes from the past to tell the story of Montréal from its founding to the present day, while the second-floor exhibit shows what life was like for individuals in the city during the 20th century.

If you walk north along Rue St-Pierre, you'll come to some imposing stone ruins. This is all that's left of one of Montréal's first hospitals, built by the Frères Charon. In 1747 it was taken over by one of the heroines of city history, Sainte-Marguerite d'Youville, founder of the Grey Nuns. Three blocks further north is Rue St-Jacques, or St. James Street, as it was known when it was the financial capital of Canada. The business barons who worked in the grand old buildings lining the street from Square Victoria to Place d'Armes controlled three-quarters of the country's wealth. And if you think they were a stodgy lot, take a closer look at the buildings. They're decorated with a fanciful array of stone cherubs, naked goddesses and lots of granite grapes and vines. Some, of course, are simply grand; the Banque Royal monolith at the corner of St-Pierre, for example, was the tallest building in the British Empire when it was completed in 1928.

Just across the street from the Banque Royal is the Centre de Commerce Mondial (World Trade Centre), one of the district's newest and most imaginative developments. It was created by glassing over Ruelle des Fortifications, a fetid, narrow alley that traced the route of the old walls. This renovation resulted in a narrow, six-storey mall linking two rows of decaying buildings (which the developers sandblasted into respectability). Throw in a luxury hotel, a link to the Métro and a magnificent black-marble fountain, and presto: a delightful interior space with a food court and a row of boutiques. The graffiti-covered slab of concrete at the east end of the centre is a section of the Berlin Wall, a gift from Berlin on the occasion of Montréal's 350th birthday in 1992.

A block east of the Centre de Commerce Mondial is the old city centre, Place d'Armes. The heroic stone figure in the middle of the square is of Paul de Chomedey, Sieur de Maisonneuve. He's surrounded by a bewildering array of architecture. The domed Greek temple behind him is the head office of the Banque de Montréal (the interior also resembles a Greek temple). The redstone building on his left is the city's first skyscraper and the soaring black tower on his right is the headquarters of the Banque Nationale. But it's the magnificent Gothic façade he's looking at that gets all the attention from tourists. This is Basilique Notre-Dame, possibly the most famous church in Canada. The interior is a vast blue cavern studded with gold-leaf stars and dimly lit by a row of stained-glass windows crafted in Limoges. The reredos, with its life-sized tableaux from the Old Testament, is a display of virtuoso wood carving. The Chapelle du Sacré-Coeur behind the main altar is as large as some churches and more ornate than most. Thousands of Montréalers have been married in that chapel. Spend an hour at the basilica before going home. If you're lucky, the Orchestre Symphonique de Montréal will be practising in the sanctuary and you can watch and listen. Or there might be a string quartet playing on the plaza in front. Alternately, you can just sit and meditate and let the colours soak into your soul.

PAUL DE CHOMEDEY

Old Port

Sean Farrell

Montréal is an island city in the middle of the St. Lawrence River and is still one of Canada's most important ports. Nowhere is the city's bond to the sea more apparent than at the lively Vieux-Port, or Old Port, along the southern edge of Old Montréal. This strip of docks is no longer the commercial heart of the city — the big container ships and bulk carriers of modern trade load and unload at more modern wharves further east — but it has become one of the most appreciated parks in Montréal.

Popular all year round, new activities and diversions seem to spring up year after year. While the relatively new Centre des Sciences de Montréal is a fabulous place to explore during any month of the year, most of the Old Port's other attractions are decidedly seasonal. In February it's the site of the annual Fête des Neiges, and its huge outdoor skating rink is used all winter long.

But the place really blossoms in summer. On warm summer days and late into the evening, the Promenade du Vieux-Port that runs the length of the waterfront from the Canal de Lachine in the west to the Quai de l'Horloge (Clock Pier) in the east is crowded with strollers, inline skaters and cyclists. Whole families glide by in pedal-driven vehicles that look like a cross between a horseless carriage and a surrey with a fringe on top. The less energetic rumble by on rented electric scooters or in little motorized trains that run tours all along the waterfront. This is also where Montréal celebrates Canada Day with concerts and dances

Old Port at night

that last well into the night.

Sometimes a wedding cake of a cruise ship will be docked at the Gare Maritime Iberville, at the western end of the Old Port just south of Pointe-à-Callière, the site of Montréal's founding in 1642. Cruise passengers are among the best accommodated of Montréal's visitors, living in floating luxury with a view of the river and Île Ste-Hélène. And all this is just an easy walk from the sights of Old Montréal. Visiting warships also use the docks when they pay courtesy calls on the city, as do the tall ships that some countries use as training vessels for their navy cadets. The latter add a real 19th-century flavour to the port.

HABITAT '67

The best way to get here is by Métro. You might want to get off at the Square-Victoria station and walk south on Rue McGill to the waterfront. It's a bit of a hike, but it's better than trying to park a car on Rue de la Commune (impossible), unless you're willing to pay for parking in one of the Old Port's lots. If you do come by Métro, a good place to start exploring the Old Port is at its western end, at Parc des Écluses (Locks), in the shadow of the great grain elevators. This spot marks the entrance to the Canal de Lachine, a 19th-century engineering marvel that took ships past the Rapides de Lachine further west. The St. Lawrence Seaway has rendered it obsolete, but its grassy banks form a kind of long, thin park that ends on the shores of Lac St-Louis. This is where Mosaïculture, a now-defunct horticultural display, set up. Open through early fall, the exhibit filled the park with colourful and meticulously crafted three-dimensional floral works of art. While the event will not be reinstated for 2005, organizers hope that funding will allow them to bring back the exhibit in 2006 under a different name.

The canal's bicycle path is also the source of many of the bikes coasting along the waterfront. Look across the Alexandra basin and you'll see a building that looks a bit like a cliffside pueblo dwelling in the American southwest. It's even the right colour to blend in with the Arizona desert. This is Habitat '67, built for the Expo '67 world's fair by architect Moshe Safdie as an experiment in modular, moderately priced housing. Its waterfront address makes it a little less modest than Mr. Safdie planned.

Habitat is the most impressive building on Parc de la Cité-du-Harve, a long, thin park that leads to the Pont de la

IMAX MOVIE THEATRE

PEDESTRIAN BRIDGE ON CANAL DE LACHINE

Concorde (Concorde Bridge) and Parc des Îles. If you walk west past the Gare Maritime Iberville on the Quai Alexandra to the Quai King-Edward at the foot of Boulevard St-Laurent, you'll find the home of the Centre des Sciences des Montréal, a building that occupies the entire pier. It is, first and foremost, a hands-on interactive museum with emphasis on audio-visual elements to encourage an exploratory approach to learning about science. It's a great place to spend a day, or at least part of one; don't leave without visiting the gift shop, where you'll find numerous unique and educational gifts and souvenirs. The centre also houses its own IMAX theatres. These special-format movies are shot with oversized film and projected on gigantic screens. The results often make you feel like you are part of the action. The theatre generally schedules a double-bill for its screenings and alternates between screenings in English and French. The films are guaranteed to assault your senses, though you might want to think twice if you suffer from motion sickness — the illusion is that effective.

The Quai King-Edward and its eastern neighbour, the Quai Jacques-Cartier, frame a marina full of pleasure craft. It's a popular place to people-watch or daydream, especially over some of the bigger yachts or sailboats berthed there. But if you want to do a bit of boating, you don't have to own one of the luxury yachts. The western side of the Quai Jacques-Cartier is lined with opportunities. You can chug along the river on an ersatz paddle-wheeler or do high-speed 360-degree turns on a speed boat. The glass-topped Bateau-Mouche — it looks a lot like those boats that cruise the Seine in Paris — offers dinner cruises on the river. And if you're looking for a day trip and money is no object, you can take a high-speed hydrofoil down the St. Lawrence and spend a few hours in Québec City before returning to Montréal in the early evening. The best deal, however, is probably the little ferries that take pedestrians and cyclists to Île Ste-Hélène and Longueuil, located on the south shore. One of the more unusual ways to tour the Old Port and Old Montréal is on the Amphi-Bus, which leaves from the Quai Jacques-Cartier. As its name suggests, this odd machine is part boat and part bus. It has both wheels and propellers and offers visitors an amphibious view of the waterfront. The Quai Jacques-Cartier also has a boutique, restaurant and washroom facilities, which makes it a good place for a pit stop.

On the east side of the Quai Jacques-Cartier is the Bassin

BONSECOURS BASSIN

QUAI DE L'HORLOGE

Bonsecours (Bonsecours Basin), where you can control a radio-operated miniature sailboat or pilot your own boat. Okay, it's only a pedal boat and you can't go beyond the boundaries of the basin, but it's a good place to laze away a summer afternoon. There's a lovely little park in the middle of the basin, a kind of grassy island linked to the mainland by narrow footbridges. It's an ideal location for the annual beer-sampling festival, one of a number of summer events held there.

The last pier is the Quai de l'Horloge on the eastern edge of the Old Port. It was once called the Quai Victoria, and it's shaped a little like a crooked thumb with the tip pointing east, down the river. If your trip so far has been uneventful and you're getting bored, the labyrinth in Shed 16 is a popular attraction that lets you get lost — and enjoy doing it. And if you need more of an adrenaline rush, check out the Saute-Moutons jet boats in the basin between the thumb and the mainland. Saute-Moutons — literally "jumping sheep" — is the French term for running the rapids, and these big, flat-bottomed boats will take you upriver for a wet and wild ride in the Rapides de Lachine. There aren't many major cities where you can do this kind of thing without going beyond the city limits. Though not cheap, it'll satisfy your taste for extreme adventure. But be warned: you will get wet.

PADDLING THE LACHINE RAPIDS

Walk along the pier — don't forget to wave to the people returning from their jet-boat ride with their hearts in their throats — to the clock tower that gives the pier its name. If you want to hear your own heart pound, climb its 192 steps for a fantastic view of the waterfront and its surroundings. You don't have to count your steps most of the way up because each stair is numbered, except for the top ones, which form a tight, spiralling staircase opening onto the top deck. There isn't room for more than a few people at a time to stand and enjoy the view, but it's worth the effort to climb all those stairs if you want to get a new and different perspective on Montréal. The tower was built in 1922 to honour the merchant mariners who kept the supply lines open to Europe during World War I.

The pier itself is the prettiest on the waterfront and now features a child's playground, where grateful parents can let their tykes burn some of that boundless energy. The little park at its western end is set aside for kite-fliers, and the benches and rock gardens at the eastern end under the clock are popular with the crowds who come out on weekends to watch the fireworks competitions. It's a good place to finish up and try to remember where you left your car.

Downtown & Ste-Catherine

Pierre Home-Douglas

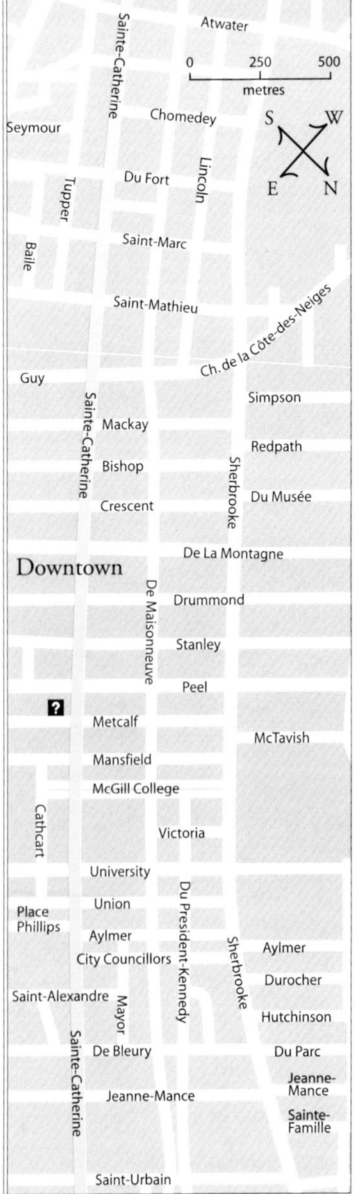

Every great city has its main street where locals and visitors throng to shop, stroll, people-watch and tap into the spirit of the town. London has its Oxford Street, New York its Fifth Avenue, Toronto its Yonge Street. In Montréal it's Rue Ste-Catherine, a gritty, jaunty strip of flash and dash that cuts a 15-kilometre swath right through the metropolis, from the affluent enclave of Westmount in the west to the factories and row housing of the working-class east end. In between lies a world of upscale boutiques, grand old department stores, seedy striptease joints, quirky shops and restaurants of every ethnic type imaginable. And people. Plenty of them. At just about any hour of the day or night you'll find Montréalers milling about, heading off to a rendezvous at a nearby bar, stopping for a café au lait, checking out the latest fashion trends or just, well, living. Rue Sherbrooke, a couple of blocks to the north, may offer more refinement, more old-world gentility, but if you want to feel the real pulse of the town, head for Ste-Catherine and take a walk.

At its western end, Ste-Catherine begins where it merges with Boulevard

Ste-Catherine

de Maisonneuve, a few hundred metres east of the Vendôme Métro station. But for most Montréalers the route kicks into high gear at Avenue Atwater, a couple of kilometres east. The intersection was once hockey mecca in this hockey-mad town. Here stands what used to be the Montréal Forum, home for more than 70 years to one of the most storied franchises in sports: the Montréal Canadiens. The fabled building closed in 1996, when the team shifted to new digs at what is now called the Bell Centre. Somehow it all seemed depressingly fitting. Once a thriving shopping and entertainment area, this stretch of Ste-Catherine seemed to suffer more than most parts of Montréal when the economy of the city turned sour during the 1980s and early 1990s. Locals watched as store after store was either boarded up or torn down. Gone were the venerable Texan Steak House and Toe Blake's Tavern. To many observers, the Forum's closing seemed the final nail in the coffin.

The Pepsi Forum

But then, Lazarus-like, the street started to make a comeback. New shops emerged, and other stores, like Garnitures Dressmaker, endured despite the economic roller-coaster ride. This shop has been at the same address since the late 1950s, sewing up a storm and dispensing craft supplies that range from wall stencils to a wide selection of feathers, beads and ribbons. And then word came that the Forum, after serving a brief stint as a key location for the $80-million feature film *Snake Eyes,* was destined to become an entertainment centre. Renamed the Pepsi Forum, it opened in 2001 and features 22 cinemas under the AMC banner and Jillian's, a three-floor complex that boasts arcade games, a bowling alley, a night club and a restaurant. And for hockey fans, the Pepsi Forum's owners added a nice touch for weary shoppers: a collection of original Forum seats from the red section. Sit down for a minute or two and imagine all the Stanley Cup–winning teams that were

Moe's

witnessed by former occupants of these seats.

If you happen to have missed breakfast, take a side trip one block north on Rue Lambert-Closse to Casse-Croûte du Coin. Regulars still call it Moe's, after its original owner. When the Forum was in full swing across the street, you would often see visiting hockey players eating huge breakfasts on game day. Regular patrons included Wayne Gretzky and Mario Lemieux — plus roadies, circus workers, even a rock star or two. Today it's still a good bet for a cheap breakfast. And it's open 24 hours a day.

Over the years, the strip from Avenue Atwater to Rue Guy has evolved into a magnet for Montréal book lovers. Some call it Bookstore Row. In addition to Mélange Magique, Québec's largest English-language occult and metaphysical bookstore, you'll find shops like Vortex, with an eclectic range of hand-picked literary titles. Nearby, the used bookstore Westcott Books stands cheek-by-jowl with Argo, a Montréal institution. There are also a couple of magazine shops that can satisfy just about any taste. Mediaphile, for example, offers hundreds of mags to hungry readers and will allow you to order from a list of 10,000 titles. The owners also indulge in a little side business, selling top-notch cigars from Cuba, Jamaica and several other countries at reasonable prices.

THE FAUBOURG

Part of the regeneration of this stretch of Ste-Catherine during the last decade or so can be found in the Faubourg. The block-long building features a good collection of ethnic take-out foods from more than a dozen nations, running the gamut from Szechuan to sushi. People who like Thai food swear by Bangkok, located in both the food court upstairs and a new restaurant setting across the street. At La Maison du Bagel, you can watch bakers pulling piping-hot bagels out of a wood-burning oven. Locals stop by the Faubourg on Sunday morning for their paper and a cup of cappuccino from Starbucks or Second Cup and sit by the windows that face out onto Ste-Catherine. Light streams in from the skylights far above the ground floor. On the way out you can pick up a tasty cinnamon bun at Saint Cinnamon or a baguette from Pagnelli's.

LA MAISON DU BAGEL

There's also evidence of new life at the intersection of Guy and Ste-Catherine, where the impressive new

Pagnelli's in the Faubourg

home of Concordia's fine arts and engineering departments is now under construction. New shops are beginning to spring up in this previously desolate neighbourhood, and there's a tangible optimism in the air.

A couple of blocks east of Guy, Ste-Catherine intersects with two streets filled with some of Montréal's best-known watering holes. Although many of the under-25 crowd have departed in the last few years for the hip bars on Boulevard St-Laurent, Rue Bishop and Rue Crescent are still hopping, particularly on Friday and Saturday nights. Among the best-known spots are Sir Winston Churchill Pub, reputedly David Letterman's favourite place to meet people in Montréal; Hurley's Irish Pub, which sells more draft Guinness than any other bar in North America; Grumpy's, where you'll often find a good collection of media types and various movers and shakers; and Brutopia, which offers live music and some of the best home-brewed beer in town.

The block between Rues Crescent and de la Montagne is dominated by Ogilvy, one of the grand dames of Montréal's department stores. Founded in 1866 by James Angus Ogilvy, the store received a much-needed facelift in the 1980s, when the five-floor edifice was converted into a series of upscale boutiques. Old-timers still bemoan the loss of the basement cafeteria, where you used to see old ladies hunched over their cup of tea as they whiled away the hours. But there have been welcome additions, including the Nicholas Hoare bookstore, which draws two thumbs up from book lovers all over town. And some traditions still endure: every day at noon a kilted bagpiper marches through the main floor playing his

Sir Winston Churchill pub

pipes, and in December locals line the snowbound sidewalk in front of the store with their children to view the elaborate antique Christmas scene on display in the Ogilvy windows.

There's more history in this area than even most Montréalers realize. Half a block south on de la Montagne stands a row of mid-19th-century townhouses. Next door to number 1181 is where Confederate President Jefferson Davis lived after the American Civil War. Davis's house was ripped down in the 1950s to make way for an alley (this was at a time when preserving the past carried little weight in Montréal), but the limestone buildings on the right that once adjoined it are identical to the ones in which Davis spent two years before leaving to live out his final years in Mississippi.

STE-CATHERINE AND PEEL

Ahead lies one of the busiest stretches of Ste-Catherine. Montréalers have long considered the intersection with Rue Peel as the absolute dead centre of town. The stores along this stretch are decidedly more upscale than those to the west. Names like Guess, Gap and BCBG display the latest fashions to the crowds strolling by. For a quick snack, pop over to the corner of Rue Mansfield and head upstairs to Basha, a Lebanese restaurant that offers tasty, filling meals such as plates of shish taouk chicken and shawarma beef for around $7. Across the street, the department store for au courant fashions, Simons, occupies the former home of the now-defunct Simpsons chain.

One block further east, take a look up Avenue McGill-College, the closest thing Montréal has to a Champs-Elysées. This is one of the best views in the city, with the copper-roofed buildings of McGill University at the top of the street, behind the curved entrance of the Roddick Gates, and Mont Royal in the background. At Christmastime, McGill-College is lit up with innumerable small red and white lights. When the snow falls softly in the evening, the street looks like a fairyland.

RODDICK GATES

A couple of blocks east you'll see another casualty of the recent shift in shopping habits of Montréalers — and Canadians as well. The imposing edifice at the corner of Ste-Catherine and Rue University was once home to Montréal's largest department store, Eaton's. The venerable

institution went belly up in the late 1990s, and the building stood empty for many years after that. In 2002, the upscale department store Les Ailes de la Mode opened in the newly renovated building.

Still, it's not all tony stores in this part of the town. The stretch from Guy to University has its share of Danseuses Nues (Nude Dancers) signs. And right across the street from the former Eaton's building is probably the best-known strip joint in town, Club Super Sexe, which features in at least one piece by Hunter S. Thompson.

The famed gonzo journalist didn't mention it, but it's hard to imagine he wasn't impressed by the fact that someone standing in front of the Club Super Sexe can divert their glance from the large red letters boldly proclaiming its attractions and catch a glimpse of one of Montréal's best-loved churches, Cathédrale Christ Church, less than half a block away. The cathedral, on Avenue Union and fronting onto Ste-Catherine, is a neo-Gothic masterpiece. It was designed in the 1850s by Frank Wills, a native of a town that has an impressive cathedral of its own: Salisbury, England. Christ Church is topped by a graceful spire made of aluminum, which replaced the original stone after it was discovered that its weight threatened the structure. In 1986 the church leaders leased the rights to their lot to developers, who then propped up the entire cathedral on huge steel posts and dug out enough space underneath to squeeze in a 100-store mall, Les Promenades de la Cathédrale. Some may have decried the move as selling out, but parishioners in the late 21st century may have the last laugh. That's when the lease expires and the promenade and the soaring glass tower called La Maison des Coopérants directly behind the cathedral become church property. Christ Church faces Carré Phillips, a small patch of green on Ste-Catherine. Also facing the square are Birks, one of Canada's oldest jewellers and a favourite for bridal registries in the city, and The Bay department store, a red sandstone beauty dating back to 1886 with a regrettably ugly steel-covered walkway that encircles the building. Birks was given a major facelift in 2001, which has brightened up the once-subdued lighting of the store.

Beyond Carré Phillips, Ste-Catherine dips down slightly to Rue Jeanne-Mance, where Place des Arts, home to the Orchestre Symphonique de Montréal, the Musée

STATUE IN CARRÉ PHILLIPS

d'Art Contemporain and the Complexe Desjardins, can fulfill many urges — for great music, contemporary arts, shopping and hotel accommodations. During the Festival International de Jazz de Montréal every July, this area is ground zero for a couple of weeks for some of the best music on the planet. The surrounding streets are wall-to-wall people as far as the eye can see, with everyone swaying to the beat of an astonishing array of free outdoor concerts.

Birks

There are still more than five kilometres to go until Ste-Catherine runs into Rue Notre-Dame at the eastern end of Montréal's docks and calls it quits. There are a few noteworthy attractions along the way. One is the Gay Village, a small but vibrant district of dance clubs, bars, clothing stores and eateries between the cross streets of St-Hubert and Papineau. A few blocks before you reach the Village, at the corner of Avenue de l'Hôtel-de-Ville, you'll pass Henri-Henri, a hat store that has been in business since 1932 and is still one of the best places in town — if not in all of Canada — to pick up a $400 Borsalino or a beret straight from France. Just ask patrons like Donald Sutherland and Charlie Sheen, who drop in here when they're filming in Montréal. Henri-Henri is exceptional — and yet it's also typical in a way: it's another little jewel that pops out on Ste-Catherine when you least expect it.

Place des Arts

Shopping on Ste-Catherine

Sherbrooke St.

James Bassil

Studded with pockets of glamour and stretches of history, the sights along Rue Sherbrooke make it a prime destination for any visitor. Attractions aside, bypassing this street would be a geographic near-impossibility: Sherbrooke spans 35 kilometres from east to west, stretching through half the island and touching upon most of downtown's diverse neighborhoods along the way.

A 35-kilometre hike doesn't fit into most travel itineraries, so where does one find the best of Sherbrooke? A good starting point might be the corner at Avenue Atwater, a surprisingly green and lush intersection in itself. To the west are 12 acres of unspoiled land encircling Dawson College, Montréal's first English-language college. To the east, equally enticing property surrounds one of the city's many convents. One of its former convents, to be precise — Le Manoir de Belmont, once a nunnery, has since been converted into a luxurious apartment complex. While this metamorphosis may strike first-time visitors as rather surprising (if not blasphemous), many religious buildings in Québec have undergone similar conversions. Throughout the 1950s, the province's powerful Roman Catholic clergy, anticipating rapid population growth, commissioned the construction

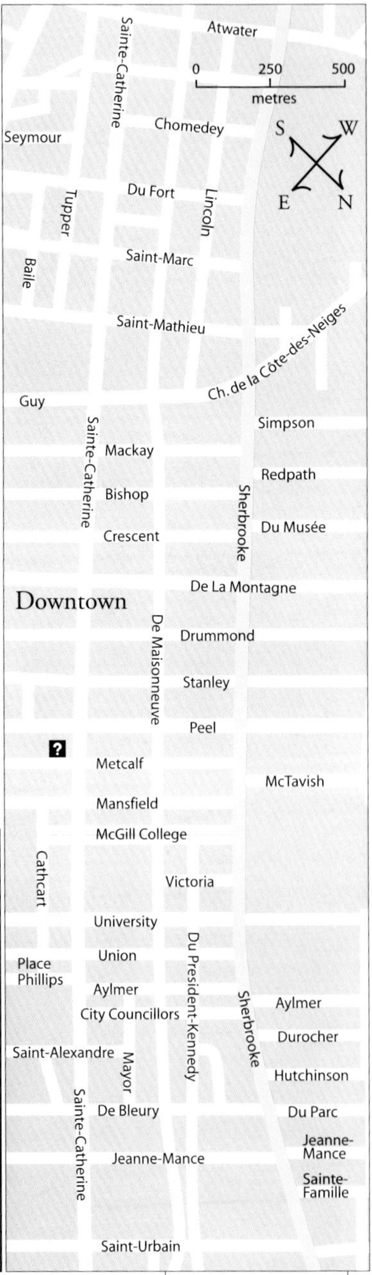

Le Manoir de Belmont

Atwater
0 250 500
metres
S W E N
Sainte-Catherine
Seymour
Chomedey
Tupper
Du Fort
Lincoln
Baile
Saint-Marc
Saint-Mathieu
Ch. de la Côte-des-Neiges
Guy
Simpson
Sainte-Catherine
Mackay
Redpath
Bishop
Sherbrooke
Du Musée
Crescent
De La Montagne
Downtown
De Maisonneuve
Drummond
Stanley
Peel
?
Metcalf
McTavish
Mansfield
McGill College
Cathcart
Victoria
University
Du President-Kennedy
Place Phillips
Union
Aylmer
Sherbrooke
Aylmer
City Councillors
Durocher
Saint-Alexandre
Mayor
Hutchinson
Sainte-Catherine
De Bleury
Du Parc
Jeanne-Mance
Jeanne-Mance
Sainte-Famille
Saint-Urbain

LE GRAND SÉMINAIRE

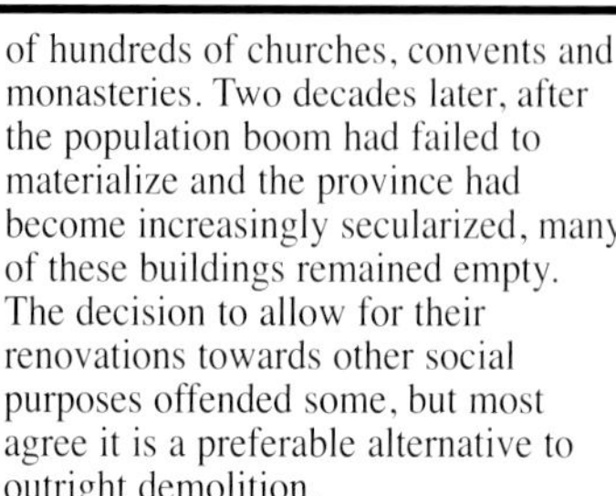

HADDON HALL

of hundreds of churches, convents and monasteries. Two decades later, after the population boom had failed to materialize and the province had become increasingly secularized, many of these buildings remained empty. The decision to allow for their renovations towards other social purposes offended some, but most agree it is a preferable alternative to outright demolition.

The profuse vegetation and recycled religious buildings continue as one proceeds east along Sherbrooke. On the north side of the street, wild growth has consumed a fence bordering the sidewalk; behind it is Le Grand Séminaire de Montréal. First used as a seminary in 1857, Le Grand Séminaire continues to operate as such and is still owned by the Roman Catholic Sulpician Order. Nonetheless, progress has spread into its grounds. Some lots on the property have been sold to corporations, making for a sharp contrast between their offices and the two stone towers looming over them, the oldest structures on the island.

Further contrast is to be found between the overgrown foliage of Le Grand Séminaire and the perfectly manicured greenery on the other side of the street. These gardens act as the entryway to Haddon Hall, a regal apartment building whose architecture recalls the early years of the 20th century. At this time, Sherbrooke served as one of the four borders for the section of the city known as the Golden Square Mile. This district was as opulent as its name suggests: the Square Mile was home to Canada's leading industrialists and businessmen, and their wealth was reflected in the mansions lining the streets.

POTTERY AT MUSÉE DES BEAUX ARTS

As Haddon Hall recalls the affluence of days past, the blocks that lie to its east showcase more current luxuries. The first glimpse of such, the Château Versailles hotel, is actually a bridge between eras. Originally built as a townhouse at the end of the 19th century, the building's Edwardian façade, along with many of its interior moldings and fixtures, has remained intact. The amenities that it offers, however, are geared towards the modern guest — Internet access, video-game

BOULANGERIE PREMIÈRE MOISSON

consoles and in-room safety deposit boxes are found in every suite.

The real-estate values continue to rise as one crosses the busy intersection at Rue Guy. On the south side of Sherbrooke is Bice restaurant, boasting one of the most magnificent dining spaces in Montréal with its glassed-in summer terrace. If the name rings familiar, it is because the restaurant is part of an international chain with branches in Tokyo, Paris, London and New York — each location offering an elegant blend of authentic and nouvelle Italian cuisine, and extravagant prices to match.

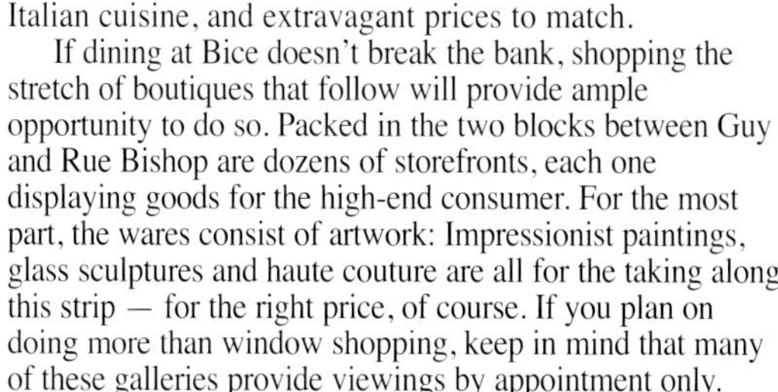

If dining at Bice doesn't break the bank, shopping the stretch of boutiques that follow will provide ample opportunity to do so. Packed in the two blocks between Guy and Rue Bishop are dozens of storefronts, each one displaying goods for the high-end consumer. For the most part, the wares consist of artwork: Impressionist paintings, glass sculptures and haute couture are all for the taking along this strip — for the right price, of course. If you plan on doing more than window shopping, keep in mind that many of these galleries provide viewings by appointment only.

Other boutiques provide less pricey indulgences, but indulgences nonetheless. Le Chocolat Belge Neuhaus specializes in Belgian pralines and other chocolate delicacies; Davidoff and La Casa del Habano cater to cigar aficionados; and Boulangerie Première Moisson offers delicious breads, pastries and quiches.

MUSÉE DES BEAUX-ARTS DE MONTRÉAL

The Musée des Beaux-Arts de Montréal comprises two buildings, one on either side of Sherbrooke. The building on the north side of the street does not host exhibitions, focusing instead on the museum's permanent collection. This collection is nothing to sneeze at: works by Picasso, Rembrandt, Monet and Cézanne are to be found alongside ancient Egyptian sculptures and Canadian landscapes. The architecture of the building on the south side of Sherbrooke (designed by Moshe Safdie) has garnered mixed reviews, but the quality of the exhibitions it houses has rarely been called into question. If scheduling permits, try to set aside at least half a day to explore all that both buildings have to offer.

Continuing east, Sherbrooke briefly takes on the appearance of Fifth Avenue as one encounters a string of posh fashion boutiques — Holt Renfrew, Hermès, Burberry and Gucci among them. Standing just past

RITZ CARLTON HOTEL

these storefronts is Montréal's most famous hotel, the Ritz-Carlton. Recently ranked among the top 100 hotels in the world, this branch of the Ritz meets the chain's reputation with its Edwardian-style décor, marble baths in each suite and fresh fruits to greet every guest. The outdoor Jardin du Ritz is open for business in the summer months; come winter, dining moves indoors to the Café de Paris, a popular spot for power lunches.

The Ritz stands on the corner of Rue Drummond. Two blocks east, at its intersection with Rue Peel, Sherbrooke begins to assume a different personality. Townhouses are replaced by highrises, and boutiques by banks. Many find the tone along this particular stretch of downtown to be a bit cold, but it does harbour some nice surprises. Zen restaurant is tucked in the basement of the Hôtel Omni, but it is accessible from the street — stop in any night of the week for the all-you-can-eat buffet. If you duck into the Sherbrooke branch of the Royal Bank and walk past the tellers, you'll find an escalator leading down to the shopping maze of Montréal's Underground City.

STATUE OF JAMES MCGILL

All this concrete and glass is nicely balanced by the lower campus of McGill University. Often referred to as the Harvard of the North, McGill is certainly Ivy League in appearance. The university was founded in 1821 and retains many of its original buildings, scattered across 80 acres of property. Walking tours are available and the Musée Redpath, an on-campus natural history museum, is open to the public, with free admission.

Beyond the buildings of the university to the north are the Gothic towers of the Hôpital Royal Victoria and the castle-like turrets of the city reservoir. South of the main gates, the university's principal road turns into Avenue McGill-College, a wide mall that leads down to busy Ste-Catherine. In summer the promenade is bright with blossoms, and the city often arranges for photo displays along its west side. In winter its trees are festooned with tiny lights and a huge Christmas tree graces the plaza of Place Ville-Marie at the Avenue's base.

MCGILL UNIVERSITY

While this portion of Sherbrooke between Atwater and McGill-College presents at least a couple of days' worth of sightseeing fodder, there are plenty of other treasures to be found on this street. Further east one finds the sparkling new buildings of McGill and the Université du Québec à Montréal, chic Boulevard St-Laurent, yet another museum and the restored monastery Le Monastère du Bon-Pasteur. Retreating west, past our starting point, one finds the ultra-plush neighbourhood of Westmount, home to the city's elite, plenty of shops and some of Montréal's finest public parks.

ST-LAURENT

SARAH LOUISE MUSGRAVE

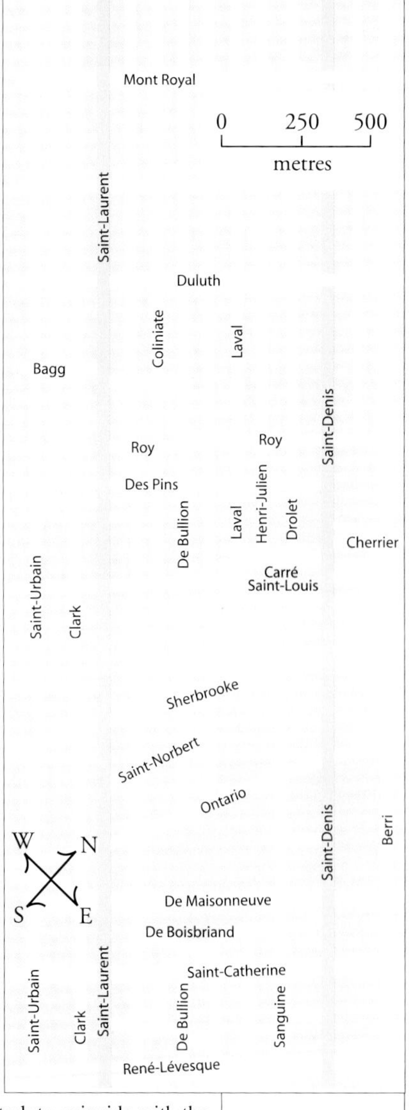

Boulevard St-Laurent is often referred to as the dividing line between Montréal's two solitudes: the French community to one side, and the English community to the other. These days, however, quite the opposite is true. While this distinctive thoroughfare still cleaves the city's addresses into east and west, it's more of a great unifier than a great divider. More than any other street, the Main, as St-Laurent is affectionately known, brings together the different languages and cultures that make up Montréal's rich heritage. A promenade along its length offers a cross-section of local life — a journey through the past, present and even the future.

A particular blend of old world and new gives St-Laurent its colourful character. This multiethnic strip has welcomed just about every wave of immigration to the province since the 1800s: speakers of Yiddish, Greek, Portuguese, Cantonese and, more recently, Spanish and Thai. Haute couture boutiques, Latin salsa bars and tattoo parlours share sidewalk space with Polish sausage counters and Jewish schmatta shops whose window displays haven't changed since the 1950s — so much so that some of them are even dusty!

Appropriately enough, St-Laurent begins where Montréal first took root, at the Old Port in the heart of the old city. Its first few blocks pass through one of the duller parts of the historical district, however. The real fun begins at Avenue Viger, where majestic red-and-gold gates announce the entrance to a small but vibrant Chinatown. Time your trek to coincide with the frenzied lunch hour, when a range of Asian aromas compete for attention: Vietnamese noodle soups, Taiwanese

CHINATOWN, ST-LAURENT

bubble teas and Chinese delicacies like fried dumplings and fresh lobster. The jumble of exotic eateries, grocery stores and gift shops extends onto Rue de la Gauchetière, a brick-lined walkway that intersects St-Laurent, where vendors hawk everything from dragon beard candy to palm readings and herbal medicines. Escape the hustle and bustle in the minimalist Dr. Sun Yat Sen Park at the corner of Rue Clark.

Continuing north, you'll tread the storied sidewalks of what was once Montréal's vaunted red-light district, back when it was the city of sin. The stretch between Boulevard René-Lévesque and Rue Ste-Catherine, where in yesteryear peeler palaces abounded, has recently been reinvented as a different kind of entertainment district: you can catch a band at Club Soda or a play at the École Nationale de Théâtre (National Theatre School). Among the few billiard halls, strip clubs and peep shows that remain from grittier days, the Montréal Pool Room is an enduring fixture. This classic dive no longer has pool tables but continues to dish out hot dogs much as it did in 1912. Its trademark *steamé* consists of a steamed wiener stuffed into a steamed bun and covered with onions, mustard and coleslaw. It's best devoured with an order of *frites* (french fries).

THE DRAGON FOUNTAIN IN DR. SUN YAT SEN PARK

A cultural institution of a different sort, the Musée Juste Pour Rire, above Boulevard de Maisonneuve, grew out of Montréal's internationally renowned Just for Laughs comedy festival. The permanent exhibit focuses on the history of humour, while the on-site cabaret regularly bills top pop-music acts. Across the street, the Godin, a new boutique hotel, stands as a testament to an increasingly upscale attitude — as the hill gets steeper here, so do the prices.

The jet-set strip awaits just across Rue Sherbrooke. Frequented by fashionistas and visiting celebs, this section of the Main is jam-packed with some of the trendiest shopping, food and nightlife in Montréal. Boutiques showcase local designers, from the sleek styles of Nevik and street sense of Space FB to the leatherware of Rugby and the whimsical creations of Scandale. Statuesque serving staff tend to the culinary cravings of the well heeled at Buona Notte and Med, while floors above, chi-chi clubs with rooftop terraces start hopping as soon as the sun goes down.

Amidst the click of high heels, the bleep of cell phones and the rev of valet parking, the Ex-Centris complex is an oasis of high-tech serenity. This imposing structure screens avant-garde films from around the world in ultra-cushy, ultra-modern facilities. It's also the primary venue for the cutting-edge Montréal International Festival of New Cinema and New Media, which runs for two weeks every fall.

THE EX-CENTRIS COMPLEX

This is an area for business types and bohemians alike to see and be seen. Before venturing north, take a short detour onto Rue Prince-Arthur, a mecca of counterculture since the 1970s. This cobblestone mall is closed to traffic — at least the motorized kind — but streams with buskers, caricaturists and acrobats, as well as budget-minded diners who flock to its patios. In keeping with the free-spirited atmosphere, most restaurants have an *apportez votre vin,* or bring your own wine, policy (meaning they don't have a liquor licence, but you can partake in your own purchases on the premises). Prince-Arthur spills into leafy Carré St-Louis, a gracious square with a central fountain surrounded by Second Empire homes built in the 19th century to house Montréal's francophone bourgeoisie.

Back on St-Laurent, the intersection of Avenue des Pins marks a crossroads of cultural chaos — in a good way. Inexpensive ethnic eats lure from every direction: lengths of links hang in the window at Slovenia, calzone emerge hot from the ovens at after-hours cafeteria Eurodeli and greasily good Portuguese chicken sandwiches are doled out at Coco Rico. La Vieille Europe, an authentic Central European grocery store, is stocked with enough cheese, salami and chocolate for a lifetime of picnics. There's food for the mind here, too. A youthful, artsy crowd populates record emporiums, handcrafted-jewellery outlets, body-piercing facilities and hip hair salons by day, then busts moves on dance floors, chills to ambient beats in lounges or swills micro-brewery products at watering holes by night.

This stretch was once the centre of Jewish life in the metropolis. In the late 19th century, thousands of emigrants from Romania, Poland and other Eastern European countries established shops, schools and synagogues in the area, creating a lively neighbourhood that later inspired the work of literary lions such as Mordecai Richler, Leonard Cohen and Irving Layton. Harking back to the good ol' days — or at least a time before the discovery of cholesterol — is the perpetually packed Schwartz's Montréal Hebrew Delicatessen, purveyor of the city's world-famous smoked meat. Order a medium-cut sandwich on rye with a cherry coke and half a sour pickle (you won't have to ask for the attitude — that's included!).

SCHWARTZ'S DELICATESSEN

BOOKSELLER S.W WELCH

The corner of Rue Marie-Anne and St-Laurent is the nexus of the Main's Portuguese enclave, encapsulated by a charming blue-and-yellow-tiled park where the community's venerable members gather to chat. Steps from an African dance club, a Jewish discount clothing store and a South American market, it's a perfect place to appreciate the remarkable diversity of the area. Another such opportunity is a St-Laurent street sale, an event that takes place periodically during summer months, when the road is cordoned off to house an absolutely bizarre assortment of merchandise: raw oysters on the half-shell, vintage clothing from fripperies, underwear by the dozen and second-hand titles from bookseller S.W. Welch.

Fans of design will revel in the span of St-Laurent north of Marie-Anne, now a high-end-décor district. Browse beautiful housewares at Côté Sud, shop for funky furniture at Biltmore or reflect on the retro stylings of Sauriol, providing home accessories to those who've cashed in on the area's condominium boom of the last decade. Signs of gentrification are also in evidence on the portion of the Main that runs through the former immigrant enclave of Mile-End, between Boulevard St-Joseph and Rue Bernard. Amid new wine bars and upmarket stores, you'll find reasonably priced Indian, Italian, Thai and Peruvian meals. Grassroots eatery Sala Rossa offers Spanish tapas in an old-style dining room, while its sister establishment, Casa Del Popolo, serves up vegetarian snacks and alternative music.

Push on a few blocks further north for a taste of Montréal's thriving Little Italy, a primo destination for foodies. The selection of restaurants and markets near Rue St-Zotique would make any nonna proud. Stop at Fruiterie Milano to browse the pasta, prosciutto, parmesan and pannetone that make this the best Italian grocery in town. For an authentic coffee-bar experience, old-school Caffe Italia comes complete with soccer paraphernalia, shaving products and some of the best espresso in the city. Sounds of merriment emerge from Piccolo Italia's numerous dining establishments any time of year, but especially during international soccer tournaments and the Montréal Grand Prix Formula One auto race.

STUDENT LIFE ALONG ST-DENIS

All the pleasures of the palate are brought together at Marché Jean-Talon, Montréal's largest outdoor farmers' market, just east of St-Laurent off Avenue Shamrock. Kiosks offer locally harvested produce, and bakeries, butcher shops and restaurants line the outer perimeter. The market caters to gourmet shoppers as well as recent arrivals from North Africa, the Middle East, Central America and almost everywhere in between. It's the perfect place to sum up the international legacy of Boulevard St-Laurent: a unifying force from one end to the other.

Excursions

Sarah Waters

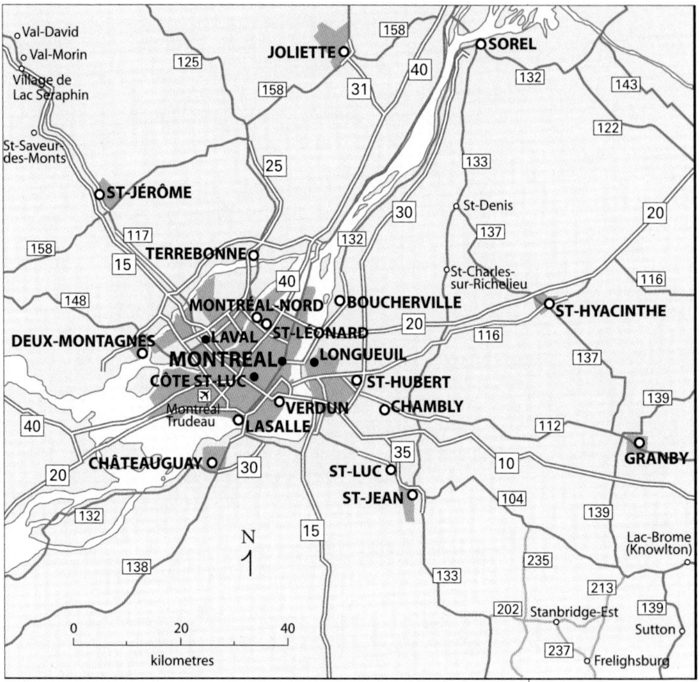

As easy as it is to get into the bustling scene in the streets of Montréal, getting out of town can be just as appealing — and surprisingly easy, too. You might drive for what seems like days in a place like Toronto and still be surrounded by suburban sprawl. Drive for just 20 minutes and you're out of Montréal and in rolling countryside; two hours and you're in the wilderness of the northern Laurentians — if the traffic's flowing on the bridges, that is. Whether you're looking for adventure or relaxation, there are plenty of choices for day trips out of Montréal.

One way to escape Montréal without really leaving is to take a cruise around the island. It takes about two hours to make a complete circle, and you're guaranteed to get a different perspective on the city as you take it in from the water. Croisières AML is a reliable cruise line operating out of the Old Port, with several tours departing daily from the Quai King-Edward.

Another watery option with an extra kick of adrenaline can be found barely 15 minutes from downtown Montréal with Les Descentes sur le St-Laurent, a company that offers raft and hydro-jet rides down the treacherous-looking Rapides de Lachine on the St. Lawrence River.

Laurentian Colour

FORTS AND PATRIOTS

One of the simplest and best excursions is to drive east (downriver) to Sorel and then follow the Rivière Richelieu south through some of the province's richest farmlands and orchards until you reach the American border crossing at Lacolle. The Richelieu was one of the most important waterways of New France. It flows north from the trading areas around Lake Champlain and the Fleuve Hudson (Hudson River) and was key in the struggle between European powers (France, Britain and Holland) vying for hegemony in the region. As a result, the valley is also rich in history.

You could start your journey with a cruise around the Îles de Sorel, an enchanting little archipelago in the St. Lawrence that's alive with waterfowl and fish. But that would take at least a couple of hours and if time is limited it might be best to start south through the valley. Follow Highway 133 towards Chambly. This route is sometimes called the Chemin des Patriotes (Patriots' Road) in honour of the men and women who joined Louis-Joseph Papineau in the 1837 rebellion against British imperial rule. The rebels faced down the British at St-Denis-sur-Richelieu and were driven off in a skirmish at St-Charles-sur-Richelieu.

There are many reminders of the revolt along the road. The route is marked with signs bearing the image of an armed rebel in a tuque and a *ceinture fléchée* (a colourful woven sash), and just outside St-Denis-sur-Richelieu on Chemin des Patriotes is an early-19th-century home that is now La Maison Nationale des Patriotes. Exhibits and audio visual shows — in French only — recount the

FORT CHAMBLY

rebellion and the battles. In St-Denis itself the insurgents' green, white and red tricolour flies over a monument erected in their honour in 1987. The nearby church has twin towers, one of which houses the liberty bell that called the rebels to battle.

The next landmark is a natural one — Mont St-Hilaire, a steep, 396-metre peak that soars abruptly out of the rolling countryside. Its lower slopes are covered with apple orchards and its upper reaches are heavily forested. Most of the mountain belongs to McGill University, but an area of about 6 square kilometres is open to the public. You can park your car halfway up the mountain and follow a series of paths to the summit for sweeping views of the valley and Montréal. The mountain was once the estate of Andrew Hamilton Gault (1882–1958), who founded Princess Patricia's Canadian Light Infantry. At the foot of the mountain is a museum dedicated to the sweetest legacy of Canada's First Nations — maple syrup. The Maison des Cultures Amérindiennes on Montée des Trente displays how sap was traditionally harvested and processed, and reveals the importance of maple products in native culture. The museum dining room serves traditional native meals.

Fort Lennox, barrack interior

Further upriver lies Chambly, an important trading and defence centre during the French regime. Captain Jacques de Chambly built the first French fort here in 1665 to defend Montréal against Indian, and later British, attacks. The stone successor of that humble wooden stockade still guards the Rapides de Chambly, the northernmost of a series of military strongholds along the river. Fort Chambly has been restored to its 18th-century appearance and stands in a pleasant park by the river. It has an interpretation centre with displays and programs illustrating military and farming life in the 18th and 19th centuries.

Chambly is also the northern end of the Canal de Chambly, a 19-kilometre waterway that skirts a series of rapids and leads to the industrial city of St-Jean-sur-Richelieu. Today it's used only by pleasure craft, and the towpath has been converted into a bicycle path. From Chambly, the road heads south through St-Jean-sur-Richelieu to the next fort on the route — Fort Lennox, built by the British in 1802. It sits on an island — Île aux Noix — in the middle of the river, and a wide moat surrounds its star-shaped fortifications. Displays and costumed actors capture the tough life of a 19th-century British citizen on colonial duty. The last fort on the river is the two-storey blockhouse at Lacolle, still pocked with bullet holes from the War of 1812.

If you're travelling with kids — and even if you're not — don't miss Lacolle's Arche des Papillons, where you can walk through a magic greenhouse surrounded by clouds of fluttering butterflies. The surrounding countryside is full of orchards and growers often make their own ciders, which you can stop and sample. Many of the village churches are quite beautiful and are decorated by some of Québec's leading artists. The ones in St-Hilaire and St-Matthias, especially, are worth visiting.

Another kid-friendly favourite is the Parc Safari, about a half-hour south of the city, just north of the U.S. border. The park is full of giraffes, elephants, leopards and other transplants from around the globe, and you can either drive your own car through it or catch a ride on one of the park's buses. A little closer to Montréal, in the town of St-Constant, is the Association Canadienne d'Histoire Ferroviaire (Canadian Railway Museum), home of the largest collection of railway equipment in Canada. This interactive museum gives visitors of all ages a chance to experience the railway adventure firsthand.

NORTHERN PLAYGROUND

Attempts in the late 19th and early 20th centuries to settle the low-lying rocky Laurentian Mountains didn't work out very well. The soil was often too thin for farming, but "Montréal's backyard" has since found its real wealth in recreation and tourism.

The hills, lakes and rivers of the region attract hikers, hunters, anglers, canoeists, kayakers, cross-country skiers and mountain bikers, not to mention artists and photographers. Downhill skiing in Canada can trace its roots to the Laurentians, which had the country's first mechanical lifts. And just in case all these natural pastimes aren't enough, entrepreneurs have filled the valleys with golf courses, go-cart tracks, bungee towers and a dizzying array of bars, boutiques and fine restaurants.

LAURENTIAN RESORT

One of the best ways to explore the region is on two wheels. Parc du P'tit Train du Nord — Québec's longest bicycle trail — follows an abandoned railway line from St-Jérôme 200 kilometres north to Mont Laurier. The trail can be easily accessed at the old railway station in Ste-Agathe or via the dozens of towns along its route. Its gentle grade takes cyclists through some of the region's prettiest countryside and most charming villages. In winter, cross-country skiers and snowmobilers glide along its length. The 20-kilometre stretch between St-Sauveur and Ste-Agathe is thick with restaurants, cafés and bed-&-breakfasts — as well as Laurentian scenery. Further north, the landscape gets wilder and the bicycle traffic thinner. North of Labelle, you can cycle for hours with just the birds for company.

But the car-bound can explore the Laurentians as well. A good place to start is St-Sauveur-des-Monts, which was once a simple ski village with a single hotel, a couple of watering holes and a few restaurants. It has developed into a major resort choked with condos, name-brand outlet stores and trendy bars that throb with life all year round. Traffic on the main street in July, when the sidewalks are full of stylish diners and shoppers, can be as thick as it is on Rue Ste-Catherine in Montréal. This might not sound like much of a wilderness escape, but it is an exciting place to be.

ST-SAUVEUR-DES-MONTS

If a slower pace appeals, you might want to consider a visit to the Polar Bear's Club, not far out of Montréal. Here you can relax in any one of a number of hot tubs along a boardwalk that overlooks a rushing stream, and if the heat is too much, just take a quick dip in the frigid stream water. If you're prepared to travel a little further, there's nothing quite like a visit to Ofuro Spa in Morin Heights. The beautiful site, with its charming Japanese wooden architecture, luscious garden and babbling waterfall, was clearly designed with ultimate relaxation in mind. The spa offers a range of massage and body-treatment packages, but you could also easily while away a day in the sauna, steam bath, whirlpool and river bath.

Ste-Agathe is a favourite for tourists and weekenders, with a number of fine hotels and restaurants. From Ste-Agathe the road snakes through Val Morin and Val David, attractive villages surrounded by hills and lakes. They too have their pleasant little restaurants and bars, plus a couple of first-class inns, but Val Morin and Val David have somehow escaped the feverish development that has marked the recent history of their more southerly neighbour.

Follow Highway 117 to St-Jovite and then take Highway 327 to the Mont Tremblant ski resort. Mont Tremblant, with a vertical drop of 650 metres, is the highest mountain in the Laurentians. Legendary travel writer and ski buff Lowell Thomas first suggested making

it into a ski hill. In September 1991 it was bought by Intrawest, the company that developed Blackcomb on the west coast. Intrawest has since spent billions of dollars turning the mountain into a year-round resort. It has opened two new mountain faces and added a gondola and several high-speed chairlifts. It has also built two spectacular golf courses, opened a half-dozen resort hotels and re-created a miniature version of Québec City at the base of the mountain. Mountain bikers use the lifts and ski trails in summer, and thousands of leaf-peepers ride the chairs to the top every fall for endless vistas of gold and crimson hills. The resort is also the setting for a summer blues festival and classical music concerts.

MONT TREMBLANT RESORT

Beyond the resort, the road turns into Parc Provincial du Mont Tremblant, a 1,500-square-kilometre wilderness of rivers, lakes and mountains. The road, which is closed in winter, follows the Rivière Diable (Devil's River), a well-named waterway punctuated with falls and rapids. Here you'll find some of the most wildly beautiful scenery in Québec. Well worth a stop are Chutes du Diable (Devil's Falls) and Chutes aux Rats (Muskrat Falls), and there's a beautiful beach on Lac Monroe. The park has hiking trails and facilities for canoeists and campers. From St-Donat-de-Montcalm, take Highway 329 south to Ste-Agathe and from there follow Highway 117 or Highway 15 (the Laurentian Autoroute) back to Montréal.

PARC PROVINCIAL DU MONT TREMBLANT

LOYALIST COUNTRY

After the American Revolution, colonists who wished to remain loyal to the British Crown fled north to Canada and settled in parts of Québec, New Brunswick and Ontario. They brought with them their language, their Protestant faith and their culture. In Québec they were allowed to establish townships in the great chunk of land along the American border between the Rivières Richelieu and Chaudière. This land was unsettled beyond the reach of the French parishes. Its gently rolling countryside made it ideal for farming, and the new settlers prospered.

The area is now known as the Cantons-de-l'Est, or Estrie (Eastern Townships), and its towns and villages resemble New England more than New France. They're full of fine brick and clapboard homes built on the British model, with central hallways and formal front rooms. The Loyalist pioneers and the British and American settlers who followed them into this region are now outnumbered by their French neighbours. The blend, however, is harmonious. Townshippers of both cultures can usually switch from one language to the other with ease and agility.

One way to get a taste of this varied and beautiful region is to drive east on Highway 10 (the Eastern Townships Autoroute) to Exit 90 and then follow Highway 243 south along the shores of Lac Brome to Knowlton, a pleasant 19th-century town full of grand brick buildings. The streets are lined with boutiques and restaurants, and there is a summer theatre that specializes in English-language comedies and mysteries. The lakeshore is lined with mansions that are the summer homes of Montréal's elite.

From Knowlton follow Highways 104 and 215 to Sutton, another pretty little Loyalist town, but the homes here are mostly white clapboard with wraparound verandahs and fanciful towers and gables. Its main street, too, has an assortment of restaurants and boutiques. Just outside town is Mont Sutton, a mountain with a major ski resort whose lifts offer summer and fall visitors a great way to view the surrounding countryside.

HIKING IN THE CANTONS-DE-L'EST

From Sutton drive west on Highway 237 through Frelighsburg, a beautiful village of brick homes cupped in the Pike River valley, to Stanbridge East, a good place to stop for a picnic. The village doesn't offer much in the way of restaurants, but it does have a delightful little Anglican church, an old grist mill and a general store and barn that are now the Musée Missisquoi of pioneer life. The land across the river from the mill has been turned into a wonderful little park.

From Stanbridge turn east again on Highway 202 and drive through Québec's wine country to Dunham. Mountains protect this gentle piece of land from the northern winds and hold the southern sun, creating a microclimate just warm enough to make the cultivation of grapes possible. Most of the vineyards along the road sell their produce in on-site boutiques and some have little

ANTIQUES IN KNOWLTON

wine bars and even restaurants.

From Dunham you can follow Highways 202 and 139 north back to the Autoroute and home to Montréal.

OTHER SUGGESTED DAY TRIPS

Terrebonne, a pretty little town on the Rivière des Mille Îles north of Montréal, is in the heart of a fertile farming area. Its wealth, however, comes from the river, which 19th-century merchants harnessed to power grist and flour mills to process grain and sawmills to cut lumber. Much of this heritage is preserved on Île des Moulins, a kind of industrial theme park — carefully preserved flour mills and sawmills as well as Canada's first industrial bakery, built in 1802 to supply hard biscuits for voyageurs and trappers. The old seigneurial office serves as an interpretation centre and the "new mill," built in 1850, houses a theatre, a cultural centre and an art gallery. These attractions are all open from mid-May until Labour Day. The industrial town of Trois-Rivières sits at the confluence of the St-Lawrence and Maurice Rivers. The Maurice splits into three channels just before it empties into the St-Lawrence, hence the town's misleading name. Its chief industry is pulp and paper, and the odour of sulphur often hangs heavy in the air, but the visitor who overcomes the olfactory assault will discover the greater charms of this place. Trois-Rivières is older than Montréal, and its historic section is full of 18th- and 19th-century treasures.

MISSISQUOI MUSÉE IN STANBRIDGE EAST

QUÉBEC CITY'S BEST

Québec City's Top Attractions

Patrick Donovan

Québec City atop Cap Diamant

I would rather be a poor priest in Québec [City] than a rich hog merchant in Chicago.
— English poet Matthew Arnold (1822–88)

Many might challenge Matthew Arnold's implied criticism of Chicago, but few would disagree with his praise for Québec City. It is unquestionably one of the most historic and beautiful cities in North America. In addition to a wealth of 18th- and 19th-century architecture, Québec City is blessed with a dramatic location atop the rugged heights of Cap Diamant (Cape Diamond). Views stretch over the widening estuary of the St. Lawrence River, with the Laurentian Mountains lending their curves to the horizon in the distance.

Château Frontenac in the snow

A nice way to get some perspective on this incredible panorama is to head for the docks and take the ferry to Lévis. When architect Bruce Price designed the Château Frontenac, the huge copper-roofed hotel that is Québec City's principal landmark, he sketched it from

CALÈCHE IN OLD QUÉBEC CITY

across the river with the intention of creating a majestic skyline for the city. In addition to offering a glimpse of the city and its castle from this intended perspective, the view from the ferry also provides a two-level history lesson. Atop Cap Diamant are the walls and turrets of Haute-Ville, or Upper Town. Along the river's edge are the narrow streets and tall stone houses of Basse-Ville, or Lower Town. The latter is where foundations for the city were laid by Samuel de Champlain in 1608. With time, governors, priests and army commanders moved to the Upper Town. The merchants, tradesmen and labourers (as well as thieves and hookers) scrabbled for a living down on the riverfront. After the 1759 British conquest little changed, except that the Upper Town aged gracefully and the Lower Town degenerated into an industrial slum, a state from which it was rescued only a couple of decades ago.

One of the best things to do in Québec is to walk around with no specific destination in mind. The steep streets of the fortified Upper Town are full of nooks, crannies and tiny laneways that shoot off at unexpected angles, with discoveries at every turn. You're bound to end up at Terrasse-Dufferin, a long wooden boardwalk hugging the cliffside by the Château Frontenac. The long walk to the end of the terrace, up the steps and along the boardwalk over to the Plaines d'Abraham has many breathtaking views. The Lower Town, containing some of the city's oldest areas, is also worth a stroll. The architecture of New France is at its most polished and obvious in Place Royale and Petit Champlain, though these areas often feel more like historical theme parks than genuine urban neighbourhoods. If the fake moccasins, Canadian-flag tote bags and cutesy mountie dolls start giving you a headache, walk west of the city walls for a taste of authentic local life. There you will find the bourgeois Quartier Montcalm, the bohemian St-Jean-Baptiste district or the rapidly-being-

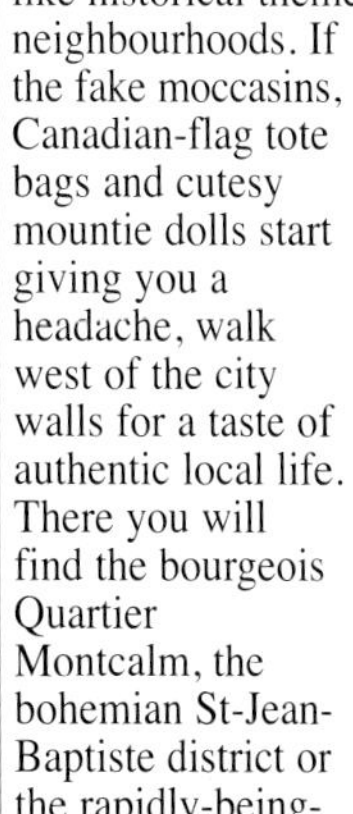

HISTORIC PETIT CHAMPLAIN

ESCALIER CASSE-COU

gentrified St-Roch neighbourhood. These lively areas are full of interesting architecture and great non-touristy cafés.

If your feet are sore, the horse-drawn wagons all over the city are generally a better option than tour buses. The latter have a hard time navigating the narrow streets. Furthermore, those who actually live downtown frequently curse these noisy eyesores under their breath. Be wary of the information calèche drivers tell you, as it often straddles the line between fact and outright nonsense. For an interesting perspective on city history that is grounded in proper research, try the excellent theatrical walking tours offered by the Compagnie des Six Associés. The tours deal with many broad themes, from medical practices in the 19th century to the evolution of crime and punishment.

Québec City has many fine museums that cover everything from history to art to ... chocolate. In the Lower Town, the huge Musée de la Civilisation focuses on Québec's relationship to the world; two excellent permanent exhibits with interactive displays cover the history of the province and its First Nations people. If you want to learn more about the history of the city itself, head to either the Centre d'Interprétation de Place-Royale or the Musée de l'Amérique Française. The latter is housed in the large Séminaire de Québec complex, Canada's first institution of higher learning, which later evolved into Université Laval in the 1850s. Many historic homes and convents are scattered throughout the city, providing various angles on local history. Among these is the Morrin Centre, which interprets local history from the perspective of its English-speaking minority. This group once represented 40 percent of the total population, and a few of its descendants are still around today to tell their tales. In addition to making available guided tours, the centre is home to a living library full of English books. The Anglo-Victorian atmosphere evokes some far-flung outpost of the British Empire between Bombay and Rangoon. Québec City's most important art museum is the Musée National des Beaux-Arts du Québec, located on the Plaines d'Abraham. For contemporary art head to Complexe Méduse in St-Roch. Finally, don't miss the tiny Choco-Musée Érico, a free museum about the origins of cocoa that should be visited if only to sample some of the best homemade ice cream and sorbet in the world.

MUSÉE DE LA CIVILISATION

Although Québec probably has more atheists per capita today than most places in the Americas, the opposite was true less than 50 years ago. The massive opulent churches that dot the landscape all over the city testify to this fact.

SAINT-JEAN-BAPTISTE

Notre-Dame-de-Québec, the large cathedral in the heart of the Upper Town, once ruled a diocese that stretched as far south as New Orleans. It has burned down and been reconstructed several times. The current cathedral dates from 1922. Older churches can be found in the Lower Town, namely Notre-Dame-des-Victoires at Place Royale and Notre-Dame-des-Anges in St-Roch. Many say the most beautiful church in Québec City is Saint-Jean-Baptiste, a monument of late-Victorian eclecticism located in the neighbourhood of the same name. Many old Anglo-Protestant congregations persist to this day: the Scottish Presbyterian Saint-Andrew's and the Anglican Cathedral of the Holy Trinity date back to the early 1800s and are worth a visit. With religion on the decline, many old churches are unfortunately being sold, converted or simply demolished. Among the rare examples of tasteful conversion is the former Anglican Saint-Matthew's church, now a public library surrounded by an interesting 18th-century graveyard.

Although Québec City is a tranquil place today, its history as a bustling military town is plainly obvious. A walk along the fortifications takes you from Parc de l'Artillerie, with its French redoubt, to the large British citadel that is still home to the Royal 22nd Régiment, with its red uniforms and large bearskin hats. Outside the walls lies Parc des Champs-de-Bataille (National Battlefields Park), site of the decisive battle between the troops of Wolfe and Montcalm that gave North America to Britain in 1759. Better known as the Plaines d'Abraham (Plains of Abraham), this park is full of winding pathways and grassy knolls, which stretch for kilometres along the cliff's edge, offering great views of the St. Lawrence. On a sunny day, do as the locals do: buy some fine Québec cheese, fresh bread and a bottle of wine from one of the many delis and boulangeries in town before strolling up to the plains for a picnic. While there, take a peek at one of the intriguing Tours Martello (Martello Towers) from the British era or the lovely French Jeanne d'Arc gardens. Walk back to the old city via the tree-lined Grande Allée, Québec's humble answer to the Champs-Elysées, with its sidewalk cafés and large nightclubs. The most interesting building along Grande Allée is the Hôtel du Parlement, or provincial parliament, with its eclectic blend of French and English architecture. To get a feel for the type of battles being fought in Québec nowadays, it's worth dropping into the Assemblée Nationale to hear all the hooting and hollering going on during question period.

MONASTÈRE DES URSULINES

PICNICKING ON THE PLAINES D'ABRAHAM

Heritage & Architecture

Sovita Chander

The walls of Québec

You can't turn around in Québec City without bumping into a story about the past. After all, this is where French colonists staked their first permanent settlement in the New World. Consequently, the city possesses a unique architectural heritage dating from its founding in the early 17th century. Most remarkably, much of this heritage is intact. For instance, it is the only city north of Mexico to have preserved its military fortifications, which comprise a wall surrounding the old city. Practically every one of the 11 square kilometres of the old city and beyond has a monument, building, park or residence with something to say. Some shout their visual wares, beckoning travellers with grandiose façades and far-flung reputations. Others sit squarely, solidly, stating their place in the history of everyday life. The rest whisper, yielding their rewards only through patient inquiry and observation.

Notre-Dame-des-Victoires

Québec City's history, and even prehistory, begins in what is now known as Basse-Ville, or Lower Town, along the banks of the St. Lawrence River. And the heart of the Lower Town, historically speaking, is Place Royale, which has been an important commercial site for at least 2,000 years. First Nations bands used it first, as a trading post, part of a vast network that covered all North America. When Jacques Cartier sailed up the St. Lawrence in 1534, he landed near the site and found the Iroquois village of

Stadacona, a thriving settlement of 500 souls. The Iroquois were gone when Samuel de Champlain arrived in 1608 to establish the first French settlement and open trade with the First Nations. Europeans were eager to establish a fur trade for a simple yet lucrative reason: fashion. Beaver fur made a luxuriously fine felt for the men's hats that were de rigueur for much of the period.

There's nothing left of Champlain's original settlement. Fire destroyed much of it in 1682 and colonial and religious officials built a church dedicated to the Virgin Mary — now called Notre-Dame-des-Victoires — on the ruins. The parishioners of the settlement had long petitioned the Church for a place of worship in the Lower Town, as the trip to the cathedral in the Upper Town was arduous in wintertime.

NOTRE-DAME-DES-VICTOIRES, INTERIOR

Looking beyond Notre-Dame-des-Victoires, we find the rest of Place Royale, which became the trading hub of New France and was where merchants lived and worked. During the British regime (from the Conquest in 1759 until Canadian Confederation in 1867), Place Royale continued to function as a commercial centre, particularly during the Napoleonic Wars. With Baltic supplies of timber cut off by Napoleon, the British navy turned to its North American colonies for shipbuilding materials. After the wars Québec City merchants and shipbuilders continued to play a key role in the domestic economy, and in time Québec City came to have the largest port in British North America. Until the 1860s, when shipbuilders began turning from wood to steel, Place Royale was at the heart of the economy of the city and the colony. From the 1860s on, the square served local needs, remaining a marketplace. Over the course of the 20th century, the area declined and Place Royale faded away into a mere shadow of its former self. In 1950 the Québec government began work on rediscovering and re-establishing this heritage site. Over the next 15 years, extensive work by archaeologists, historians and museum professionals returned Place Royale to its former standing as a vibrant public space.

The information centre for Place Royale in the Maisons Hazeur and Smith on Rue Notre-Dame is also an annex of the Musée de la Civilisation. This

MAISON THIBAUDEAU

new museum inside two stone houses named after former owners Lord François Hazeur, a wealthy merchant in 1682, and Charles Smith, a butcher and landowner in the early 1800s, traces the history of Place Royale through exhibits on its construction and inhabitants. Guided tours are available year-round (reservations are required out of season), as are tours of the surrounding buildings.

Interesting nearby sites include Maison Chevalier, featuring a display of 17th- and 18th-century domestic life; Maison Paradis, featuring artisans displaying work and demonstrating techniques; and Parc de l'UNESCO, a small playground built when UNESCO declared the old city a world heritage site, featuring structures based on a maritime theme.

TOP: MAISON CHEVALIER
INSET: MAISON CHEVALIER, INTERIOR

From Place Royale you can easily walk to Rue du Petit-Champlain, the first street in Québec City. In the 17th and 18th centuries, this narrow lane was the main street of the town, with businesses and residences lining each side. Nowadays, after the 1977 revival of the street and surrounding neighbourhood by artisans and business people, you can find high-quality crafts made in Québécois, Native and Inuit traditions. From Petit-Champlain, you can cut across to Rue Dalhousie, where the Lévis-Québec ferry docks. The ferry itself may not be of historic interest, but it does offer a spectacular view of old Québec. In winter, the ride turns into suitable entertainment for children (and some adults), as they watch the boat glide through the ice floes. Although the chunks of ice are blasted down to a safe, navigable size, they are still large enough to be awesome.

RUE PETIT-CHAMPLAIN

Further along Dalhousie is the Musée de la Civilisation, the province's main ethnographic museum. It was designed by architect Moshe Safdie to echo the heritage of Québec City. Three historic buildings were integrated into the museum: Maison Estèbe, Maison Pagé-Quercy and the site of the Ancienne Banque de Québec. Maison Estèbe and Maison Pagé-Quercy were both built after 1750 by local merchants for use as their residences; at the time, merchants would have stored their goods at home. The Banque de Québec was founded in 1818, but the original building, not to mention the bank itself, had long since disappeared by the time the museum was built. The terraced waterfall at the main entrance makes reference to the city's natural landmarks — the river and the cliff. Lastly, the bell tower, or *campanile*, evokes the church steeples scattered throughout the old city.

The Funicular

From the Lower Town, there are two picturesque ways to reach the Upper Town. The first is to walk up the Escalier Casse-Cou (Breakneck Stairs), one of more than 20 staircases that link the Upper Town and the Lower Town. The stairs, which are as steep as their name suggests, ascend from Rue du Petit-Champlain. The ironwork was constructed in 1893, designed by the architect Charles Baillairgé (who was descended from a prominent Québec City family of master builders and architects going back to the previous century), but the staircase has been in use since the 17th century.

From these stairs, you have to walk another couple of hundred metres uphill along the Côte de la Montagne. If this prospect sounds intimidating, you have a second option: the funicular, or cable car, which was renovated in the late 1990s. The lower station on Petit-Champlain is known as Maison Louis-Jolliet. The house was built in 1683 by Louis Jolliet, the first European to reach the Mississippi River. The upper station opens onto Place Terrasse-Dufferin, built in 1878 and named for the governor general of Canada in 1872 through 1878. Lord Dufferin persuaded city officials to launch the beautification project that ended up preserving the fortified walls surrounding the city.

Terrasse-Dufferin

The multilayered, copper-roofed structure adjacent to Terrasse-Dufferin is the Château Frontenac. This landmark was built as a luxury hotel in 1893 by the Canadian Pacific Railway. The site had previously housed several generations of governors under both French and British regimes. Up the hill from Terrasse-Dufferin is the Promenade des Gouverneurs, flanked by the Château Frontenac and two residential streets. Originally enclosed and part of the governor's residence during the 18th century, it is now a public park. The Wolfe-Montcalm monument at the entrance to the park commemorates the generals of both sides in the 1759 Conquest, when the colony passed from French to British hands. From this location you can head in a number of different directions to see several key religious structures.

BASILIQUE NOTRE-DAME-DE-QUÉBEC

When religion played a greater role in public life these buildings were important symbols of status, power and prestige. The cathedral of the Roman Catholic archbishop of Québec is the Basilique Notre-Dame-de-Québec on Rue de Buade. The original church was built in 1647, but one look will tell you that this is not a 17th-century structure. The church has been rebuilt several times, most recently in 1922 after a fire. The Ursuline convent on Rue Donnacona houses the Ursuline nuns, a teaching order. They run the oldest private girls' school in North America, founded in 1639. Much of the grounds is off-limits to visitors, but you can visit the chapel and the museum. The Anglican Cathedral of the Holy Trinity on Rue des Jardins was built in 1804 to serve the spiritual needs of the English elite. Captain William Hall and Major William Robe, both of the Royal Artillery, designed the cathedral in the classical tradition embodied by two London churches: St. Martin-in-the-Fields and Marylebone Chapel, both by architect James Gibbs. (Many colonial builders were inspired by Gibbs's 1728 *Book of Architecture,* in which he published his technical drawings.)

The Séminaire de Québec on Côte de la Fabrique is a vast assembly of buildings that used to house Université Laval before it moved to the suburb of Ste-Foy. The seminary was founded in 1663 by Québec's first bishop, François de Laval, to train priests locally; it is the oldest post-secondary teaching institution in North America. At least two portions of the complex are of interest to visitors. The first, the Vieux-Séminaire, is made up of three wings — the Aile de la Procure, the Aile de la Congrégation and the Aile des Parloirs — that date from the late 17th century, with some portions having been rebuilt over the course of the 19th century. The other site worth a visit is the Musée de l'Amérique Française, which comprises four seminary buildings; the entrance is located on Rue de l'Université. The museum, which is now affiliated with the Musée de la Civilisation, is home to a collection of religious artifacts, including rare 18th- and 19th-century silver objects from England, France and Québec. Also part of the museum is the seminary's Chapelle Extérieure, which was deconsecrated in 1992. Many original features of the late-19th-century reconstruction of the chapel, including the spectacular *trompe-l'oeil* ceiling and stained-glass windows, remain in excellent condition.

SÉMINAIRE DE QUÉBEC

Moving west through the old city, you'll find the Literary and Historical Society of Québec, founded by

Lord Dalhousie in 1824. The society was one of a few institutions to attract both English and French elites to its meetings and lectures. The library of the society also had a surprising number of women among its members. In Victorian times it was rare for proper women of the middle and upper classes to venture beyond the domestic sphere, but lending libraries like this one provided some intellectual stimulation. The society is housed in a former prison completed in 1814. The architect François Baillairgé, an ancestor of the Charles Baillairgé who designed the Breakneck Stairs, constructed the prison in accordance with the enlightened principles of the day, following the ideas of British prison reformer John Howard.

THE LIBRARY OF THE LITERARY AND HISTORICAL SOCIETY OF QUÉBEC

At the western edge of the Upper Town, down the hill from the Literary and Historical Society, you will find Parc de l'Artillerie, which provides an ideal introduction to the military history of the city, including detailed information about the fortifications and walls. The fortifications form a 4.6-kilometre wall around Haute-Ville, extending from the Citadelle on the Plaines d'Abraham to the Prescott gate in the east to the St-Jean, Kent and St-Louis gates to the west.

The Federal Arsenal at the main entrance to the park houses a scale model of Québec City dating from 1808. From the old city, exit at the St-Louis gate and follow the Grande Allée; you'll find yourself at the parliament buildings. Several buildings and monuments make up this historic site. The imposing main parliament building was completed in 1886, designed by the architect Eugène-Étienne Taché in the French Empire style. The statues surrounding the quadrangle's outer walls are a veritable who's who of Québec history, ranging from Comte de Frontenac, one of the first governors of New France, to Robert Baldwin, co-premier of the United Canadas in the mid-19th century. The interior is open to the public through guided tours.

MANÈGE MILITAIRE

Beyond the old city and its impressive adjuncts such as the parliament buildings, there are subtle rewards for people who decide to wander off the beaten tourist track. At the bottom of Côte d'Abraham, you'll find the Jardin St-Roch, a peaceful square surrounded by some of the city's more modern developments. This is where you'll find the Complexe Méduse, a string of row houses that was

converted into a fascinating new complex with numerous art galleries by a few artists' collectives in the mid-1990s, now the city's foremost venue for contemporary art.

St-Jean-Baptiste, adjacent to the Upper Town, is an old working-class district that has been gradually gentrified. To get to this neighbourhood, follow Rue St-Jean outside the St-Jean gate across the Autoroute Dufferin-Montmorency, and you'll find that the street narrows and the shops and restaurants get funkier and more interesting. At the corner of Rues St-Augustin and St-Jean lies Saint-Matthew's, the Anglican church that was converted to a branch of the municipal library in 1980. Surrounding the converted church is Parc St-Matthew, formerly the Québec Protestant Burying Ground, which was in use from 1771 to 1860. Captain Thomas Scott, the younger brother of Sir Walter Scott, is buried just inside the main entrance. The park is open from May to November.

ST-JEAN-BAPTISTE DISTRICT

Further along St-Jean, the local Catholic parish church, Église Saint-Jean-Baptiste, occupies the block between Rues Ste-Claire and Deligny. The current building was completed in 1884, designed by Joseph Ferdinand Peachy, after a fire destroyed its predecessor. The ornate exterior, designed in the French Second Empire style, echoes aspects of Parisian churches from the same period. It can accommodate up to 3,000 worshippers. If you wander through the residential part of the neighbourhood, be sure to head down the hill to the Tour Martello on Rue Lavigueur, just to the west of Rue Racine. It is one of the least-known, least-publicized parts of the fortifications; the interior of the tower is not open to the public, but there is a lookout.

MARTELLO TOWER ON RUE LAVIGEUR

A guidebook can get you oriented in Québec City, but you're sure to discover even more by exploring on your own. You could spend months here and still find surprises at the end of your stay.

Festivals & Events

Sarah Waters

Fêtes de la Nouvelle France

Many people in traditionally Catholic countries or regions tend to enter the penitential season of Lent with a hangover and something worth repenting. That's because they've partaken of that grand tradition — the pre-Lenten carnival, or Mardi Gras. This one last, glorious blowout, often lasting a couple of weeks, once prepared the devout to endure the 40 days of fasting and mortification that led up to the glory of Easter.

Lent is less rigorous than it used to be and not as widely observed, even in devout countries, but the carnival tradition persists. There are street parties, fireworks and parades — often featuring thousands of nubile young women dressed in little more than glitter and spangles — and people eat too much, drink too much, sing too much and pursue romance with commendable vigour. All this is very well in places like New Orleans, Rio de Janeiro and Nice. But Québec City has managed to create a similar bacchanalia, complete with street parties and parades, each year towards the end of January and into the first couple of weeks of February — in one of the harshest climates in the world.

Dozens of imitators have sprung up across Canada —

Montréal's Fête des Neiges and Ottawa's Winterlude, for example. But Québec City's party, the Carnaval de Québec, is the granddaddy of them all. The first winter carnival was held in 1894. It was a fairly modest event with some religious overtones. But it had a parade, as well as a ball for the elite and street parties for humbler folk. The round of parties and suppers with the occasional sporting event made for a pleasant and heart-warming break in the middle of a brutal winter, and the city kept up the tradition sporadically for several decades.

BONHOMME CARNAVAL

But it wasn't until 1955 that the Québec Winter Carnival became an annual event, thanks to members of the city's chamber of commerce who were looking for a way to perk up the anemic midwinter economy and attract some visitors. The chamber beefed up the parade and the balls and introduced Bonhomme Carnaval, the event's endearing mascot. He's supposed to be a snowman, and his tuque and *ceinture fléchée* (a colourful woven sash) add a dash of Québec patriotism.

Both Bonhomme and the Carnaval are endearing symbols of Québec's hardy resolve to enjoy life, and they continue to brighten the dead of winter with two weeks of parties and sporting events that attract more than 100,000 fun seekers. That's not to say that the Carnaval hasn't had its problems, but since 1996 the organizers have been making serious efforts to revitalize their big party and clean up its sometimes riotous image. One of the oddest changes has been to name the Carnaval after some of the world's biggest food companies. Each year the organizers manage to entice one of these corporations to climb aboard as a sponsor. That means a definite emphasis on good, clean family fun, so along with the traditional balls and street parties, there are more kid-friendly activities: slides and rides at the ice park built on the Plaines d'Abraham, for example, and junior lessons in ice sculpting. Each evening, an ice palace located across from Québec's parliament building is illuminated with a dazzling array of lights. Also each night, a large parade, complete with magnificent floats, great bands and hilarious clowns, winds through the streets of the old city. Bonhomme Carnaval, the pudgy snowman with the big smile, pops up everywhere, including at the big evening parade. Most of the carnival's traditional events — dogsled races, ice-sculpture-carving contests, boat races across the half-frozen St. Lawrence, ski and

DOGSLED RACES AT CARNAVAL DE QUÉBEC

snowmobile races, street parties — are still going strong.

The two other most venerable events on Québec City's social calendar are the Concours Hippique de Québec (the Québec Horse Show) in late June through early July and Expo-Québec, the province's biggest agricultural fair, in the last two weeks of August. The horse show is the first event in the equestrian World Cup, and it attracts some of the best horsemen and horsewomen in the country and, indeed, the world. They gather on the Expo-Cité grounds for five days of exquisite dressage. This is pretty serious, classical stuff, and a lot of the finer points might well be lost on all but the cognoscenti. But the setting and the steeds are magnificent, and the jumping competitions are spectacular.

Expo-Québec has marked the end of summer in Québec for more than 90 years. With more than 300,000 visitors each year, the event features some of the region's prime livestock, especially beef cattle, and agricultural exhibits. It comes with all the usual bells and whistles of a major country fair: a midway, shows and horse pulling contests. Expo runs in conjunction with the Carrefour Agro-Alimentaire, a kind of food fair that showcases all the culinary specialties of the region. It includes competitions, demonstrations by some of the province's best chefs and, of course, tastings.

Top and bottom: Expo-Québec

A newer event that has grown into the city's biggest party is the summer festival, Festival d'Été de Québec, held in early July. This is the largest festival of French-language performing arts and street theatre in North America. There are hundreds of acts — singers, dancers, jugglers, clowns, acrobats, magicians — and most of the shows are free of charge and in the open air. The narrow streets and cobbled squares of the old city as well as the open parkland of the Plaines d'Abraham provide some of the finest stages in North America for this sort of event. Other summer events are the Fêtes de la Nouvelle France in early August, which recalls the era of the 17th- and 18th-century French regime with military displays, parades and re-enactments as well as storytellers, musicians, singers, dancers and street performers; Plein Art, a 10-day crafts exhibition held in a tent on the esplanade near the parliament buildings; and the Festival International de Musiques Militaires. Military bands from across Canada and Europe perform in and around the Upper Town in late August. At the conclusion of the four-day event, trumpets blare and drums beat as the troops parade through the old city, winding up at Terrasse-Dufferin, where they perform their last outdoor concert.

A couple of events held just outside the city are also worth considering. The Grands Feux Loto-Québec take place at the end of July and the beginning of August. These fireworks displays are staged in a spectacular setting, on parkland at the foot of Chutes Montmorency. One of the best observation points is the St. Lawrence River, so the area around the falls fills with boats whose lights twinkle and flash in the darkness, adding to the show.

FÊTES DE LA NOUVELLE FRANCE

If you're in town around the second week of September, you might want to explore the Festival des Journées d'Afrique. With a variety of free concerts for the whole family and a number of indoor concerts by acclaimed international artists, the festival is a fantastic opportunity to acquaint yourself with heartwarming tropical beats from around the globe.

Just a few miles further downstream lies the shrine of Sainte-Anne-de-Beaupré, built in honour of the mother of the Virgin Mary. St. Anne's Feast Day is celebrated on July 26 with due religious ceremony — solemn Masses and rosary recitations — but it is also something of a festival. Gypsies and some First Nations bands hold St. Anne in particular esteem, and they flock to the site in late July. Many of the First Nations celebrate in traditional costumes and the Gypsies often arrive in caravans of mobile homes. The last major event of the summer is the Festival International du Film de Québec, a weeklong celebration of some of the best Canadian and foreign films. It starts in late August and ends around Labour Day.

Fall comes relatively early to the Québec City region, and the leaves start to turn as early as mid-September. The city celebrates this change with a Festival des Couleurs on nearby Mont Ste-Anne, an 800-metre-high ski hill that affords a dramatic view of the surrounding countryside. Another fall event that has been turned into a festival is the return of the snow geese. Great clouds of these magnificent white birds, which spend their summers at the northern tip of Baffin Island, descend on the marshes and farmlands near the city to stock up on carbohydrates before continuing their flight to their winter nesting grounds on the Atlantic shores of the Carolinas. One of their favourite stopovers is Cap Tormentine, and the local residents celebrate the visit with the Festival de l'Oie des Neiges de Saint-Joachim. Every morning the birds fly off in thousands to forage for food and every evening they return to spend the night in huge colonies. Sandwiched between those two natural events are shows, craft displays and guided walking tours of the birds' favourite haunts.

FESTIVAL D'ÉTÉ DE QUÉBEC

SHOPPING

LORRAINE O'DONNELL

SHOPPING ON RUE TRÉSOR

You know what really makes this city tick? It's money, of course. Don't be fooled by the grand edifices of religion and learning and governance. Québec City also thrives on commerce, and it is full of stores. To really know the place, then, you have to go shopping. You'll discover all kinds of hidden treasures when you do; Québec has wonderful things to buy, especially local products that make good souvenirs. There are antique and newly handcrafted household goods brimming with character. There is clothing made and worn by Quebeckers because it suits their boiling summers and freezing winters. And there are the fruits of many artists and artisans: paintings, sculpture, jewellery.

But shopping somewhere new is about more than buying things. It also gives you a glimpse of real life, the chance to encounter local people going about their business and to see what they eat, wear and use to work and play. It can take you off the beaten track and into interesting neighbourhoods. This is especially true of Québec City, with its range of markets and malls, department and discount stores, running the gamut from humble to upscale, dusty to dazzling.

RUE ST-LOUIS

The brief guide that follows introduces you to some of the best places to shop in Québec City. It is organized by district, starting with the old city centre, where you will most likely be spending a lot of time, and moving outwards to some of the other areas that are also worth a look.

OLD CITY CENTRE

You can find all kinds of souvenirs in the upper part of the old city centre. For kitschy knick-knacks and T-shirts, look into the shops on Rue St-Louis. Nearby in the landmark Château Frontenac is Lambert & Co., featuring

CHARLEVOIX SOCKS AT LAMBERT & CO.

regional crafts like colourful striped wool socks in the old Charlevoix style. Rue du Trésor is a fun open-air market of locally produced prints and paintings, many of the city itself. At the end is Rue de Buade, site of the well-known tobacconist J.E. Giguère, with its Québec-made pipes and Cuban cigars. Over on Côte de la Fabrique is a small branch of the famous Simons department store, founded in Québec and known for its house brands of women's and men's clothing, especially cozy sweaters and hats. Down the street, you can buy fine handmade sweaters and moccasins at La Corriveau and high-end jewellery at Zimmermann. Now turn onto the main shopping street of the area, Rue St-Jean. Here, you'll find everything from candy to more clothes. The chic Librairie Pantoute sells English-language guidebooks for the region. Boutique L'Échelle is jam-packed with toys.

Shopping in the lower section of the old city is more varied. Although the Quartier du Petit-Champlain may look discouragingly touristy, in fact many locals come here to buy high-quality, handcrafted goods. There are Québec designer clothes at Oclan. On Rue du Petit-Champlain, all kinds of handicrafts, ranging from lace to glassware to art, including sculpture and paintings, are sold. Sculpteur Flamand features wood carvings in the traditional Québécois style, while down the street La Soierie Huo sells graceful, modern hand-painted silk and wool scarves.

RUE ST-JEAN

In the Old Port area is Rue St-Paul, famous for its shops selling antiques and decorative items. Gérard Bourguet Antiquaire sells 18th- and 19th-century pine furniture, while Décenie features great pieces from the 1960s, such as modern dishes and vinyl chairs. Nearby is the Marché du Vieux-Port on Quai St-André, open from March through November. Although somewhat sterile and stuck out in the middle of nowhere, the farmers' produce is fresh, nice handicrafts such as handwoven table linens are available and it's right on the river.

Antiques on Rue St-Paul

Basse-Ville (Lower Town)

The differences between the old city centre and the Lower Town are many, and nowhere does this become more apparent than in the stores. If you consider the old centre too upscale and spic-and-span, then gritty Basse-Ville is the place for you. It's an old working-class district, now also populated by artists, students and immigrants, and many of its stores are unpretentious and eclectic.

This being said, parts of Rue St-Joseph E. are being returned to their former glory. Once Québec City's main shopping street, it suffered a giant setback in the 1960s, when new suburban shopping centres enticed its clientele away. To compete, five blocks of St-Joseph E. were enclosed and turned into a hideous mall during the next decade, but this "improvement" only hastened the area's decline. Finally, in 2000, the roof was taken off three blocks (between Rues de la Couronne and St-Dominique) and a frenzy of renovation marked the launch of a process to return the street to its standing as the city's true downtown. Check out the revamped Laliberté, whose fur coats are famous (you can even visit the shop's fur workshop); Baltazar, with its hip decorative objects; brand-new Mountain Equipment Co-op, known for excellent outerwear; and then make your way to the westernmost sign of change, bookstore Librairie Pantoute.

Further west on St-Joseph E., you'll find Basse-Ville bargains. X20 sells its own line of funky streetwear. A worthwhile detour: see and sample the bright rows of cupcakes and other baked goods at Royaume de la Tarte (on Avenue des Oblats at Rue Durocher). On Rue St-Vallier O. are a number of East Asian and Latin American import stores. There's also Magasin Latulippe, with its enormous selection of camping, fishing and hunting gear and sturdy outdoor wear.

If you follow this street back to its east end, you'll come to the wonderful thrift shop Comptoir Emmaus: four giant floors of inexpensive used clothing, books, furniture and housewares. Here you can find that pineapple-shaped ashtray you've always wanted. Be sure to check out the second-floor pneumatic-tube system for making change!

Suit at Oclan

HANDMADE PAPER AT COPISTE DU FAUBOURG

HAUTE-VILLE (UPPER TOWN)

Right outside the old city walls is the shopping centre Place Québec on Avenue Honoré-Mercier. It houses some 20 stores, restaurants and useful services like a post office, but its dreariness might put you off.

Much more engaging is Rue St-Jean west of Côte d'Abraham, the colourful commercial heart of the friendly St-Jean-Baptiste neighbourhood. Cafés peacefully co-exist here with upscale sex shops (gay and straight) and stores selling cool clothing and local and imported furniture and decorative items. You'll also find purveyors of fine food, including the oldest grocery store in North America, J.A. Moisan. Of special note are the astonishing arrays of fun, cheap rubber stamps at Paradis des Étampes and handmade paper at Copiste du Faubourg.

Continuing west down Rue St-Jean until it changes its name to Chemin Ste-Foy, you come to Avenue Cartier, which serves the richer, older, more orderly clientele of the Montcalm neighbourhood. As well as many restaurants, cafés and specialty food shops, Cartier has a number of good women's fashion boutiques. One with consistently attractive collections is Boutique Paris Cartier. The mini-mall Halles le Petit Cartier will interest gourmets. On Boulevard René-Lévesque E. just east of Cartier are some exclusive Québec designer shops. Pop into Autrefois Saïgon to see an intriguing line of women's clothing made here but possessing an East Asian flavour.

SUBURBS

To really cover the Québec shopping scene, follow the locals to the suburban malls. These centres are omnipresent, enormous and convenient. They sell all kinds of clothing, household items and food, and they have good parking facilities as well as services like stroller loans. Plus they offer shelter and entertainment when it's too cold to be outside. What they lack is local flavour and charm. Probably the most interesting is Galeries de la Capitale; it has an enormous indoor playground featuring a rollercoaster. For sheer size, visit Place Laurier in the suburb of Ste-Foy. Weighing in at 350 stores, it's the largest shopping centre in eastern Canada. Close by, Place Sainte-Foy has big department stores, including another Simons, while the huge Ailes de la Mode offers a shuttle service to downtown hotels.

But all is not hopelessly suburban in Ste-Foy. Witness the lively outdoor food and flea market on Avenue Roland-Beaudin, open every Sunday from May to early October. You can browse and haggle your way through reams of the lovely stuff cast off by people anxious to mine new treasures at (where else?) the nearby malls.

Dining

Patrick Donovan

It comes as no surprise that Québec City has the highest density of French restaurants on the continent. Some of the finest chefs in the country ply their trade in very sumptuous locales here. The city also boasts an array of humbler bistros serving tasty soups, baguettes and plenty of coffee.

The city's finest and most expensive restaurants are located within the fortified city and its immediate environs. Further from the walls, Grande Allée has many charming terraces, but most restaurants on this stretch offer subpar overpriced tourist fare. Your best bets for a good concentration of mid-price restaurants serving excellent food are Avenue Cartier and Avenue Maguire (in Sillery). Cheaper café food is to be found all over town, but the most interesting places are on or near Rue St-Jean.

Haute Cuisine

Although similar to what one would find in France, Québécois haute cuisine uses local ingredients in very interesting ways. In addition to beef and pork, the selection of meat dishes may include caribou or venison. These morsels may come braised in maple syrup, marinated in arctic tea leaves or served with Saguenay berries.

For years, La Grande Table de la Maison Serge Bruyère on Rue St-Jean was considered the city's best restaurant. Many new rivals now grace the culinary scene.

Two wonderful restaurants serving eclectic haute cuisine are the Laurie Raphaël on Rue Dalhousie and Le Saint-Amour on Rue Ste-Ursule. The former is run by Daniel Vezina, who was named chef of the year in 1997.

Terrace Dining

Inside Laurie Raphaël

Le Saint-Amour

Vezina refers to his cooking as *cuisine du marché* (market cuisine), since menus change regularly in accordance with the availability of fresh produce in the market. He also puts obscure plants growing in the Québécois wild to very imaginative use. Le Saint-Amour is also run by an award-winning chef. Jean-Luc Boulay took in Québec's provincial prize for best cuisine three years in a row. His food tastes as poetic as its sounds, with dishes like "Western beef filet mignon with Maniguette peppercorns / raw-milk blue cheese and Port wine reduction / Belles de Fontenay and caramelized cippolinis." The glass-roofed courtyard out back provides one of the most romantic settings in the city. If that's not enough to stimulate romantic appetites, the restaurant also has its own chocolaterie, which serves up many fine desserts.

Le Continental on Rue St-Louis ranks in the same category as the aforementioned spots in terms of quality and atmosphere. The food, however, is closer to traditional French fare. Filet mignon is the specialty of the house; it is served flambéed by the chef before your eyes.

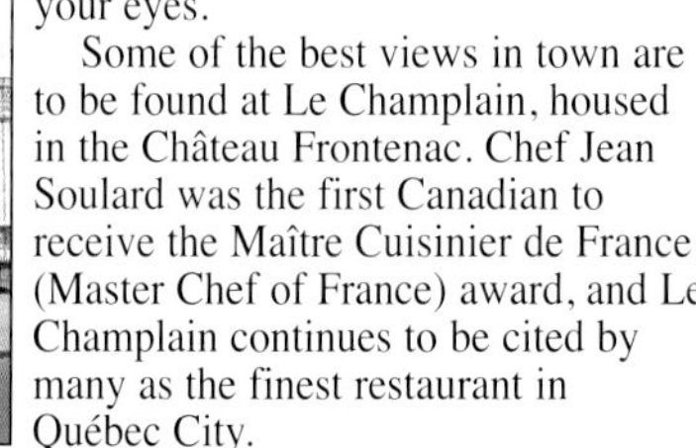

Le Continental

Some of the best views in town are to be found at Le Champlain, housed in the Château Frontenac. Chef Jean Soulard was the first Canadian to receive the Maître Cuisinier de France (Master Chef of France) award, and Le Champlain continues to be cited by many as the finest restaurant in Québec City.

If you're interested in sampling Québécois haute cuisine at affordable prices, try Le Café du Clocher Penché on Rue St-Joseph E., home to Chef Eric Vilain. A three-course lunch will set you back less than $15, while evening prices hover in the $17 to $24 range. Try the salade au confit de canard, made with conserve of duck. The café also has a fine selection of Russian teas.

Le Café Clocher Penché

Italian cuisine

Québec City boasts many excellent Italian restaurants. The best is probably Le Michelangelo on Chemin St-Louis. Unfortunately, this restaurant is located far out in the suburbs (in Ste-Foy) in a surreal white stucco building near the Pont de Québec (Québec Bridge) and Aquarium. Closer to the heart of the action lies Au Parmesan on Rue St-Louis, a wildly atmospheric place with a wandering accordionist and loads of bottles and knick-knacks lining the walls. This is one of the few restaurants along the touristy stretch of Rue St-Louis that provides superb food. Cuisine from the Parma region of Italy is featured and the chef makes his own prosciutto and smoked salmon on site. Other notable establishments offering Italian cuisine include Le Graffiti on Avenue Cartier and the little-known Ciccio Café on Rue Claire-Fontaine, which has excellent pasta dishes. For more affordable Italian food, try Les Frères de La Côte, a Mediterranean restaurant specializing in wood-fired pizzas that is run by two boisterous brothers from the south of France.

Le Graffiti

Cafés, Bistros and Brasseries

The most quintessentially French bistro in Québec City is without a doubt Le Café du Monde on Rue Dalhousie, a huge sprawling place in the ferry terminal of the old port. Quiches, moules-frites and pâtés grace the menu, and the atmosphere of a Parisian brasserie is unmistakable. The service will remain friendly as long as you refrain from snapping your fingers and yelling "Garçon!"

If you're looking for something more cozy, there are many smaller cafés worth sneaking into for a bowl of coffee. Chez Temporel on Rue Couillard is a favourite with local students, serving up affordable soups and excellent croûtons (baguettes covered with white wine and melted cheese). Le Petit Coin Latin on Rue Ste-Ursule has one of the loveliest terraces in Québec City. The specialty here is Swiss raclette: cheese and meats grilled on a small portable oven. Finally, Le Hobbit and Le Grand Méchant Loup (both on Rue St-Jean) are also great little neighbourhood cafés in the artsy St-Jean-Baptiste district.

Les Frères de La Côte

If you feel like you're about to overdose on French food, travel down Rue St-Jean to Pub Sainte-Alexandre, which offers excellent British pub grub in a fairly authentic

atmosphere. It has a good selection of sausages and pours the best Guinness in town.

Non-Western Cuisine

Although Québec is not a very multi-cultural city, there are still a few establishments that dish out excellent non-Western food.

A beautiful presentation from Yuzu Sushi Bar

The Aviatic Club on Rue de la Gare-du-Palais, located in the old train station, serves up worthwhile French, Asian and Tex-Mex food in a classy atmosphere. This is where Québec City's yuppies meet after work. The crispy orange beef is the best in town, and the aviolles are a tasty dessert (they're sugary, fried tortillas served with chocolate or caramel sauce and homemade ice cream).

The Aviatic Club

There are many restaurants serving good, affordable Thai, Cambodian and Vietnamese food all over town. The best of the lot is probably the Cambodian-run Restaurant L'Apsara on Rue d'Auteuil, located in an old bourgeois mansion next to the city walls. It's a bit more expensive than the others, but the food is well worth the price.

If you're looking for sushi, the classiest place in Québec City is the chic and very expensive new Yuzu Sushi Bar on Rue de l'Église, recently nominated as having the nicest restrooms in Canada! More affordable Japanese food can be found at Le Tokyo on Rue St-Jean. Don't let the run-down exterior mislead you; this is Québec's oldest Japanese restaurant, and it still offers excellent food.

The best place for a taste of North Africa is probably Le Carthage on Rue St-Jean. On certain nights, belly-dancing shows accompany the tajine and couscous. For more modest fare, the small Tunisian-run Salon de Thé Le Sultan is located nearby and serves up delicious mint tea and sandwiches. Shisha-smoking takes place on cozy cushions in the back room.

For North-American Indian cooking, Nek8arre at the Village-des-Hurons treats its guests to interesting Huron food. Don't come expecting an authentic atmosphere; it's a touristy place in the middle of a reconstructed Huron village, but it nevertheless provides an interesting cultural experience. Buffalo, caribou, deer and clay-baked fish are served up with corn and wild rice.

Last but Not Least . . .

A section on dining in Québec City would be incomplete without mentioning poutine, a staple of Québécois junk food. Although the dish is now available nationwide, even in big chains like McDonald's, this artery-clogging concoction of French fries, brown sauce and squeaky cheddar cheese curds is best sampled in Québec City. Ask any resident where the best poutine in town is and most will point you to local fast-food chain Chez Ashton (many locations).

QUÉBEC CITY BY AREA

LOWER TOWN

PATRICK DONOVAN

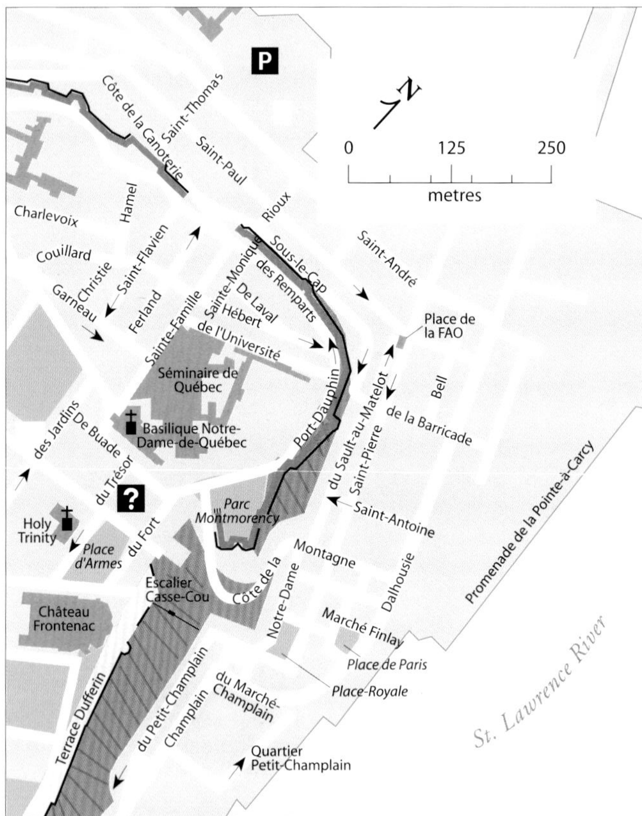

PLACE ROYALE, PETIT CHAMPLAIN AND VIEUX-PORT

To many people, Vieux-Québec means the walled city on the hill with its warren of narrow, twisted streets spreading out from the castle-like bulk of the Château Frontenac. In fact, Haute-Ville, or Upper Town, is the newer part of the old city. To introduce yourself to Québec City's real birthplace, you can stand on Terrasse-Dufferin at the edge of the Upper Town and look over the wrought-iron guardrail. The steep roofs below cover some of the oldest buildings in North America. In 1608 Samuel de Champlain landed down there on the narrow strip of land between the St. Lawrence River and the cliff, cut down some trees and built himself a trading post. That first rude settlement comprised a moated manor house and some storehouses and outbuildings. Fire and war have destroyed any trace of Champlain's post, but many of the walls and foundations of the current buildings date to the prosperous days of the early 1700s.

The year 1608 also saw Jean Duval tried and found guilty of treason for trying to kill Samuel de Champlain

Notre-Dame-des-Victoires

and take over the new French colony. Champlain had Duval beheaded. The head was then displayed as a warning to others, and it is said that this grisly event ushered a darker element into the city's history. You can investigate this more mysterious side of the city's past after dark by taking a walking excursion with Ghost Tours of Quebec. By lantern light, your costumed guide will lead you through Old Québec's haunted sites, filled with the promise of spectres and tales of revenge.

As recently as the 1960s, the Lower Town by the harbour was a rundown slum. Revitalization work began at Place Royale, a gathering place where various First Nations bands met as early as 2,000 years ago. The new settlers began to use it as a marketplace in 1673. The restorers certainly succeeded in recapturing the look of the French regime, but unfortunately, they also managed to suck much of the life out of the place. It now looks rather like a film set, and on most summer days it's difficult to find anyone in the vicinity who isn't carrying a camera.

Still, the humble church on the square, Notre-Dame-des-Victoires, is worth battling the crowds to see. Built in 1687, it was a favourite of New France's first bishop, François de Laval. Hanging from the ceiling is a replica of the boat *Brézé,* one of the few remaining examples of ex-voto offerings left by devout sailors who arrived in Québec. When caught in one of the frequent storms in the Gulf of the St. Lawrence, they would promise to build an exact replica of their boat if providence saved them.

Place Royale

Just down the hill from Place Royale towards the harbour is Place de Paris, a once bustling market now dominated by a chunk of modern sculpture that, according to rumour, has been repeatedly mistaken for a public washroom. It was a gift from the city of Paris and provides a little comic relief for tourists and locals who wonder whether the real gift is inside this large white box. Behind this odd monolith are several houses and the reconstructed Batterie Royale, topped with 10 French cannons. Notice the different types of roofing on the houses, selected by the restoration crew to give a didactic presentation of roofing styles in New France.

Batterie Royale

Many of the original houses in this part of the city were built out of wood and had shingle roofs. Because of the rough winter climate, large fires had to be kept up indoors, which sent sparks flying through the air. Given the flammable nature of the building materials, the city burned down time after time. After the umpteenth fire, the governor required that all new buildings be constructed of stone and have tin roofs; also, every other building had to have a ladder for means of escape. To learn more about the early days of New France, you can visit the new Centre d'Interprétation de Place-Royale, housed in the two interesting postmodern buildings on the square.

Quartier du Petit-Champlain

Between 1797 and 1897, Québec City's 40 shipyards turned out 2,500 ships. The Quartier du Petit-Champlain, hugging the cliff to the west beyond the funicular and the Breakneck Stairs, was where the shipsmiths, spar- and block-makers, riggers, chandlers and tow-boat owners lived, most of them poor Irish immigrants. Restored by a citizens' co-operative a decade after Place Royale, this area is worth a wander for the craft shops, cafés and atmosphere.

On the other side of the Lower Town, the modern port offers something of a relief from the tourist throngs at Place Royale. Sit down on one of the benches facing the water and watch the yachts, freighters and cruise boats dodge each other. Stubby blue-and-white ferries plough back and forth between the port and Lévis on the south shore. For just a few dollars, the ferry ride gives you an unparalleled view back at the city. If you walk east along the shore, you can rent a bicycle near the Agora (an outdoor amphitheatre) and ride the extensive bike paths all around the port and, if you like, right out to Beauport.

The magnificent Nouvelle Douane, or "new" Customs House (actually built in 1856), on Quai St-André is still what it claims to be, and it glares across at the equally magnificent Société des Ports Nationaux building (built in 1914) on Rue de Quercy. Between them is a restful little park with fountains and rows of mountain ash trees.

The New Customs House

Going back towards the cliff, the imposing buildings of the old financial district tower over the narrow Rues du Sault-au-Matelot, St-Antoine and St-Pierre. Until the 1960s, this was the Wall Street of Québec;

Nouvelle Douane

it even had its own stock exchange for a few years. Now there's not a bank to be seen — just restaurants, hotels, art galleries and one of the most interesting museums in Canada, the Musée de la Civilisation on Rue Dalhousie.

The museum, built in 1988, was designed by Moshe Safdie (who also conceived Montréal's Habitat '67 and Ottawa's National Gallery) to blend in with the old buildings that surround it. With a special mission to explore Québécois culture and its relationship to the world, the museum consists of 11 exhibition spaces arranged around a vast bright entrance hall, which in turn is dominated by a cement sculpture featuring pools of water that represent the spring breakup on the St. Lawrence River. Aside from permanent, temporary and travelling exhibitions, the space hosts concerts, film screenings, poetry readings and political debates: the museum has managed to turn itself into a truly vibrant cultural centre. The pièce de résistance is the fabulous dressing-up room in the basement, with extraordinarily creative costumes available for adults and children alike to try on for size.

Across the street, Robert Lepage, Québec's internationally renowned playwright and filmmaker, was inspired to add some blocks of black granite to the back of the old fire station. The building is now the home of his production company, Ex Machina. All his shows are created, rehearsed and produced here, but this is not a performance space.

Musée de la Civilisation

Nearby, you'll find the small Place FAO, which has won scores of architectural prizes for having transformed an ordinary street corner into a unique public space. From here, walk down Rue St-Paul, renowned for its excellent antique shops. If you duck into one of the narrow passageways between houses on this street, you'll discover Rue Sous-le-Cap, one of Québec City's hidden gems: a dark, narrow street that hugs the cliff and is criss-crossed with picturesque stairways and galleries. When the river was higher, this was the only route around the shore.

The Centre d'Interprétation du Vieux-Port on Rue St-André, an eyesore run by Parks Canada, reflects the importance of Québec City's maritime history as both a port and a shipbuilding centre. In the 19th

century it was one of the five most important ports in the world. In 1833 the *Royal William*, built here, was the first ship to cross the Atlantic powered solely by steam. The Marché du Vieux-Port is the next stop. Here you can buy a snack from the farmers of Île d'Orléans, whose ancestors sold their wares at Place Royale during the French regime. As you munch your apple, take a look at the railway and bus station, built to resemble a château. If you step inside and look up at the magnificent skylight, you'll see its stained-glass map of North America.

Above: Vieux-Port
Below: Marché du Vieux-Port

St-Roch and St-Sauveur

Beyond the Dufferin-Montmorency viaduct is another part of the Lower Town, vibrant with life, devoid of tourists and changing as fast as Shanghai. As recently as 1990, St-Roch was a bleak urban wasteland with decaying buildings punctuated by empty parking lots. Since then, the neighbourhood has undergone one of the most thorough revitalization cures imaginable. It now contains pricey sushi bars, hip nightclubs and some of the most expensive condos in the city. At the moment, it is an interesting place where wealthy urban bachelors in chic lofts rub shoulders uncomfortably with bohemian artists and much of the old working-class population. Many are worried that the gentrification will go too far and rising rents will drive the latter populations away. Walk through the neighbourhood and judge for yourself.

A good place to begin is the Jardin St-Roch at the bottom of Côte d'Abraham. This is where the city's revitalization efforts began. Inaugurated in 1992, this tree-filled square, with its lovely waterfall, was initially a strange oasis surrounded by grim parking lots. Today, many tasteful new buildings frame it. Among these is Complexe Méduse, the premier venue for contemporary art in Québec City. In the mid-1990s, several artists' collectives came together to convert

Railway and bus station

a string of row houses into a vibrant complex that now houses numerous art galleries.

From the park, walk down towards Rue St-Joseph, the main commercial artery of St-Roch. Until a few years ago, St-Joseph was listed in the *Guinness Book of World Records* as the "longest covered street in the world." Despite this honour, it was also one of the dreariest places in the world: a strip of shops on the verge of bankruptcy under a low, claustrophobia-inducing roof that concealed many interesting 19th-century buildings. The roof, built in 1972, was an urban renewal error, and most of it was demolished at the turn of the millennium. This made way for a pedestrianized street with many new chic shops, excellent bakeries and unique art galleries.

The massive Église Saint-Roch, a church built during World War I, deserves a peek for its impressive stained glass. Further down St-Joseph is the city's main library, the very modern Bibliothèque Gabrielle-Roy, built in 1983. Nearby is the beautifully restored Édifice de la Fabrique on Boulevard Charest E., an industrial brick building with a prominent turret and clock tower. It now houses Université Laval's faculty of fine arts, though many still refer to it as Dominion Corset. Don't laugh: in its heyday, this factory employed over 1,000 single women, who produced as many as 21,000 corsets and brassieres per day.

The smaller back streets of St-Roch and the neighbouring St-Sauveur district are worth exploring. The tightly packed housing on streets such as Jérôme, Arago and du Roi in St-Roch and Aqueduc, des Oblats and Victoria in St-Sauveur are a jumble of styles. Tiny old houses with mansard roofs are jammed in among those from every successive era.

In the heart of this working-class neighbourhood is a large complex that dates back to the French regime and contains the oldest surviving church in the city. The Hôpital Général on Boulevard Langelier was founded in 1693 by Québec's second bishop and still looks after the poor and dying. With a little advance notice, sisters from the Augustinian order will give you a guided tour of the museum and the beautiful Notre-Dame-des-Anges chapel (built in 1673), Québec City's best-kept secret. At the cemetery outside, the remains of the Marquis de Montcalm were recently re-interred next to the soldiers who fell with him on the Plaines d'Abraham.

Wall mural in St-Roch neighbourhood

Upper Town

Mary Ann Simpkins

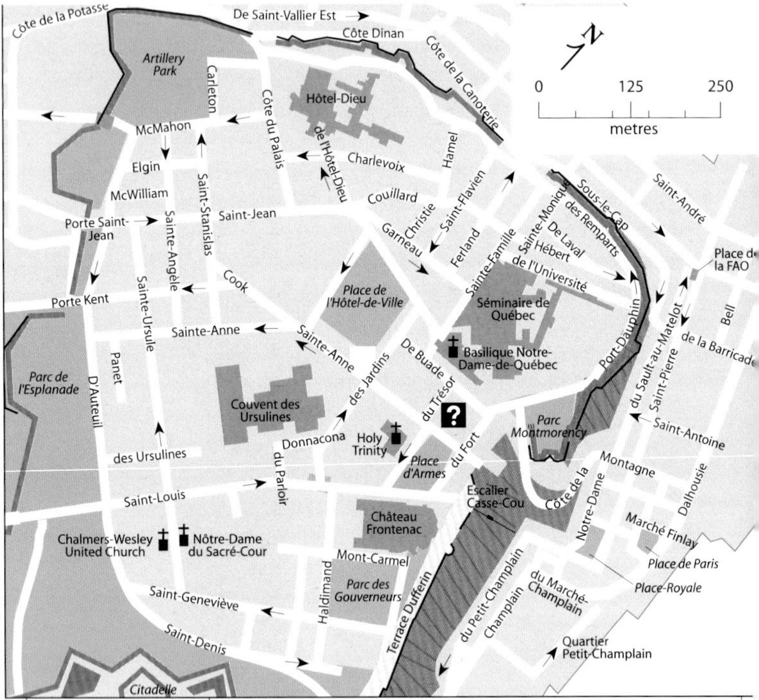

The doughty French settlers who founded Québec City in the 17th century built their homes and warehouses with convenience in mind, not security. Theirs was a trading venture, after all, and what better place to build it than on the banks of the St. Lawrence River, where boats and canoes could easily land? A few skirmishes with English fleets, however, revealed their vulnerability, and soon the colonists hacked a trail up the sheer rock face of the heights and founded Haute-Ville, or Upper Town, in 1620. At the top, Samuel de Champlain built a small fortress, where his statue now stands between the Château Frontenac hotel and a wildly modernistic globe that commemorates UNESCO's decision to designate the entire old city a world heritage site. Champlain's statue faces Place d'Armes, a space that served as a military parade ground during both the French and British regimes. The park is a good starting point for touring the Upper Town. And there's really only one way to accomplish this: on foot. Most tour buses are too big to navigate the more interesting streets and the horse-drawn calèches cover only part of the route.

Château Frontenac

So lace up your most comfortable shoes, pick up a free city map at the tourist bureau facing the square and set out.

CATHEDRAL OF THE HOLY TRINITY

You can easily walk the route in an hour, but that won't include stops along the way. Better to set aside most of a day and do the place thoroughly.

Start at the turreted Musée du Fort on the corner of Place d'Armes, where taped commentary and lights flashing on a panoramic model of the city chronicle Québec's military conflicts. Much livelier is Québec Expérience on Rue du Trésor. Blazing guns, gushing water, three-dimensional figures and other special effects give you dramatic snapshots of the city's history, from the first explorers to the present day. The English-speaking population of Québec City has dwindled since the mid-1800s, dropping from half the population to less than 2 percent today, yet three of the churches in Upper Town are anglophone. The one you see backing onto the northeast corner of Place d'Armes is Cathedral of the Holy Trinity, the mother church of the Anglican diocese of Québec and the first Anglican cathedral built outside the British Isles. King George III, no doubt unclear on Canada's timber resources, shipped over oak from Windsor Castle's royal forest for construction of the pews. A balcony pew has been reserved since 1810 for royalty or royalty's representative. Guided tours of the cathedral, offered daily from May to Thanksgiving in October, recount the fascinating history behind some of the memorial plaques and the burial of the Duke of Richmond under the main altar. Craftspeople set up shop on the church grounds in the summertime, but artists hang their paintings and engravings of Québec City year-round on the walls lining Rue du Trésor, which leads eastward from Place d'Armes and was where the early colonists came to pay their taxes to the governor of New France.

BASILIQUE NOTRE-DAME-DE-QUÉBEC

At the end of this short street, turn left on Rue de Buade to reach the entrance to the Basilique Notre-Dame-de-Québec, the cathedral of the Roman Catholic archdiocese. The glorious

interior is lavishly decorated with statues, stained glass and a sumptuous gilded canopy over the main altar. The church's side chapel holds a resting bronze figure representing Québec's first bishop, François de Laval, who is entombed, with more than 900 other souls, in the church's crypt. In summer the church stages Feux Sacrés, an impressive sound-and-light show that focuses on the building's architectural and religious history. The ornate iron gate next to the cathedral guards the Séminaire de Québec, founded by Bishop Laval in 1663 to train priests for the parishes of New France. The first institution of post-secondary education in North America, it eventually evolved into Université Laval. In 1954, the university moved to modern quarters in suburban Ste-Foy, but the old Séminaire still houses the architecture school. It also houses the Musée de l'Amérique Française, which traces more than three centuries of French history and culture in North America through temporary and permanent exhibitions that include ornate silver chalices, carved wood religious sculptures and Canadian and European paintings. Don't miss the seminary's stunning external chapel, with its Second Empire *trompe-l'oeil* interior and Canada's largest collection of relics.

TOP: BASILIQUE NOTRE-DAME-DE-QUÉBEC, INTERIOR
INSET: AN ORNATE IRON GATE GUARDS THE SÉMINAIRE DE QUÉBEC

RIGHT: MUSÉE DE L'AMÉRIQUE FRANÇAISE

Opposite the basilica, Québec's city hall once again flies the Canadian flag. After the failure of the Meech Lake constitutional amendments to recognize the province of Québec as a distinct society within Canada, Mayor Jean-Paul L'Allier ordered the flag removed. Angered by this action, three French Canadian veterans rose early each morning for a brief flag-raising ceremony.

HÔTEL DE VILLE (CITY HALL)

A new council voted in 1998 to reinstate Canada's national emblem.

Follow the seminary's high stone wall down Rue Ste-Famille to the street's end. At this point, if you turn right on Avenue des Remparts you'll come to Parc Montmorency, which has been lined with a row of British cannons since 1832. The guns had enough force to shoot cannonballs across the St. Lawrence River into Lévis, from which the British had bombarded the city in 1759, destroying many houses. Those facing the river were mainly rebuilt in the same architectural style, using the original foundations and walls.

The home of the Marquis de Montcalm

If you turn left at the end of Ste-Famille, you'll reach one house that survived the British bombardment, the home of the Marquis de Montcalm, the general in charge of the French forces. A plaque identifies the burgundy-coloured house. The wood facing was installed over the stone around 1850 as protection against the fierce northeasterly winds. Go back up Rue Ferland and just before turning the corner onto Rue Couillard, you'll see a small doorway on your right. It leads into the convent of the Bon-Pasteur and was used by unwed mothers-to-be who needed the nuns' help but wanted to avoid the prying eyes on the more public Rue Couillard. The 19th-century convent is now a museum, and you can enter through the front door no matter what your condition. Rotating and permanent exhibits fill three floors, and friendly nuns will play an English video about their order for you and answer questions about the displays ranging from the cloth-enclosed nuns' rooms to religious art.

Convent of the Bon-Pasteur

A block away, at the corner of Rue St-Flavien and Couillard, is one of the few historic homes open to the public. Stuffed with Victorian furniture and decorations, including a Christmas tree adorned with period ornaments, the Maison François-Xavier Garneau retains the typical decor of a 19th-century bourgeois home. Built in 1864, the two-storey neoclassical home topped with a widow's walk is named after French Canada's first historian, its most famous occupant — his statue sits near the St-Louis gate. On weekends, you might run into the man responsible for preserving the home, former Canadian national cycling champion (now owner of an international cycling products company) Louis Garneau.

It's hard to avoid the influence of nuns in Québec City. After the church established a presence in the colony,

HÔTEL-DIEU

dozens of religious orders poured into the city. One of the first to arrive was a group of Augustinian nuns, who opened a hospital in 1644, the first in North America north of Mexico. Hôtel-Dieu still operates, as does the adjoining convent and its museum on Rue Charlevoix next to the small church at the side of the massive greystone hospital. Note that the museum is undergoing renovations, expected to be finished by 2008, and only displays a few paintings and some old medical instruments.

Rue St-Jean was the city's fashionable shopping street from the late 1800s to the 1950s, but now it's a mishmash of souvenir shops, clothing stores and restaurants. Walking past these towards the St-Jean gate, you'll reach Parc de l'Artillerie on the right. This national historic site run by Parks Canada transports you back into Québec's military history, a passage reinforced by guides acting as characters from the different periods. The reception centre for the complex is the Federal Arsenal, a turn-of-the-century munitions factory that closed in 1964. A short walk away looms the imposing Dauphine redoubt. The French began building the whitewashed fort in 1712, later turning it into barracks. Inside you'll find French soldiers, but also a cook from the Royal Artillery Regiment. After the Conquest, the redoubt housed British troops. Be sure to visit all four floors: each represents a separate era. A British military captain of the 1830s lives amidst elegant furnishings in the cottage on another side of the parade grounds.

On the other side of St-Jean, Rue d'Auteuil runs parallel to the city's walls. The Upper Town was the preserve of religious organizations, the city's administration and the wealthy, as you can see at 69 d'Auteuil, considered the Upper Town's most beautiful house. Any similarity between it and Ottawa's parliament buildings is understandable: this was the residence of their builder, Thomas McGreevy. In contrast to the flamboyance of McGreevy's home, Chief Justice Sewell chose the stolid English Palladian style for his residence, erected in 1803 at the corner of d'Auteuil and Rue St-Louis.

PARC DE L'ARTILLERIE

The St-Louis gate on Rue St-Louis is the principal entrance to Vieux-Québec. When the British garrison departed, the city tore down many gates. Some people clamoured for the walls to be demolished as well, but the governor general at the time, Lord Dufferin, persuaded them to save the walls and had this gate and others rebuilt. The road to the left of the gate leads to the Citadelle. On the right, dug into the wall, is the magazine the British used to

NO. 69 RUE D'AUTEUIL

store gunpowder. It serves as an interpretation centre and has a scale model of the city depicting the evolution of the walls, from those constructed by the French in 1690 to those put up by the British in 1790. Back on St-Louis, head for the city centre. At Rue Ste-Ursule, make a short detour to your right and take a peek into the church of Notre-Dame-du-Sacré-Coeur. Its richly coloured stained-glass windows diffuse a gentle light onto walls crammed with marble plaques giving thanks for favours granted. Across the street, Chalmers-Wesley United Church offers free Sunday-night concerts in summer on its century-old organ.

Returning to St-Louis, keep your eyes peeled for a souvenir of the British bombardment: a cannonball lodged in the base of a tree. If you turn left on Rue Donnacona, you'll come to the great sprawl that is the Monastère des Ursulines, home to an order of nuns who arrived in Québec City in 1639, led by the indomitable Marie de l'Incarnation. Its stone walls still house the oldest continuously operating girls' school in North America, a beautiful chapel and a delightfully eclectic museum. The four rooms of the Musée des Ursulines display the parchment signed by Louis XIII approving the opening of a monastery and school in New France; altar cloths finely embroidered with silk and gold thread; and porcupine-needle baskets. Further down St-Louis are some of Haute-Ville's oldest houses. The white house with the steep red roof, for example, was constructed in 1677. It's now the restaurant Aux Anciens Canadiens. The stately white building with blue trim was built about 1650 and is where the French formally surrendered the city to the British in 1759. Oddly enough, it now houses the French consulate.

THE ST-LOUIS GATE

The Château Frontenac only emerged as the city's most recognizable symbol in 1893. William Van Horne and other businessmen had the turreted, copper-roofed hotel constructed on the site of the demolished governor's palace. Actually, there were two palaces here. French governors had greatly expanded Champlain's small fort and reinforced it with stone. The English governor, however, refused to live in the château and had another built. The wooden boardwalk in front of the château is called Terrasse-Dufferin, fitting recognition for Lord Dufferin's foresight in saving the only fortified city remaining in North America.

THE WALLS AND BEYOND

SARAH WATERS

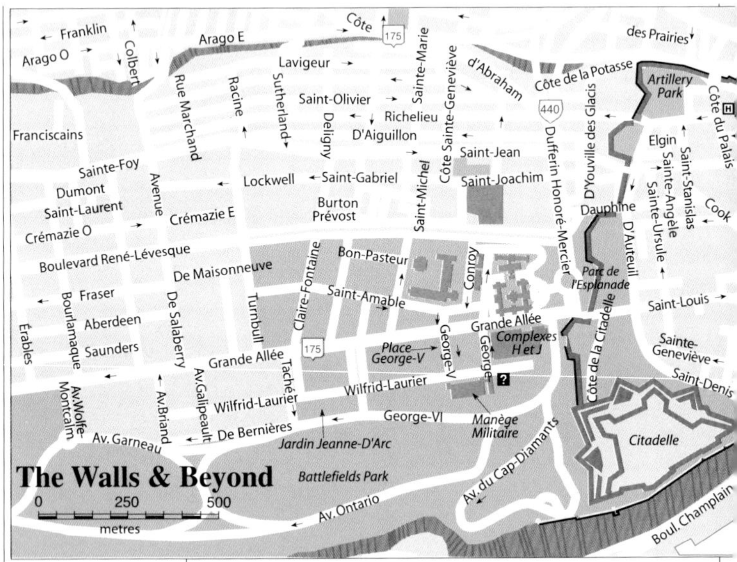

There's something very seductive in the grey stone walls of Vieux-Québec. Tourists have been known to disappear behind the St-Louis gate, never to re-emerge until it's time to go home. And they no doubt have a wonderful time exploring the cobbled streets and 18th-century buildings of the old city. But their view of Québec remains somewhat skewed and one-dimensional. Staying behind the walls is a delightful but limiting experience. To get the whole picture, you may want to step beyond the sheltering walls and explore the other facets of the city.

A good way to start would be to skirt the edges of the historic city and examine its fortifications before you

CANNONS ALONG THE WALLS OF QUÉBEC

venture out onto unprotected turf. There are two parts to this exploration: the walls and the citadel. Let's start with the walls. The city has always been fortified (a lack of protection would have been madness), but the French authorities didn't begin the present walls in earnest until after British troops took Louisbourg on Cape Breton Island in 1745. The construction turned out to be a bit late. The walls were still unfinished when General James Wolfe conquered the city in 1759, so it was left to the British to complete them. By the late 19th century, North America was a fairly peaceful place and the walls didn't really have much military purpose any more. But Lord Dufferin, Canada's governor general from 1872 to 1878, thought they added a certain romance to the old city and insisted they be preserved. In fact, he ordered that they be refurbished and all the advance defences be torn down to expose the splendour of the walls. So Québec City owes much of its French-regime charm to the whimsical tastes of an English aristocrat.

FORTIFICATIONS OF QUÉBEC

At the interpretation centre attached to the wall on Rue St-Louis, Parks Canada gives an excellent overview of the history of the fortifications and their construction. You can take a 90-minute walking tour from here, or explore on your own. It's just a short stroll over to the St-Louis gate, and there you can begin to get a real feel for the ramparts. This is the most impressive section of the fortifications. It faces west over what was once open ground and the most vulnerable to attack. The wall here is 1.5 metres thick and close to 5 metres high. Two ornate main gates (the St-Louis and the St-Jean) puncture its stone solidity. At the northern end of the section is Parc de l'Artillerie, a pleasant green space that holds relics of some of the oldest sections of the fortifications. The park's old foundry has a beautiful scale model of what Québec City looked like at the beginning of the 19th century. Nearby is the Redoute Dauphine, parts of which date to 1713. Beyond the park the fortifications swing east along the clifftops overlooking the Lower Town. The cliffs provided a natural defence, so the walls here are not much more than chest high, but they're studded with

THE ST-JEAN GATE

REDOUTE DAUPHINE

cannons and mortars. The walls along Avenue des Remparts eventually lead to the Château Frontenac. Just in front of the château is Terrasse-Dufferin, a wide boardwalk along the cliffs that leads to the narrower and more precipitous Promenade des Gouverneurs, which in turn leads you to the next stop on the tour: the Citadelle de Québec.

This star-shaped fortress straddles the old city and the wider metropolis beyond. Part of Vieux-Québec, it is linked to the rest of the city because it is part of the fortifications that extend beyond the walls: it's a post-Conquest addition. The British built the citadel between 1820 and 1831 to defend the city against an American attack that never came. It represents the apogee of 19th-

The Van Doos Band on parade

century fortifications, with low-lying walls half-hidden behind gentle grassy slopes designed to absorb cannon shot and force attackers to expose themselves to relentless fire from the fort. It is still an active military post, home to the Royal 22e Régiment (the "Van Doos"), who keep a battalion on station year-round. Two unflinching infantrymen in red tunics and tall bearskin hats guard the handsome main gate (the Dalhousie gate), and visitors must join a guided group to tour the interior. What you can see, however, is somewhat limited. The chapel (once a powder magazine) and the governor general's residence are off-limits, as are the barracks. Visitors do tour an old military prison that now houses part of the Van Doos'

Former Governor General's residence

MONUMENT ON THE PLAINES D'ABRAHAM

museum (arms, uniforms, medals, etc.) and get a magnificent view of the old city from the King's Bastion and a sweeping one of the river from the Prince of Wales's Bastion.

The western walls of the fort overlook the Plaines d'Abraham, now Parc des Champs-de-Bataille (National Battlefields Park), naturally the next stop. This is the biggest urban park in Canada, with 107 hectares of gently rolling greenery laid out on the clifftops overlooking the St. Lawrence River. If it's a fine day, plan to spend a couple of hours exploring its nooks and crannies as you wander westward. It could be said that Canada's fate was sealed on this pleasant tract of land on September 13, 1759, when General James Wolfe and his battle-hardened Scots and English soldiers defeated a French garrison force commanded by the Marquis de Montcalm. The battle claimed the lives of both commanders and essentially ended French dreams of a North American empire.

Reminders of the park's martial past litter the landscape in the form of old cannons, plaques and monuments to both leaders and several panels describing the battle. Two later military relics are the Tours Martello (Martello Towers), one of which now houses exhibits on military engineering and (of all things) meteorology. At the other, immerse yourself in 1814 military life. Enjoy a meal typical of the period while helping British soldiers solve a mystery (this activity is held in English on Friday evenings). These round stone towers, named for the man who designed them, were cutting-edge military technology when built in the early 1800s as outer defences for the citadel. The walls that face away from the citadel are solid and thick to fend off attack. The walls facing the citadel, however, are much thinner and could be easily destroyed by the citadel's cannon so that attackers could never use them for defence.

For something a little less militaristic, pause at the Jardin Jeanne d'Arc. This flower-filled oasis, with its statue of the Maid of Orléans, is located at the entrance to the park between Avenue Taché and Place Montcalm. It certainly looks peaceful, but it was planted in honour of the soldiers of Nouvelle France who died fighting General Wolfe. The saint it's named for led an army and is entrusted with guarding the valour of French arms.

To find out more about the park and its history, you have a choice. At the turreted former naval reserve backing onto the park, close to the pedestrian bridge leading to the citadel, the Maison de la Découverte offers a glimpse of battles and other conflicts fought here through an

MARTELLO TOWER ON THE PLAINES D'ABRAHAM

MUSÉE DU QUÉBEC

entertaining three-dimensional film. On another floor, an interactive exhibit examines the flora, fauna and geology of the plains. Right in the middle of the park, at the old Musée du Québec on Avenue Wolfe-Montcalm, is the Centre d'Interprétation du Parc des Champs-de-Batailles. The ground floor of the museum's handsome Édifice Baillairgé features a mock-up of the battle and exhibits on the evolution of the site. It also offers guided tours of the park.

The Musée National des Beaux-Arts du Québec is itself well worth a visit. It has one of the finest art collections in Canada, with more than 22,000 pieces that illustrate the development of painting, sculpture and decoration in Québec from the 18th century to the present. One of its treasures is Charles Alexander Smith's *Assemblée des Six Comté*. It's an important portrayal of Canadian history that shows rebel-leader Louis-Joseph Papineau addressing a crowd during the 1837–38 insurrections against British colonial rule. Besides a permanent retrospective of two Québec artists, Jean Paul Lemieux and Jean-Paul Riopelle, the museum displays landscapes, portraits and a fascinating exhibit of religious art and artifacts drawn from churches all over the province. But the Musée du Québec is not all art. One of its two buildings (the Édifice Baillairgé, a beautiful Renaissance-revival structure) was designed in 1871 by renowned architect Charles Baillairgé to serve as a prison. The museum has preserved an entire cell block and uses it to portray prison life in the 19th century.

CAFÉ ON GRANDE-ALLÉE

When you emerge from the museum (and to do the place justice, this should be several hours after you enter), walk down Avenue Wolfe-Montcalm and turn right onto Grande Allée to head back towards the old city. This stretch of Grande Allée is about as stately and elegant a street as any in North America. It's lined with some fine old homes, churches and public buildings in styles that range from neo-Gothic to Beaux-Arts, with a heavy dose of Second Empire, which was very

Maison Krieghoff

popular with the 19th-century bourgeoisie who made their homes here. Recent commercial and government efforts to participate in this architectural display have marred the grace of the street somewhat with contributions from the glitter-and-glass school of architecture (commercial) and the bunker style of construction (government). But it's easy to look past these structures and focus on the gems.

At No. 115, for example, is something that resembles a country cottage with its steep roof and dormer windows but is, in fact, a city house built in 1850. It's named Maison Krieghoff for its most famous resident, the painter Cornelius Krieghoff, who lived in it off and on in 1859 and 1860. Next door is the graciously proportioned Ladies' Protestant Home, with its massive cornice and lantern. No. 82 is a piece of pure Regency, the Maison Henry-Stuart, with its row of French windows and massive overhanging roof. Maison Henry-Stuart and its pretty gardens are open to the public, and afternoon tea is served here. The fanciful jumble of towers and battlements at 530 Grande Allée that looks a little like a fortress is actually the church of Saint-Coeur-de-Marie, built by Eudist priests in 1919. Further west and just two blocks north of Grande Allée on Rue de la Chevrotière is a far more significant religious building. It's the mother house of the Soeurs du Bon-Pasteur (Sisters of the Good Shepherd), a religious order dedicated to the education of abandoned and delinquent girls. Its austere walls hide one of the most exuberantly beautiful places of worship in the city, a neo-Baroque chapel designed by Charles Baillairgé. Its narrow nave soars several storeys and a beautifully gilded 18th-century retable rests on the main altar.

Maison Henry-Stuart

Just across the street from the nuns' residence is one of those ugly government buildings, Édifice Marie-Guyart. This one, however, has a saving grace. Its top floor, the 31st (at 221 metres high), is an observatory with a magnificent, 360-degree view of the city and the surrounding countryside. There's a fee to get in, but it's worth it.

If you head back to Grande Allée and continue the trek east, you'll come to the very heart of the Québec government, the Hôtel du Parlement, where the province's legislature — the Assemblée Nationale — meets in Second Empire splendour. The building faces the walls, so to get to the main entrance you have to skirt its southern side. The grim bronze personage standing in the garden is one of Québec's most notorious premiers, Maurice (Le Chef)

Soeurs du Bon-Pasteur chapel

Duplessis, who governed the province for much of the 1930s, '40s and '50s.

You'll appreciate the beauty of the Hôtel du Parlement if you walk all the way down to Avenue Dufferin. Turn left and walk to the front gates for a visual history lesson. Eugène-Étienne Taché, the architect who designed the building in 1875, went out of his way to showcase the men and women who built the province. Bronze statues of people such as Samuel de Champlain; Paul de Chomedey, Sieur de Maisonneuve; Marguerite Bourgeoys; and Jeanne Mance fill 22 niches along the façade and up the sides of the central tower. A First Nations family in bronze poses at the main door and just below them, a First Nations fisherman stands at the edge of a fountain, his spear poised to catch a fish. In less politically correct times (say, in the late 1970s), this door was called the Porte des Sauvages, or Door of the Savages. You don't hear that term much any more.

TOP: HÔTEL DU PARLEMENT
INSET: DETAIL ON STATUE

There are frequent tours of the building and it's worth going inside even if only to see the two parliamentary chambers. The ornate Red Room on the left of the main door is where the appointed Legislative Council used to meet. When it was disbanded, the room became the main meeting room of parliamentary commissions and committees. Nowadays, laws are actually hammered out in the Blue Room on the right of the main door. This isn't quite as ornate as the Red Room and the colour scheme is a little less florid, but it's pretty fancy. The painting above the speaker's chair depicts the Debate on Languages in 1793 that resulted in French gaining official status in what was a British territory. Between the two chambers is a hall that has served as the parliamentary dining room since 1917, currently named Le Parliamentaire; it is open to the public.

When you exit the Hôtel du Parlement you'll nearly be back at the St-Louis gate, but before you return to the charms of the old city, look across Grande Allée at the Manège Militaire, or Armoury. It too was designed by Eugène-Étienne Taché. The pleasant green space in front of it is Place George V, and there a monument honours the memory of two British soldiers who died fighting a fire in Faubourg St-Sauveur in 1889.

MANÈGE MILITAIRE

EXCURSIONS

MARY ANN SIMPKINS

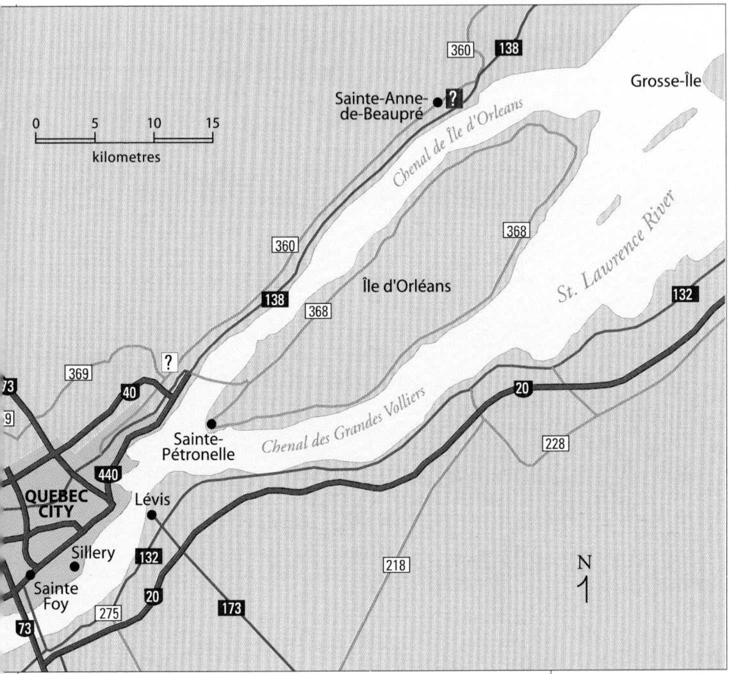

The area around Québec City, beyond the old walls and Grand Allée, is rich in history and natural beauty. Within a short distance of the citadel are marvellous gardens, a waterfall higher than Niagara Falls, a shrine that attracts pilgrims from all over the world and a traditional First Nations village.

Take Sillery, for example, just west of the Plaines d'Abraham, where the governor general of the United Province of Canada had his home in the 1800s. In those days, nearly half the city's population was English-speaking and the wealthy ones lived in grand homes near the vice-regal residence. Fire destroyed the residence in 1966 and the grounds became a public park — the Bois-de-Coulonge on Chemin St-Louis, which is filled with flower gardens and walkways to some great viewing spots over the St. Lawrence River.

THE BOIS-DE-COULONGE

Fire also wrecked a smaller home on the estate. A replica was erected in 1929. Villa Bagatelle is a rare example of rural Québec Gothic architecture. The barren, modernized interior that features rotating exhibits on aspects of Québec society is overshadowed by the English-style garden, which demonstrates the diversity possible in a small space. The wooded oasis is crammed

VILLA BAGATELLE

DOMAINE CATARAQUI

with more than 350 varieties of exotic and indigenous plants, from apple trees to forsythia, along with two rock gardens, a stream and a pond.

The governor general's summer residence was a few kilometres away, in the centre of Sillery. Additions over the years have turned Domaine Cataraqui on Chemin St-Louis into an elegant neoclassical villa. Purchased by the provincial government after the death of the last owner, Catherine Rhodes, the house was restored to the style of the 1930s, when Rhodes lived here with her husband, the artist Henry Percyval Tudor-Hart. Some furnishings, photographs and paintings belonging to the couple remain in the house, which also serves as the provincial government's official reception centre and an art gallery, hosting three major exhibitions a year.

Just as elegant are other buildings on the estate, such as the stable and Tudor-Hart's studio. The artist treated the front lawn as a canvas, using dynamite to duplicate the contours of the waves that ripple over the St. Lawrence, visible at the end of the property. You can easily spend an hour wandering among the flower beds and along trails through a forest of catalpa, Japanese ginkgo and other species. This is an idyllic setting for the various musical groups that perform Wednesday evenings and Sunday mornings in summer.

Nearly directly below, at the base of the cliff on Chemin du Foulon, is the Maison des Jésuites. The Jesuits set up their first permanent mission in North America beside the St. Lawrence where First Nations people fished for eel. Fire demolished the original home. The present stone house was built around 1730, with the second floor being added about 100 years later. Inside are photographs, amulets and other artifacts unearthed on digs here, and a copy of a 1769 romance novel written by a resident, Frances Brooke — the first English-language book published in Canada. The Jesuits tried to persuade the Montagnais, Algonquin and Attikamek nations to settle among them, but only a few stayed here permanently. The Amerindian camp in the backyard is a reminder of their presence, as are the wooden crosses across the street in the First Nations cemetery.

MAISON DES JÉSUITES

Back up the cliff, nearly adjacent to the bridges connecting the north and south shores, is the Aquarium du Québec. The collection of more than 3,500 specimens ranges from pythons to piranhas. Small outdoor pools are the year-round home of the seals that perform in two shows

Laval University

a day. Rivalling thc exhibits is the aquarium's location on the edge of a forested cliff. There's an excellent view of the river and the Pont de Québec (the Québec Bridge, the world's longest cantilevered bridge). A stroll through the woods brings you to a picnic area, a hatchery for rainbow trout, a skeleton of a whale at the exhibit on the St. Lawrence and the old toll station for crossing the river.

A few blocks north, opposite three large shopping centres, is Université Laval's Jardin Roger Van den Hende on Boulevard Hochelaga, named for its founder, a professor of ornamental horticulture. The garden ranks as one of eastern Canada's most beautiful. From May to September the public can tour the 6 hectares, filled with more than 2,000 plant species from Europe, Asia and North America; the arboretum; and the water garden. The highlight for many visitors is the extensive rose garden. The more than 200 different types, from shrub to hybrid teas, have unusually vibrant colours, a result of the area's cold nights.

In Charlesbourg, the Jardin Zoologique du Québec on Rue de la Faune is popular not just with children but also with photographers looking for a place to shoot wedding pictures. That's because the zoo is also the site of a horticultural park with flower beds, a lake inhabited by flamingos, two waterfalls and a river populated with ducks and swans. Trolley rides begin at the entrance and circle the park without stopping. Walk instead, following moose tracks and bear paws painted on the paths. The 6-kilometre route goes by most of the 600 animals. Besides moose, polar bears and pythons, there are farm animals and a petting zoo. A guide inside one old stone house — left from the days when a mink farm was located here — might also offer you a chance to caress an African cockroach. Falcons and vultures soar overhead in the summer birds-of-prey show.

On leaving the zoo, drive east to reach the Réserve Indienne de Wendake, the only Huron reserve in Canada. Converted by the Jesuits and allied with the French, the Huron left what is now Ontario more than 300 years ago to settle here. A wooden palisade circles the re-created traditional Huron village, which offers

Traditional Huron-Wendake Village

a glimpse into the lives of the ancestors of the present residents. Inside the longhouse, a full-sized doe hangs from the rafters and someone might be tanning a beaver skin by the smokehouse. In one building, costumes help explain the differences between the various nations. The village restaurant serves typical aboriginal food, and its row of tiny shops sell everything from herbal remedies to recordings of Huron music. The Traditional Huron-Wendake Village is open year-round, with dance and song performances from May to September.

Île d'Orléans

Île d'Orléans, a small island that is a 15-minute drive east of Québec City, remains rooted in the past. The entire island was named a historic district by the Québec government in 1970. The first settlers arrived in 1649 and most buildings date from the 18th and 19th centuries. Driving the 67-kilometre road around the island reveals a bucolic landscape, a vista of farms, stone manors and churches interspersed with a few artisans practising time-honoured crafts.

When he set out to conquer Québec in 1759, General James Wolfe set up his headquarters at the western tip of Île d'Orléans, in Ste-Pétronille, the smallest of the island's six parishes. His takeover of the island wasn't always peaceable. The Manoir Mauvide-Genest in St-Jean, for example, rated the finest example of rural architecture under the French regime, still bears the pockmarks of British cannon fire in its stone walls. The Norman-style manor is today a museum and restaurant.

Elsewhere on the island, the Parc Maritime de St-Laurent celebrates the shipbuilding heritage of St-Laurent parish with exhibits and on-site demonstrations of wooden boat-building; a blacksmith demonstrates traditional techniques at the Forge à Pique-Assaut; and weavers spin rugs at the Economusée du Tapis in St-Pierre. To see other works by local craftspeople, visit the parish church, Canada's oldest village church.

Chutes Montmorency

On the mainland, just east of the Île d'Orléans bridge, the Pont d'Île, Chutes Montmorency plunges 83 metres, a drop nearly one and a half times greater than that of Niagara Falls. For a superb view, cross the pedestrian bridge suspended over the

BASILIQUE SAINTE-ANNE-DE-BEAUPRÉ

falls. The cable car offers another panorama, as well as an alternative to climbing the 400 stairs connecting the upper and lower boardwalks. Perched on top of the cliff close to the falls is a Palladian-style villa, a replica of the original constructed around 1783 for the governor of Québec, later rented by the Duke of Kent. A small museum tells the history of the graceful white wooden building, which also houses an art gallery, bar and restaurant. The Sunday buffet is popular with local residents.

Further east along Highway 138 sits Basilique Sainte-Anne-de-Beaupré. Pilgrims have been coming to this site since 1658; it is considered the oldest Christian shrine in North America. And they're still coming, more than 1 million of them a year, to pray inside the most recent church on this site: a concrete edifice warmed by glimmering mosaics, carved stones and 200 stained-glass windows. In summer, evening candlelight processions sometimes wind over the nearby hillside, where life-sized bronze figures line the Way of the Cross. On the opposite side of the basilica, the round Cyclorama features a museum and a panoramic painting of Jerusalem. One floor covers the history of the pilgrimages, displaying photographs along with earrings, necklaces and other offerings to St. Anne. The second floor displays the church's treasures, from silver chalices to an 18th-century gilded altar.

The shrine and its little town sit at the foot of Mont Ste-Anne, an 800-metre-high mountain that offers some of the best alpine and cross-country skiing east of the Rockies. The resort has 56 downhill trails totalling 84 kilometres. Thirteen percent of them are classified as extremely difficult. The cross-country network, the largest in Canada, has 223 kilometres of trails, while a large funpark and two halfpipes lure snowboarders. At the base of the mountain are a skating rink and ski museum. In summer, mountain bikers and hikers take over the trails, sightseers ride the lifts and golfers play on the two courses that grace the foot of the mountain.

SKIING AT MONT STE-ANNE

In summer, take the ferry from Québec City to Lévis and catch one of the shuttle buses that meander around the city. Among the stops is Fort No. 1, built early in the 19th

Celtic Cross

century to fend off an American attack that never came. The guides who lead tours wear costumes modelled on the uniforms of the Royal Engineers, but the fort is no longer a military installation. It was used as a storage depot for ammunition through two world wars and was finally decommissioned in 1948.

East of Lévis, close to the town of Montmagny, sits Grosse Île. For more than 150 years the small island was the main gateway to Canada for thousands of immigrants and the quarantine station for those afflicted with cholera, typhoid and black plague. A sense of sadness pervades this final destination for so many. The largest graveyard is known as the Irish Cemetery. Most of the more than 5,000 men, women and children buried here were fleeing the Irish potato famine. The sightseeing trolley also visits the Celtic Cross, the Catholic church, the hospital and the Disinfection Building, where pipes over narrow shower stalls sprayed each ship passenger with mercury chloride. The only way to reach this island, operated by Parks Canada, is on licensed boats. Tour operators offer packages from Montmagny, nearby Berthier-sur-Mer and Québec City. The tours last around three hours. There are picnic tables and the hotel has a cafeteria.

East of Ste-Anne-de-Beaupré, villages cling to cliffs overlooking the St. Lawrence River. This area has long been a magnet for artists — even the smallest village boasts a gallery. The scenic landscape leads to Pointe-au-Pic, where a turreted stone castle, Manoir Richelieu, was recently renovated to celebrate its 100th anniversary. Opposite the hotel, try your luck at the casino. Or hop aboard a boat for a whale-watching tour or a ride down the majestic Saguenay fjord.

Golf at Mont Ste-Anne

LISTINGS: CONTENTS

GETTING THERE

MONTRÉAL

Located along the shores of the St. Lawrence River, Montréal is easy to get to by air, highway, rail and water.

BY AIR

Pierre Elliott Trudeau International Airport: Located 18 kilometres west of downtown Montréal, the airport is accessible from Highways 20 and 40 and by commuter train or shuttle bus. It is a 20-minute drive from the city centre. The airport handles regular scheduled flights from local and international destinations. Some 20 major airlines offer regularly scheduled flights.

BY ROAD

By car or by bus, travellers can reach Montréal by several major routes. Highways 20 and 40 enter Montréal from the west. Hwy. 20 also enters Montréal from the northeast, hugging the north shore of the St. Lawrence River. Hwy. 10 enters Montréal from the east over the Pont Champlain (Champlain Bridge). Hwy. 15 runs towards Montréal from Québec's southern border, shared with New York State, and from the north. Out-of-town buses arrive and depart from the Montréal Bus Terminal (formerly the Terminus Voyageur), at 505 Boul. de Maisonneuve E. (corner of Berri). Adirondack Trailways and Greyhound Lines offer rides to New York City, and Orléans Express covers Québec City and other destinations in the province. From May to October, the Rout-Pass entitles holders to unlimited bus travel for 15 consecutive days in Québec and Ontario. Call the station at 514-842-2281 for bus company fares and schedules.

BY RAIL

Train travellers arrive at Gare Centrale (Central Station), 895 Rue de la Gauchetière O. Montréal is served by the VIA Rail Canada system, the network that provides all rail service throughout Canada. Amtrak provides daily service to New York and Washington. VIA Rail offers a Canrailpass, valid for one month, which allows the holder 12 days of train travel across Canada. Central Station is located directly beneath the posh Hôtel La Reine-Élisabeth (Queen Elizabeth Hotel) and across from the Hilton Montréal Bonaventure. The station also serves commuter rail lines and is connected by indoor tunnels to Montréal's subway system and several underground shopping centres. Call 1-800-561-3949 or 514-989-2626 for train schedules and fares.

QUÉBEC CITY

Located 253 kilometres northeast of Montréal along the St. Lawrence River, Québec City is easily accessible by air, road and rail.

BY AIR

Jean Lesage International Airport: The airport is located 16 kilometres west of downtown Québec City along Route 138 and Autoroute 540. The airport offers scheduled flights with Air Alliance, Air Canada, Air Nova, Air Atlantic, Northwest Airlink and charter flights with Aeropro, Aviation Portneuf and Aviation Roger Forgues. For information on flights, call 418-640-2700. There is no longer any bus shuttle service available from the airport into the city. A taxi costs about $27 from the airport to downtown.

BY ROAD

Québec City is served by Highway 20 along the south shore of the St. Lawrence River and Hwy. 40 from the north. Buses arrive at the Bus Terminal, 320 Rue Abraham-Martin. Intercar Côte-Nord links Québec City with a number of northern towns, and Orléans Express Coach Lines links the city with the rest of Québec. From May to October, the Rout-Pass entitles holders to unlimited bus travel for 7, 14 or 18 consecutive days in Québec and Ontario. Call 418-525-3000 for information.

BY RAIL

Via Rail Canada offers daily service between Québec City and Montréal with regular and first-class cars. Call 1-888-842-7245 for information and reservations. Trains arrive and depart from Gare du Palais, 450 Rue de la Gare-du-Palais in downtown Québec City. Call 418-524-4161 for information.

TRAVEL ESSENTIALS

MONEY

Currency can be exchanged at any bank at the prevailing rate. If you use a small local branch, it's best to call ahead to confirm its capacity to exchange, on the spot, any currency other than American funds. There are currency exchange booths at the airport. Banks are generally open from 10 A.M. to 4 P.M. Units of currency are similar to those of the United States, except for the Canadian one-dollar (loonie) and two-dollar (toonie) coins.

Most major North American credit cards and bank cards, including American Express, Carte Blanche, Diners Club, EnRoute, MasterCard and Visa, are accepted almost everywhere. Travellers' cheques can be cashed in major hotels, some restaurants and large stores. Many stores and services will accept U.S. currency, but the exchange rate they offer may vary greatly. Since there are no laws enforcing foreign currency rates of exchange, it is strongly recommended that you convert to Canadian funds before you make your purchases.

American visitors may also use bank or credit cards to make cash withdrawals from automated teller machines that are tied into international networks such as Cirrus and Plus. Before you leave home, check with your bank to find out what range of banking services its cards will allow you to use.

PASSPORTS

American citizens are required to carry proof of citizenship, such as a U.S. passport or a birth certificate, plus photo identification. Naturalized U.S. citizens should carry a naturalization certificate, plus photo identification. Permanent U.S. residents who are not citizens are advised to bring their Alien Registration Card (Green Card) or a valid 1551 stamp in their passport. Note that other documents such as a driver's licence or voter registration card will not be accepted as proof of U.S. citizenship. Visas are not required for U.S. tourists entering Canada from the U.S. for stays up to 180 days.

Citizens of most other countries must bring a valid passport. Some may be required to obtain a visitor's visa. For details, please consult the Canadian embassy or consulate serving your home country.

CUSTOMS

Arriving

As a non-resident of Canada, you may bring in any reasonable amount of personal effects and food, and a full tank of gas. Special restrictions or quotas apply to certain specialty goods, and especially to plant-, agricultural- and animal-related materials. All items must be declared to Customs upon arrival and may include up to 200 cigarettes, 50 cigars, 200 grams (6.5 oz.) of manufactured tobacco and 200 tobacco sticks. Visitors are also permitted 1.14 litres (40 oz.) of liquor or 1.5 litres of wine or 8.5 litres (24 x 12-oz. cans or bottles) of beer.

You may bring in gifts for Canadian residents duty-free, up to a value of $60.00 (Canadian) each, provided they do not consist of alcohol, tobacco or advertising material. For more detailed information, call the Canada Border Services Agency's Automated Customs Information Service (ACIS) at 1-800-461-9999, or visit the Canada Border Services Agency on-line at www.cbsa-asfc.gc.ca

Departing

For detailed customs rules for entering or re-entering the United States, please contact a U.S. Customs office before you visit the province of Québec. Information is also available on the U.S. Customs and Border Protection (CBP) Web site at www.customs.ustreas.gov. Copies of the U.S. Customs information brochure *Know Before You Go* are available from U.S. Customs offices or on the CBP Web site (under "Publications"). It is generally recommended that you try to pack the things you'll need to declare separately.

Travellers from other countries should also check on customs regulations before leaving home.

TAXES

Most goods and services are subject to a federal tax (GST) and a provincial tax (PST) in Québec. Foreign residents may be entitled to certain tax rebates on tourism-related goods and services. If you keep all sales slips from your visit you will be able to claim tax rebates upon your departure. For more information, visit the "Tax Refund for Visitors" page at www.cra-arc.gc.ca/tax/nonresidents/visitors/tax-e.html, or phone 902-432-5608 or 1-800-668-4748 (Canada).

Goods and Services Tax (GST, or TPS in French)
The federal Goods and Services Tax is 7%. This is a value-added tax that applies to most goods, purchased gifts, food/beverages and services, including most hotel and motel accommodation.

Provincial Sales Tax (PST, or TVQ in French)
The Québec provincial sales tax is 7.5% of the original price plus GST. A PST refund form can also be obtained by contacting Revenue Québec at 514-873-4692, or ask a retailer for a form.

GETTING ACQUAINTED

TIME ZONE

Montréal and Québec City fall within the Eastern Standard Time Zone.

CLIMATE

Here are average Montréal temperatures, highs and lows; fluctuations from the norm are common:

January	21°F to 5°F –6°C to –15°C
February	25°F to 7°F –4°C to –14°C
March	28°F to 19°F –2°C to –7°C
April	52°F to 34°F 11°C to 1°C
May	66°F to 45°F 19°C to 7°C
June	73°F to 55°F 23°C to 13°C
July	79°F to 59°F 26°C to 15°C
August	77°F to 57°F 25°C to 14°C
September	68°F to 48°F 20°C to 9°C
October	55°F to 39°F 13°C to 4°C
November	41°F to 28°F 5°C to –2°C
December	27°F to 12°F –3°C to –11°C

Average annual rainfall:
28.98in./73.63 cm.

Average annual snowfall:
89.6in./226.2 cm.

Average temperatures are
5.4°C (41°F) in spring,
19.4°C (66.2°F) in summer,
11.4°C (51.8°F) in autumn,
–6.1°C (21.2°F) in winter.

Here are the average Québec City temperatures, highs and lows:

January	18°F to 1°F –8°C to –17°C
February	21°F to 3°F –6°C to –16°C
March	32°F to 16°F 0°C to –9°C
April	46°F to 28°F 8°C to –2°C
May	63°F to 41°F 17°C to 5°C
June	72°F to 50°F 22°C to 10°C
July	77°F to 55°F 25°C to 13°C
August	73°F to 54°F 23°C to 12°C
September	64°F to 45°F 18°C to 7°C
October	52°F to 36°F 11°C to 2°C
November	37°F to 25°F 3°C to –4°C
December	23°F to 9°F –5°C to –13°C

Average annual rainfall:
34.69in./88.13 cm.

Average annual snowfall:
132.6in./337 cm.

Average temperatures are
3.2°C (37.4°F) in spring,
17.7°C (64.4°F) in summer,
9.5°C (50°F) in autumn, and
–8.3°C (17.6°F) in winter.

GUIDES AND INFORMATION SERVICES

Tourisme Québec operates more than 200 tourist information offices province-wide to provide regional information and seven Maisons du Tourisme, with more extensive services. For information call 1-877-266-5687 (Canada and the United States); fax 514-864-3838; e-mail info@bonjourquebec.com; or write to Tourisme Québec at P.O. Box 979, Montreal, QC H3C 2W3. Also, visit Tourisme Québec's Web site at www.bonjourquebec.com for comprehensive information about accommodations, camping and attractions throughout the province of Québec.

MONTRÉAL

- L'Hôtel de Ville de Montréal (Montréal City Hall). 275 Rue Notre Dame E., Montréal, QC H2Y 1C6; 514-872-1111. For a guided visit, e-mail bam@ville.montreal.qc.ca.
- Infotouriste Centre. 1001 Square Dorchester, Montréal, QC H3B 1G2; 514-873-2015 or 1-877-266-5687 (North America). Near the Peel Métro station, the Infotouriste Centre handles travel planning, hotel reservations, car rentals, attractions and guided bus tours. Visit www.tourisme-montreal.org for regional information.
- Tourisme Montréal's Greater Montréal Convention and Tourism Administration Bureau. 1555 Rue Peel, Suite 600, Montréal, QC H3A 1X6; 514-844-5400; fax 514-864-3838. Regional information is available at www.tourisme-montreal.org/meet, or visit www.montrealcam.com to see Montréal in real time via the Greater Montreal LiveCam Network.
- Tourist Information Centre of Old Montréal. 174 Rue Notre-Dame E. Located near the Champs-de-Mars Métro station, the centre supplies bus maps, road maps, telephone cards, museums passes and bicycle-path passes as well as brochures about attractions. www.oldportofmontreal.com.

QUÉBEC CITY

- Ville de Québec (Québec City Hall). 43 Côte de la Fabrique, Québec City, QC G1R 5M1; 418-641-7010. Ground floor houses the Urban Life Interpretation Centre of the Ville de Québec, 418-641-6172.
- Maison du Tourisme. 12 Rue Ste-Anne. Located across from the Château Frontenac, the Infotouriste Centre provides extensive local information plus hotel and car rental reservations. Visit www.bonjourquebec.com.
- Office du Tourisme et des Congrès de la Communauté Urbaine de Québec. 399 Rue St-Joseph E., Second Floor, Québec City, QC G1K 8E2; 418-641-6654; fax 418-641-6578.
- Vieux-Québec Tourist Information Bureau. 835 Avenue Wilfrid-Laurier, Québec City, QC G1R 2L3; 418-641-6290; fax 418-522-0830; www.regiondequebec.com

LANGUAGE

Most Montrealers speak English, but when travelling through some areas of the province, you might as well be in France. But unlike speaking French in Paris, using a phrase or two *en français* will most likely get a cheer of praise by most French-speaking Quebeckers.

GETTING AROUND

TRAVELLING IN MONTRÉAL AND QUÉBEC CITY

Montréal is an island connected to the mainland by bridges to the north and south of the city. The city is served by the Ville-Marie Expressway, which leads to Highways 10, 15 and 20, travelling west and east. The Decarie Expressway leads to Hwy. 40, travelling north and west.

If you're a member of any recognized auto-club affiliates (AAA, CAA, etc.), the CAA-Québec will provide all club services. In Montréal, call 514-861-1313, and elsewhere in Québec, call 1-800-222-4357. CAA-Québec also has a Web site: www.caaquebec.com

PUBLIC TRANSPORTATION

MONTRÉAL

The Société de Transport de Montréal (STM) operates from 5:30 A.M. to

12:30 or 1:00 A.M., depending on the Métro line. Some bus lines run all night. The subway system consists of four Métro lines and covers 65 kilometres across 65 stations, with free transfers to the STM bus network of 163 daytime and 20 nighttime service routes. Exact fare is required. Free maps, discount tickets and day passes are available at all stations and in many convenience shops. At the time of publication, one adult ticket is $2.50 and six tickets are $11.25. The Tourist Card, which allows unlimited travel for one day for $8 or for three days for $16, is available year-round at the Berri-UQAM, Bonaventure and Peel Métro stations (and at various other stations in the summer months). Call 514-280-5507 for more details; call 514-786-4636 for bus lines, schedules and additional information; fax 514-280-5666; e-mail commentaires@stm.info; visit www.stcum.qc.ca

Commuter Buses and Trains
Regular train service to Montréal's suburbs operates from Gare Centrale (Central Station) and Gare Windsor. Call 514-287-8726 for commuter-train schedules for both stations. Regular bus service on the South Shore runs from Métro Longueuil (450-463-0131) and in Laval from Métro Henri Bourassa (450-688-6520).

A ferry service offers rides to pedestrians and cyclists from the Old Port to Parc des Îles, Longueuil, Promenade Bellerive in East Montréal and Île Charron from mid-May to mid-October. Call 514-281-8000 for information.

QUÉBEC CITY

The Société de Transport de la Communauté Urbaine de Québec operates bus lines throughout Québec City. Fares at the time of publication are $2.50 for adults and free for children. Students and children over five need to present a valid student card for access at a reduced rate of $1.40. Day passes are available. Call 418-627-2511 for information.

A Winter Shuttle, the HiverExpress, operates daily from downtown Québec City to Ste-Foy hotels and a number of outdoor activity sites. Call 418-525-5191 for reservations.

The Société des Traversiers du Québec operates year-round daily ferry services from Québec City to Lévis, across the St. Lawrence River. For information call 418-644-3704; fax 418-643-5178; or visit www.traversiers.gouv.qc.ca

CARS AND RENTALS

Most foreign driver's licences are valid in Québec. Non-resident drivers and passengers of automobiles licensed in Québec are entitled to the same compensation from the Société de l'Assurance Automobile du Québec as Québec residents if they are injured in an accident in the province. Other non-resident accident victims, including pedestrians, cyclists and drivers of cars not licensed in Québec, can be compensated in inverse proportion to. their responsibility for any accidents. Owners of vehicles driven in Québec must have at least $50,000 in liability coverage. For additional information, contact the Societé de l'Assurance Automobile du Québec at 514-873-7620 (in Montréal), 418-643-7620 (in Québec City), or toll free at 1-800-361-7620, or visit www.saaq.gouv.qc.ca

Distances are indicated in kilometres and speed limits in kilometres per hour. One kilometre equals about five-eighths of a mile. To convert from kilometres to miles, multiply kilometres by 0.6. To convert from miles to kilometres, multiply miles by 1.6. Metric measurements are used for motor fuel. One litre equals about one-quarter of an American gallon, or about one-fifth of an Imperial gallon.

Speed limits on highways and main roads are 100 km/h maximum and 60 km/h minimum. The provincial police prohibit possession of a radar detector, whether connected or not, and fines range from $500 to $1,000. Turning right on a red light is permitted throughout Québec except on the island of Montréal and at intersections where road signs prohibit such turns. Seatbelt use by passengers and drivers is mandatory.

MONTRÉAL

- Alamo Rent-a-Car, Pierre Elliott Trudeau International Airport.

514-633-1222 or 1-800-327-9633; www.alamo.com
- Avis Car and Truck Rental. Pierre Elliott Trudeau International Airport; 514-636-1902. Downtown, 1225 Rue Metcalfe; 514-866-2847; www.avis.com
- Hertz Canada Ltée. 1073 Rue Drummond; 514-938-1717; www.hertz.com
- Pelletier Car and Minibus Rental. 3585 Rue Berri; 514-281-5000; www.pelletierrentacar.com
- Sako Location d'Autos Inc. 2350 Rue Manella; 514-735-3500; www.sako.com

Consult the Yellow Pages for more agencies.

QUÉBEC CITY

- Discount Location. 12 Rue Ste-Anne; 418-655-2206 or 1-800-263-2355; www.discountcar.com
- Hertz Canada Ltée., Jean Lesage International Airport. 418-871-1571 or 1-800-263-0600; www.hertz.com
- Via Route. 450 Rue de la Gare-du-Palais; 418-692-2660; www.viaroute.com

Consult the Yellow Pages for more agencies.

TOURS

MONTRÉAL

- Autocar Connaisseur Grayline. 1140 Rue Wellington; 514-934-1222; www.coachcanada.com. Sightseeing tours on board a replica of Montréal's streetcars of the past.
- Autocar Impérial. Infotouriste Centre, 1001 Square Dorchester; 514-871-4733; fax 514-871-9786; e-mail info@autocarimperial.com; www.autocarimperial.com. Bilingual city tours, some on double-decker buses.
- Aventure Boréale Inc. 514-271-1230 or 1-877-271-1230; fax 514-271-3153; e-mail info@borealtours.com; www.borealtours.com. Day trips to the countryside. Downtown departures for canoeing, fishing and hiking in the summer, and dogsledding, ice fishing, snowmobiling and snowshoeing in the winter. Transportation and meals included.
- La Balade du Vieux-Port. 514-496-7678. A bilingual guided tour of the Old Port's past, departing from the Quai Jacques-Cartier.
- Bateau-Mouche au Vieux-Port de Montréal. 514-849-9952 or 1-800-361-9952; fax 514-849-9851; e-mail info@bateau-mouche.com; www.bateau-mouche.com. Tour the city in a glass-roofed boat offering spectacular views. Five daytime excursions and a Parisian-style dinner cruise with gourmet menu and live entertainment leave daily from the Quai Jacques-Cartier.
- Delco Aviation Ltée. 450-663-4311 or 514-984-1208; fax 450-975-8965; www.delcoaviation.com. See Montréal from a seaplane in summer or try hydroskis in winter.
- Flowers Aviation Inc. 6324 3e Ave.; 514-727-6486. Cessna 206 seaplanes tour regions throughout the province.
- Guidatour. 514-844-4021 or 1-800-363-4021; e-mail info@guidatour.qc.ca; www.guidatour.qc.ca. Daily walking tours of Old Montréal from June through October. Tickets on sale at Basilique Notre-Dame. Private guided tours of Montréal and environs available in several languages.
- Montréal AML Cruises. 514-842-9300 or 1-800-563-4643; www.croisieresaml.com. Sail the St. Lawrence River on guided tour boats or dinner cruises. Bilingual guides.
- Montréal Guide Service. 514-342-8994; e-mail info@montrealguideservice.com; www.montrealguideservice.com. Multilingual guided tours tailored for individuals or groups.
- Old Montréal Ghost Trail. 514-868-0303 or 1-800-363-4021; e-mail fantom.montreal@videotron.net; www.phvm.qc.ca. Meet some of the city's most famous ghosts on an evening walking tour.
- Les Services des Calèches et Traîneaux Lucky Luc. 514-934-6105. Tour Montréal in your own horse-drawn carriage, sleigh or long coach. Door-to-door.
- Vélo Aventure Montréal Inc. 514-847-0666; www.veloaventure.com. Rentals and sales of bicycles and in-line skates plus bicycle tours. Located at the Quai Convoyeurs in the Old Port.

- Vélo-Tour Montréal. 514-259-7272; www.velomontreal.com. Bicycle rentals and tours in English, French and Spanish.

QUÉBEC CITY

- Pro Aviation Inc. 710 7e Ave., Ste-Foy; 418-872-0206; www.proaviation.net. See the city by seaplane.
- Belle Époque Calèches. 418-687-6633. Horse-drawn buggies offer tours for small groups.
- Calèches du Vieux-Québec. 418-683-9222. Horse-drawn-carriage tours of the Old Town.
- Corporation du Tourisme Religieux de Québec. 418-694-0665; www.patrimoine-religieux.com. Walking tours of religious sites.
- Gray Line and Dupont offer a variety of bus tours. 418-649-9226 or 1-888-558-7668; fax 418-525-3044; www.graylinequebec.com
- Héli-Express. 418-877-5890; www.heliexpres.com. See Québec City from above on a helicopter tour.
- Old Québec Tours. 1-800-267-8687; www.oldquebectours.com. Bus tours of the city and environs for small groups. Whale watching tour available.
- Québec Historical Society. 418-692-0556; www.societehistoriquedequebec.qc.ca. Walking tours to discover the city's past.
- Visites Historiques de Québec. 418-656-4245. Bus tours cover historical landmarks.

ACCOMMODATION

What follows is a good cross-section of the accommodation options Montréal and Québec City offer.

Montréal has more than 23,000 rooms to suit every taste and every budget. The Greater Montréal area offers comfortable and convenient accommodations for groups of any size in hotels, motels, apartment hotels, bed-and-breakfast homes, college dormitories, campgrounds and resorts. The major hotel chains are represented in the city, as well as a range of lesser-known but equally comfortable establishments.

The majority of these establishments are located in the downtown core, near the subway system. Many are within walking distance of the major convention sites and shopping areas.

The Québec government is responsible for regulating and supervising hotel establishments and campgrounds, as well as issuing permits.

Non-Canadian residents can receive a cash rebate of the federal Goods and Services Tax (GST) and the Provincial Sales Tax (PST) on short-term accommodations and on some purchases.

Infotouriste offers a hotel reservation service for Montréal and Québec City. Contact the office at 1001 Square Dorchester, Montreal, QC H3B 4V4; 514-873-2015 or 1-877-266-5687 (North America).

Approximate prices are indicated, based on the average cost, at time of publishing, for two persons staying in a double room (excluding taxes): $ = $50–$90; $$ = $90–$180; $$$ = above $180.

For the locations of downtown hotels in Montréal, see the map on pages 8–9.

MONTRÉAL

Hotels: Pierre-Elliott Trudeau International Airport

- Day's Inn Montréal Aéroport. 4545 Chemin Côte-Vertu O., Ville St-Laurent, QC H4S 1C8; 514-332-2720; fax 514-332-4512; www.daysinn.com. Conference rooms, public transportation nearby. $$
- Econo Lodge Aéroport. 6755 Chemin Côte-de-Liesse, Ville St-Laurent, QC H4T 1E5; 514-735-5702 or 1-877-424-6423; fax 514-340-9278. Airport shuttle, conference room, outdoor swimming pool, nearby golf course. $$
- Four Points Hotel Dorval. 6600 Chemin Côte-de-Liesse, Ville St-Laurent, QC H4T 1E3; 514-344-1999 or 1-800-325-3535; fax 514-344-6720. Five minutes from airport. Family and corporate rooms. Indoor pool and waterslide, nearby golf course. $$
- Holiday Inn Aéroport-Montréal. 6500 Chemin Côte-de-Liesse, Ville St-Laurent, QC H4T 1E7; 514-739-3391 or 1-800-465-4329;

fax 514-739-6591; e-mail holidayinnap@rosdevhotels.com; www.rosdevhotels.com. Free airport shuttle. Tropical garden, indoor and outdoor pools, sauna, whirlpool, nearby golf course. $$

- Hotel Ramada Aéroport Montréal. 7300 Chemin Côte-de-Liesse, Ville St-Laurent, QC H4T 1E7; 514-733-8818 or 1-800-318-8818; fax 514-733-9889. Airport shuttle, conference rooms, outdoor pool, nearby golf course. $$
- Montréal Aéroport Hilton. 12505 Chemin Côte-de-Liesse, Dorval, QC H9P 1B7; 514-631-2411 or 1-800-445-8667; fax 514-631-0192; www.hilton.com. Free airport shuttle, nearby golf course. $$$
- Quality Hotel Aéroport Montréal. 7700 Chemin Côte-de-Liesse, Ville St-Laurent, QC H4T 1E7; 514-731-7821 or 1-800-361-6243; fax 514-731-7267; e-mail info@qualityhoteldorval.com; www.qualityhoteldorval.com. Airport shuttle, babysitting, conference rooms, nearby golf course, spa and fitness centre, outdoor pool. $$

Hotels: Downtown

- Appartements Touristiques du Centre-Ville. 3463 Rue Ste-Famille, Suite 008, Montréal, QC H2X 2K7; 514-845-0431 or 1-877-845-0437; fax 514-845-0262; www.appartementstouristiques.com. Fitness centre, indoor pool, some rooms with cooking facilities, indoor parking, laundry room on main floor. $$, Map 1
- Auberge de la Fontaine. 1301 Rue Rachel E., Montréal, QC H2J 2K1; 514-597-0166 or 1-800-597-0597; fax 514-597-0496; www.aubergedelafontaine.com. Conference room, continental breakfast buffet, laundry service, Internet station. $$, Map 2
- Auberge le Jardin d'Antoine. 2024 Rue St-Denis, Montréal, QC H2X 3K7; 514-843-4506 or 1-800-361-4506; fax 514-281-1491; www.hotel-jardin-antoine.qc.ca. Airport shuttle. $$, Map 3
- Best Western Europa Centre-Ville. 1240 Rue Drummond, Montréal, QC H3G 1V7; 514-866-6492 or 1-800-361-3000; fax 514-861-4089; e-mail info@europahotelmtl.com; www.europahotelmtl.com. Airport shuttle, spa/fitness centre, conference rooms. $$, Map 4
- Best Western Ville-Marie Hôtel et Suites. 3407 Rue Peel, Montréal, QC H3A 1W7; 514-288-4141 or 1-800-361-7791; fax 514-288-3021; e-mail info@hotelvillemarie.com; www.hotelvillemarie.com. Conference rooms, some rooms with cooking facilities, fitness centre. $$, Map 5
- Le Centre Sheraton. 1201 Boul. René-Lévesque O., Montréal, QC H3B 2L7; 514-878-2000 or 1-800-325-3535; fax 514-878-2305; www.sheraton.com/lecentre. Business centre, Internet service in all rooms (charge), spa/fitness centre with indoor pool and lounge, non-smoking floors. $$$, Map 6
- Château Royal Hotel Suites. 1420 Rue Crescent, Montréal, QC H3G 2B7; 514-848-0999 or 1-800-363-0335; fax 514 848-1891; www.chateauroyal.com. Cooking facilities in all rooms, conference rooms, indoor parking. $$$, Map 7
- Days Inn Montréal Centre-Ville. 215 Boul. René-Lévesque E., Montréal, QC H2X 1N7; 514-393-3388 or 1-800-668-3872; fax 514-395-9999; www.daysinnmontreal.com. Conference rooms, free Internet access, non-smoking floors. $$, Map 8
- Delta Centre-Ville. 777 Rue University, Montréal, QC H3C 3Z7; 514 879-1370 or 1-877-814-7706; fax 514-879-1831; www.deltahotels.com. Indoor pool, fitness centre, near amenities. $$$, Map 9
- Fairmont La Reine Élizabeth Hotel. 900 Boul. René-Lévesque O., Montréal, QC H3B 4A5; 514-861-3511 or 1-800-257-7544; fax 514-954-2296; e-mail queenelizabeth.hotel@fairmont.com; www.fairmont.com/queenelizabeth. Conference rooms, airport shuttle, fitness centre, express check in/out, indoor pool, non-smoking and private concierge floors. The Beaver Club dining room. $$$, Map 10
- Four Points by Sheraton Hôtel & Suites Montréal Centre-Ville. 475 Rue Sherbrooke O., Montréal, QC H3A 2L9; 514-842-3961 or 1-888-

625-5144; fax 514-842-0945; www.fourpoints.com. Conference rooms, business centre, fitness centre, pet policy. $$, Map 11

- Hilton Montréal Bonaventure, Place Bonaventure. 900 de la Gauchetiere O., Montréal, QC H5A 1E4; 514-878-2332 or 1-800-445-8667; fax 514-878-3881; www.hiltonmontreal.com. Airport shuttle, conference rooms, rooftop garden with indoor and outdoor pools. $$$, Map 12
- Holiday Inn Montréal-Midtown. 420 Rue Sherbrooke O., Montréal, QC H3A 1B4; 514-842-6111 or 1-866-655-4669; fax 514-842-9381; e-mail himidtown@rosdevhotels.com; www.rosdevhotels.com. Airport shuttle, indoor pool, conference rooms, fitness centre, Internet access, pet policy. $$$, Map 13
- Hôtel Château Versailles. 1659 Rue Sherbrooke O., Montréal, QC H3H 1E3; 514-933-8111 or 1-888-933-8111; fax 514-933-6867; www.versailleshotels.com. European charm, gym and sauna, babysitting, airport shuttle, near museums. $$$, Map 14
- Hôtel Courtyard Marriott Montréal. 410 Rue Sherbrooke O., Montréal, QC H3A 1B3; 514-844-8855 or 1-800-449-6654; fax 514-844-0912; www.courtyardmontreal.com. Airport shuttle, indoor pool, spa and fitness centre. $$$, Map 15
- Hôtel de la Couronne. 1029 Rue St-Denis, Montréal, QC H2X 3H9; 514-845-0901; fax 514-845-4165; www.hoteldelacouronne.ca. Airport shuttle, breakfast included, parking, some rooms with shared bathrooms. $, Map 16
- Hôtel Delta Montréal. 475 Ave. du Président-Kennedy, Montréal, QC H3A 1J7; 514-286-1986 or 1-877-286-1986; fax 514 284-4342; www.deltamontreal.com. Conference rooms, children's activity centre, indoor and outdoor pools, spa and fitness centre, underground parking. $$$, Map 17
- Hôtel de Paris. 901 Rue Sherbrooke E., Montréal, QC H2L 1L3; 514-522-6861 or 1-800-567-7217; fax 514-522-1387; www.hotel-montreal.com. Airport shuttle, youth hostel and apartment-hotel rates also available. $$, Map 18
- Hôtel des Gouverneurs Place Dupuis. 1415 Rue St-Hubert, Montreal, QC H2L 3Y9; 514-842-4881 or 1-888-910-1111; fax 514-842-1584; www.gouverneur.com. Airport shuttle, babysitting, conference rooms, indoor pool. $$$, Map 19
- Hôtel du Fort. 1390 Rue du Fort, Montréal, QC H3H 2R7; 514-938-8333 or 1-800-565-6333; fax 514-938-3123; e-mail reserve@hoteldufort.com; www.hoteldufort.com. Conference rooms, Internet access, fitness centre. $$$, Map 20
- Hôtel du Manoir Saint-Denis. 2006 Rue St-Denis, Montréal, QC H2X 3K7; 514-843-3670 or 1-888-567-7654; fax 514-844-2188; e-mail hotel@manoirstdenis.com; www.manoirstdenis.com. Restaurant on premises. $, Map 21
- Hôtel Dynastie. 1723 Rue St-Hubert, Montréal, QC H2L 3Z1; 514-529-5210 or 1-877-529-5210; fax 514-529-7170. Near amenities, bicycles at no charge (upon availability). $, Map 22
- Hôtel Inter-Continental Montréal. 360 Rue St-Antoine O., Montréal, QC H2Y 3X4; 514-987-9900 or 1-800-361-3600; fax 514-847-8730; www.montreal.intercontinental.com Conference rooms, babysitting, indoor pool, fitness centre. $$$, Map 23
- Hôtel Le St-Paul. 355 Rue McGill, Montréal, QC H2Y 2E8; 514-380-2222; fax 514-380-2200; www.hotelstpaul.com. Luxury boutique hotel in Old Montréal. $$$, Map 24
- Hôtel Lord Berri. 1199 Rue Berri, Montréal, QC H2L 4C6; 514-845-9236 or 1-888-363-0363; fax 514-849-9855; e-mail info@lordberri.com; www.lordberri.com. Airport shuttle, conference rooms, near bus terminal, fitness centre. $$, Map 25
- Hôtel Maritime Plaza. 1155 Rue Guy, Montréal, QC H3H 2K5; 514-932-1411 or 1-800-363-6255; fax 514-932-0446; e-mail info@hotelmaritime.com; www.hotelmaritime.com. Airport shuttle, conference rooms, indoor pool. $$$, Map 26
- Hôtel de la Montagne. 1430 Rue de la Montagne, Montréal, QC H3G

1Z5; 514-288-5656 or 1-800-361-6262; fax 514-288-9658; www.hoteldelamontagne.com. Airport shuttle, conference rooms, outdoor pool, underground parking, swanky lobby bar. $$$, Map 27

- Hôtel Montréal Crescent. 1366 Boul. René-Lévesque O., Montréal, QC H3W 2R4; 514-938-9797; fax 514-938-9797. Conference room, near amenities. $$, Map 28
- Hyatt Regency Montréal. 1255 Rue Jeanne-Mance, P.O. Box 130, Montréal, QC H5B 1E5; 514-982-1234 or 1-800-361-8234; fax 514-285-1243; www.hyatt.com. Business centre, coffeemaker, Internet access. Iron and ironing board in every room. $$$, Map 29
- Loews Hôtel Vogue. 1425 Rue de la Montagne, Montréal, QC H3G 1Z3; 514-285-5555 or 1-800-235-6397; fax 514 849-8903; www.loewshotels.com. Two televisions, a fax machine and an oversized safe in every room. Conference rooms, babysitting, fitness centre. $$$, Map 30
- Montréal Marriott Château Champlain. 1050 Rue de la Gauchetière O., Montréal, QC H3B 4C9; 514-878-9000 or 1-800-200-5909; fax 514-878-6761; www.marriott.com. Airport shuttle, massage, hairdresser, sauna and fitness centre, indoor pool and babysitting. $$$, Map 31
- Novotel Montréal Centre. 1180 Rue de la Montagne, Montréal, QC H3G 1Z1; 514-861-6000 or 1-800-221-4542; fax 514-861-0992; www.novotelmontreal.com. Airport shuttle, conference rooms, babysitting, fitness centre. $$$, Map 32
- Quality Hotel. 3440 Ave. du Parc, Montréal, QC H2X 2H5; 514-849-1413 or 1-800-465-6116; fax 514-849-6564; wwww.choicehotels.ca. Pet policy, restaurant on premises. $$, Map 33
- Residence Inn by Marriott Montréal Westmount. 2170 Ave. Lincoln, Montréal, QC H3H 2N5; 514-935-9224 or 1-800-678-6323; fax 514-935-5049. Indoor pool, gym, free Internet access, fully equipped kitchens. $$$, Map 34
- Ritz-Carlton Montréal. 1228 Rue Sherbrooke O., Montréal, QC H3G 1H6; 514-842-4212 or 1-800-241-3333; fax 514-842-3383; www.ritzcarlton.com. Old-world elegance; shops, restaurant serving breakfast, lunch, dinner and afternoon tea. $$$, Map 35

Bed & Breakfasts

Montréal has hundreds of bed-and-breakfast rooms available in many locations. There are also several services that cater to finding visitors accommodations that suit their needs. Stay in a loft in Old Montréal or a Victorian mansion in Westmount as an alternative to hotels.

- Angelica Blue Bed & Breakfast. 1213 Rue Ste-Élisabeth, Montréal, QC H2X 3C3; 514-844-5048 or 1-800-878-5048; fax 450-448-2114; e-mail info@angelicablue.com; www.angelicablue.com. Non-smoking, located in the heart of downtown Montréal. $$
- Auberge Bonsecours. 353 Rue St-Paul E., Montréal, QC H2Y 1H3; 514-396-2662; fax 514-871-9272. Located in Old Montréal, charming accomodation in renovated stables. $$
- B A Guest B&B. 2033 Rue St-Hubert, Montréal, QC H2L 3Z6; 514-738-9410 or 1-800-738-4338; fax 514-735-7493; e-mail info@bbmontreal.com; www.bbmontreal.com. The main guest home in a small network of B&Bs that range from downtown condominiums to Victorian mansions in tony Outremont and Westmount. $–$$
- Bed & Breakfast de Chez-Nous. 3717 Rue Ste-Famille, Montréal, QC H2X 2L7; 514-845-7711; fax 514-845-8008; www.studios montreal.com. Near Rue Prince-Arthur. Studios and fully furnished apartments can accommodate as many as six people for short-term or longer visits. $$
- Bonheur d'Occasion. 846 Rue Agnès, Montréal, QC H4C 2P8; 514-935-5898; fax 514-935-5898; www.bbcanada.com/526.html. Meals, no credit cards. $
- Carole's Purrfect B&B. 3428 Rue Addington, Montréal, QC H4A 3G6; 514-486-3995; e-mail info@purrfectbnb.com; www.purrfectbnb.com. Vegetarian breakfast, ask ahead about pets, no credit cards, non-smoking rooms. $

- Chambres avec Vue/Bed and Banana. 1225 Rue de Bullion, Montréal, QC H2X 2Z3; 514-878-9843; fax 514-878-3813; e-mail bed@bedandbanana.com. Meals, no credit cards, non-smoking rooms. $
- Couette et Café Cherrier. 522 Rue Cherrier, Montréal, QC H2L 1H3; 514-982-6848 or 1-888440-6848; fax 514-982-3313; e-mail couette@sympatico.ca; www.bbcanada.com/2073.html. Meals and bistro on premises. $–$$
- Downtown Bed & Breakfast Network. 3458 Ave. Laval, Montréal, QC H2X 3C8; 514-289-9749 or 1-800-267-5180; fax 514-287-7386; e-mail mariko@bbmontreal.qc.ca; www.bbmontreal.qc.ca. Downtown, Old Montréal, Latin Quarter locations. Non-smoking rooms and handicapped facilities. 50 rooms. 6 suites. $
- Gîte Toujours Dimanche. 1131 Rue Rachel E., Montréal, QC H2J 2J6; 514-527-2394; fax 514-527-6129; e-mail info@toujoursdimanche.com; www.toujoursdimanche.com. Meals, non-smoking rooms. $$
- La Maison du Jardin. 3744 Rue St-André, Montréal, QC H2L 3V7; 514-598-8862; fax 514-598-0667; e-mail maisonjardin@yahoo.com; www.bbcanada.com/jardin. Meals, no credit cards. $
- A Montréal Oasis. 3000 Chemin de Breslay, Montréal, QC H2X 2G7; 514-935-2312; fax 514-881-7231; e-mail bb@aei.ca; www.bbcanada.com/694.html. Downtown, Old Montréal and Latin Quarter locations with or without private bath. Open fireplace, terrace and gourmet breakfast. 20 rooms. $
- Relais Montréal Hospitalité. 3977 Ave. Laval, Montréal, QC H2W 2H9; 514-287-9635 or 1-800-363-9635; fax 514-287-1007; e-mail b_b@martha-pearson.com; www.martha-pearson.com. Rooms near Old Montréal for smokers and non-smokers in furnished apartments rented on short- and long-term basis. $
- Welcome Bed & Breakfast. 3950 Ave. Laval, Montréal, QC H2W 2J2; 514-844-5897 or 1-800-227-5897; fax 514-844-5894; e-mail info@bienvenuebb.com; www.welcomebnb.com. Country inn ambience, located downtown. $

Hostels & College Residences
Almost all the residences listed below are available in summer only, but they provide a safe, economical alternative to hotels. Make sure to book in advance.

- Auberge Alternative du Vieux-Montréal. 358 Rue St-Pierre, Montréal, QC H2Y 2M1; 514-282-8069; e-mail info@auberge-alternative.qc.ca; www.auberge-alternative.qc.ca. Open year-round. $
- Auberge de Jeunesse l'Hôtel de Paris. 901 Rue Sherbrooke E., Montréal, QC H2L 1L3; 514-522-6861 or 1-800-567-7217; fax 514-522-1387; e-mail questions@hotel-montreal.com; www.hotel-montreal.com. Open year-round, no curfew. $
- Auberge de Jeunesse de Montréal/Hostelling International. 1030 Rue Mackay, Montréal, QC H3G 2H1; 514-843-3317 or 1-866-83-3317; fax 514-934-3251; e-mail info@hostellingmontreal.com; www.hostellingmontreal.com. Open year-round. $
- Chez Jean. 4136 Rue Henri-Julien, Montréal, QC H2W 2K3; 514-843-8279; www.aubergechezjean.com. Breakfast included, no credit cards, pet policy. $
- Collège Français. 5155 Rue de Gaspé, Montréal, QC H2T 2A1; 514-270-4459; fax 514-278-7508; e-mail vacancescanadamd@videotron.ca; www.montrealplus.ca/portalf/infosite/122548/1.html. Summer only, dormitory. $
- Concordia University. 7141 Rue Sherbrooke O., Montréal, QC H4B 1R6; 514-848-2424, x.4758; fax 514-848-4780; e-mail lcleduc@alcor.concordia.ca; www.residence.concordia.ca/summer.html. Summer only, dormitory, meals served daily. $
- Gîte du Parc Lafontaine. 1250 Rue Sherbrooke E., Montréal, QC H2L 1M1; 514-522-3910; fax 514-844-7356; e-mail info@hostelmontreal.com; www.hostelmontreal.com. Open year-round, meals. $
- McGill University Residences.

3935 Rue University, Montréal, QC H3A 2B4; 514-398-5200; fax 514-398-6770; e-mail reserve.residences@mcgill.ca; www.mcgill.ca/residences/summer. Summer only, dormitory. $

- Résidence Lallemand, Collège Brébeuf. 5625 Ave. Decelles, Montréal, QC H3T 1W4; 514-342-1320; fax 514-342-6607; e-mail residence@brebeuf.qc.ca; www.brebeuf.qc.ca. Summer only, dormitory. $
- Université de Montréal, Services des Résidences. 2350 Boul. Édouard-Montpetit, Montréal, QC H3T 1J4; 514-343-6531; fax 514-343-2353; e-mail residence@sea.umontreal.ca; www.resid.umontreal.ca. Summer only. $
- Université du Québec à Montréal. 303 Boul. René-Lévesque E., Montréal, QC H2X 3Y3; 514-987-6669 or 1-888-987-6669; fax 514-987-0344; www.residences-uqam.qc.ca. Summer only, cooking facilities, indoor pool, group rates. $
- Y.W.C.A. 1355 Boul. René-Lévesque O., Montréal, QC H3G 1T3; 514-866-9942; fax 514-861-1603; e-mail info@ydesfemmesmtl.org; www.ydesfemmesmtl.org. Recently renovated Y Hotel. $

QUÉBEC CITY

Hotels: Downtown

- Delta Québec. 690 Boul. René-Lévesque E., Québec, QC G1R 5A8; 418-647-1717 or 1-877-814-7706; fax 418-647-2146; www.deltahotels.com. Airport shuttle, conference rooms, non-smoking rooms, outdoor pool, spa and fitness centre. $$–$$$
- Fairmont Château Frontenac. 1 Rue des Carrières, Québec, QC G1R 4P5; 418-692-3861 or 1-800-257-7544; fax 418-692-1751; e-mail chateaufrontenac @fairmont.com; www.fairmont.com/frontenac. The crème de la crème of old-world style. Airport shuttle, babysitting, conference rooms, non-smoking rooms, indoor pool, fitness centre. $$$
- Holiday Inn Select Quebec City-Downtown. 395 Rue de la Couronne, Québec, QC G1K 7X4; 418-647-2611 or 1-800-267-2002; fax 418-640-0666; e-mail reservation@hiselect-quebec.com; www.holiday-inn.com. Airport shuttle, kids eat free, conference rooms, non-smoking rooms, indoor pool, fitness centre. $$
- Hôtel Château Bellevue. 16 Rue de la Porte, Québec, QC G1R 4M9; 418-692-2573 or 1-800-463-2617; fax 418-692-4876; e-mail bellevue@vieuxquebec.com; www.vieux-quebec.com/bellevue. Mid-sized hotel, babysitting, near transportation. $$
- Hôtel Château Laurier. 1220 Place George V O., Québec, QC G1R 5B8; 418-522-8108 or 1-800-463-4453; fax 418-524-8768; e-mail laurier@vieuxquebec.com; www.vieux-quebec.com/laurier. Wireless Internet access, 9 deluxe rooms with fireplace and therapeutic bath, babysitting, non-smoking rooms. $$
- Hôtel Clarendon. 57 Rue Ste-Anne, Québec, QC G1R 3X4; 418-692-2480 or 1-888-222-3304; fax 418-692-4652; www.hotelclarendon.com. Airport shuttle, conference rooms, health spa, near transportation. $$–$$$
- Hôtel Dominion 1912. 126 Rue St-Pierre, Québec, QC G1K 4A8; 418-692-2224 or 1-888-833-5253; fax 418-692-4403; e-mail reservations@hoteldominion.com; www.hoteldominion.com. Mid-sized hotel, conference rooms, non-smoking rooms. $$$
- Hôtel du Capitole. 972 Rue St-Jean, Québec, QC G1R 1R5; 418-694-4040 or 1-800-363-4040; fax 418-694-1916; e-mail hotel@lecapitole.com; www.lecapitole.com. Small but luxurious hotel, babysitting, conference rooms, non-smoking rooms. $$$
- Hôtel Loews Le Concorde. 1225 Place Montcalm, Québec, QC G1R 4W6; 418-647-2222 or 1-800-235-6397; fax 418-647-4710; e-mail loewsleconcorde@loewshotels.com; www.loewshotels.com/leconcorde home.html. Airport shuttle, babysitting, conference rooms, non-smoking rooms, outdoor pool, fitness centre. $$–$$$
- Hôtel Manoir Victoria. 44 Côte du

Palais, Québec, QC G1R 4H8; 418-692-1030 or 1-800-463-6283; fax 418-692-3822; e-mail admin@manoir-victoria.com; www.manoir-victoria.com. Airport shuttle, babysitting, conference rooms, non-smoking rooms, indoor pool, fitness centre. $$–$$$

- Hôtel Palace Royal. 775 Ave. Honore-Mercier, Québec, QC G1R 6A5; 418-694-2000 or 1-800-567-5276; fax 418-380-2553; www.jaro.qc.ca/en/palace. Conference rooms, indoor tropical garden with pool, sauna and whirlpool bath, fitness room, babysitting. $$$
- Québec Hilton. 1100 Boul. René-Lévesque E., Québec, QC G1R 4X3; 418-647-2411 or 1-800-445-8667; fax 418-647-2986; www.hilton.com. Babysitting, conference rooms, non-smoking rooms, outdoor pool, spa and fitness centre. $$–$$$

Hotels: Suburbs

- Days Inn, Québec Ouest. 3145 Ave. des Hôtels, Québec, QC G1W 3Z7; 418-653-9321 or 1-800-463-1867; fax 418-653-2666; email dayssf@globetrotter.net; www.daysinn.com. $$
- Hôtel Clarion Québec. 3125 Blvd. Hochelaga, Ste-Foy, QC G1V 4A8; 418-653-4901 or 1-800-463-5241; fax 418-653-1836; e-mail hotel@clarionquebec.com. Indoor pool, restaurant on premises, health club. $$
- Hôtel Classique. 2815 Blvd. Laurier, Ste-Foy, QC G1V 4H3; 418-658-2793 or 1-800-463-1885; fax 418-658-6816; e-mail info@hotelclassique.com; www.hotelclassique.com. Indoor pool, meeting rooms, free parking. $$
- Hôtel Lindbergh. 2825 Blvd. Laurier, Ste-Foy, QC G1V 2L9; 418-653-4975 or 1-800-567-4975; fax 418-651-8805; e-mail hotel-lindbergh@jaro.qc.ca; www.jaro.qc.ca/en/linbergh. Indoor and outdoor pools, business centre, conference rooms, babysitting. $$
- Hôtel Quality Suites. 1600 Rue Bouvier, Québec, QC G2K 1N8; 418-622-4244 or 1-800-267-3837; fax 418-622-4067; www.choicehotels.com. Babysitting, conference rooms, free continental breakfast, non-smoking rooms. $$

Bed & Breakfasts

- Acceuil B&B Bourgault Centre-Ville. 653 Rue de la Reine, Québec, QC G1K 2S1; 418-524-9254 or 1-866-524-9254; fax 418-524-9254; e-mail gbourgault@bnbbourgault.com; www.gites-classifies.qc.ca/accbou.htm. Meals, garden terrace. $$
- À la Maison Tudor. 1037 Rue Moncton, Québec, QC G1S 2Y9; 418-686-1033; fax 418-686-6066; e-mail ckilfoil@lamaisontudor.com; www.lamaisontudor.com. Meals, apartments with cooking facilities for longer stays, non-smoking rooms. $$
- B&B Cafe Krieghoff. 1091 Ave. Cartier, Québec, QC G1R 2S6; 418-522-3711; fax 418-647-1429; e-mail info@cafekrieghoff.qc.ca; www.cafekrieghoff.qc.ca. Meals, neighbourhood cafe on premises. $
- Chez Monsieur Gilles. 1720 Chemin de la Canardière, Québec, QC G1J 2E3; 418-821-8778; fax 418-821-8776; e-mail mgilles@sympatico.ca; www.chezmonsieurgilles.com. Pool room, hot tub on rooftop terrace, near skiing and golf course. $$
- Hayden's Wexford House B&B. 450 Rue Champlain, Québec, QC G1R 2E3; 418-524-0524; fax 418-648-8995; e-mail haydenwexfordhouse@videotron.net; www.haydenwexfordhouse.com. Meals, heritage home, non-smoking, near skiing. $$
- La Maison d'Élizabeth et Emma. 10 Rue Grande-Allée O., Québec, QC G1R 2G6; 418-647-0880; www.bbcanada.com/699.html. Meals, non-smoking rooms. $
- La Maison Historique James Thompson. 47 Rue Ste-Ursule, Québec, QC G1R 4E4; 418-694-9042; e-mail jamesthompson@canada.com; www.bedandbreakfastquebec.com. Meals, heritage building inside the walls of Old Québec, no credit cards. $

Hostels & College Residences

- Association Y.W.C.A. de Québec. 855 Ave. Holland, Québec, QC

G1S 3S5; 418-683-2155; fax 418-683-5526; e-mail ydesfemmes@ywcaquebec.qc.ca. Sauna, pool, cooking facilities, near transportation. $

- Auberge de la Paix. 31 Rue Couillard, Québec, QC G1R 3T4; 418-694-0735; e-mail alapaix@clic.net; www.aubergedelapaix.com. Breakfast included, no credit cards. $
- Auberge Internationale de Québec. 19 Rue Ste-Ursule, Québec, QC G1R 4E1; 418-694-0755; fax 418-694-2278; e-mail reservation@hostellingquebec.com; www.cisq.org. Café serves meals in summer. Dorms or private rooms. $
- Résidence du Collège Mérici. 757, 759, 761 Rue St-Louis, Québec, QC G1S 1C1; 418-683-1591; fax 418-682-8938; e-mail information@college-merici.qc.ca; www.college-merici.qc.ca. Open seasonally. Cooking facilities in all rooms. $

DINING

MONTRÉAL

Montréal boasts some of the finest restaurants in North America. With huge cultural diversity, there is something for everyone. The following is a select list of the restaurants available. The restaurants are listed alphabetically by ethnicity (e.g., French) and by general type (e.g., Brunch).

Approximate prices are indicated, based on the average cost, at time of publication, of dinner for two including wine (where available), taxes and gratuity: $ = under $45; $$ = $45–$80; $$$ = $80–$120; $$$$ = $120–$180; $$$$$ = over $180. Meals served are indicated as: B = breakfast; L = lunch; D = dinner; S = snacks; Late = open past midnight. Credit cards accepted are also indicated: AX = American Express; V = Visa; MC = MasterCard. Restaurants to which patrons may bring their own wine = BYOB.

American

- Hard Rock Café. 1458 Rue Crescent; 514-987-1420. Rock and roll–themed restaurant featuring classic American cuisine, memorabilia, music and really cool merchandise. L/D, Late, $, AX/MC/V.
- Nickels. 1384 Rue Ste-Catherine O.; 514-392-7771. Céline Dion's chain features burgers and smoked meat extraordinaire. B/L/D, Late, $, AX/MC/V.
- Upstairs Jazz Bar & Grill. 1254 Rue MacKay; 514-931-6808; www.upstairsjazz.com. One of Montréal's top live jazz venues. D, Late, $–$$, AX/MC/V.

Chinese

- Aux Délices de Szechuan. 1735 Rue St-Denis; 514-844-5542. Sumptuous décor, culinary artwork, efficient service. D, $, AX/MC/V.
- Chez Chine (Holiday Inn Select Montréal Centre-Ville). 99 Ave. Viger O.; 514-878-9888 or 1-888-878-9888; www.hiselect-yul.com. Authentic Chinese cuisine in a spectacular dining room. B/L/D, $–$$, AX/MC/V.

French

- Alexandre. 1454 Rue Peel; 514-288-5105. Twelve imported beers on tap. Regional cuisine. Typical Parisian brasserie. L/D, Late, $$, AX/MC/V.
- Café de Paris/Le Jardin du Ritz (Ritz-Carlton Montréal Hotel). 1228 Rue Sherbrooke O.; 514-842-4212; www.ritzcarlton.com. Welcoming atmosphere and impeccable service, afternoon tea. B/L/D, $$, AX/MC/V.
- Claude Postel Restaurant. 443 Rue St-Vincent; 514-875-5067. Exquisite French cuisine and excellent crème brûlée. Located in Old Montréal. L/D, $$, AX/MC/V.
- La Colombe. 554 Rue Duluth E.; 514-849-8844. Elegant North African-influenced French cuisine in a cozy room. BYOB, D, $$, AX/MC/V.
- La Trattoria. 5563 Chemin Upper Lachine; 514-484-5303. Many inventive pizzas and pastas. BYOB, L/D, $, V/MC.
- Restaurant Le P'tit Plateau. 330 Rue Marie-Anne E.; 514-282-6342. Elegant but cozy spot where dishes from the south of France are served. BYOB, non-smoking, D, $, V/MC/No Interac.

GREEK

- La Cabane Grecque, 102 Rue Prince-Arthur E.; 514-849-0122; fax 514-849-3879; www.lacabanegrecque.com. A family restaurant with steak and seafood specialities. BYOB, L/D, Late, $, AX/MC/V.
- Hermès (Himalaya). 14 Rue Jean-Talon O.; 514-272-3880. Great Greek food, open late. L/D, $, MC/V.
- Restaurant Minerva. 17 Rue Prince-Arthur E.; 514-842-5451 or 514-842-5452. Steak, seafood, Italian and Greek cuisine. L/D, Late, $, AX/MC/V.

INDIAN

- Bombay Palace. 2201 Rue Ste-Catherine, O.; 514-932-7141; fax 514-932-7143; www.bombaypalace restaurant.com. Culinary specialties from Bombay, including Tandoori Lamb Chops and Tiger Prawn Masala. Excellent buffet. L/D, $$, AX/MC/V.
- Punjab Palace. 920 Rue Jean-Talon, O.; 514-495-4075; www.punjabpalace.ca. Inexpensive homestyle cooking with fantastic vegetarian and meat dishes. L/D, $, AX/MC/V.
- Raga Buffet Indien. 3533 Chemin Queen-Mary; 514-344-2217; fax 514-845-8348. Vegetarian and tandoori cuisine. Worth the hike for the buffet. L/D, $, AX/MC/V.

ITALIAN

- Bocca d'Oro. 1448 Rue St-Mathieu; 514-933-8414. Exotic menu, romantic atmosphere, great food. L/D, $, AX/MC/V.
- Brontë. 1800 Rue Sherbrooke O.; 514-934-1801 or 1-888-933-8111; www.versailleshotels.com. High-end Italian restaurant. Breakfast for guests of the Meridien/Chateau Versailles only. B/L/D, $$, AX/MC/V.
- Hostaria Romana. 2044 Rue Metcalfe; 514-849-1389. Serving continental cuisine, fish and seafood for the past 30 years. Features music nightly. L/D, $, AX/MC/V.
- Il Cavaliere (Hôtel Lord Berri). 1199 Rue Berri; 514-845-9236; fax 514-849-9855. Cozy atmosphere, exceptional Italian cuisine. B/L/D, $, AX/MC/V.
- Weinstein & Gavino's Pasta Bar Factory. 1434 Rue Crescent; 514-288-2231. A place to see and be seen, this bustling restaurant regularly accommodates up to 700 patrons. L/D, $–$$, AX/MC/V.

JAPANESE

- Higuma. 3807 Rue St-Denis; 514-842-1686. Simple place, great sushi. L/D, $, AX/MC/V.
- Katsura. 2170 Rue de la Montagne; 514-849-1172; fax 514-849-1705; www.bar-resto.com/katsura. Traditional cuisine, private tatami rooms, sushi bar. L (weekdays only)/D, $$, AX/MC/V.
- Kaizen Treehouse Sushi Bar & Restaurant. 4120 Rue Ste-Catherine O. (in Westmount); 514-932-5654; e-mail info@70sushi.com; www.kaizen-sushi-bar.com. Sushi and sashimi, with tasting menus for vegetarians and fish lovers alike. Live jazz from Sun. to Tues. L/D, $$, AX/MC/V.

RUSSIAN

- La Métropole. 1409 Rue St-Marc; 514-932-3403. Great food, excellent Russian tea and pastries, weekend music shows. L/D, $$, AX/MC/V.
- Troïka. 2171 Rue Crescent; 514-849-9333. Flavoured vodkas, Russian musicians. D, $$, AX/MC/V.

SPANISH

- Casa Galicia. 2087 Rue St-Denis; 514-843-6698; fax 514-843-9159; www.casagaliciamontreal.com. Lively weekend flamenco shows and tasty appetizers and main dishes. L/D, $$, AX/MC/V.
- Casa Tapas. 266 Rue Rachel E.; 514-848-1063. A friendly restaurant with rustic Spanish décor. Offers a new twist on tapas. D, $$, AX/MC/V.

BRUNCH

- Beauty's. 93 Ave. du Mont-Royal O.; 514-849-8883. This hip hangout and Montréal breakfast institution serves up tasty diner fare. B/L, $, AX/MC/V.
- Café Santropol. 3990 Rue St-Urbain; 514-842-3110; fax 514-284-4256; www.santropol.com.

Massive portions served in this urban oasis that opens a garden terrace in summer months. L/D, $, Interac only.

- Chez Cora Déjeuners. 1425 Rue Stanley; 514-286-6171; www.chezcora.com. One location of a chain serving hearty breakfasts with plenty of fresh fruit. B/L, $, AX/MC/V.
- Dusty's. 4510 Ave. du Parc; 514-276-8525. Diner specials, tasteful and simple, since 1950. B/L, $.
- Maison Kam Fung. 1111 Rue St-Urbain; 514-878-2888. Dim sum delights. B/L/D, $, AX/MC/V.
- Restaurant Lotte. 1115 Rue Clark; 514-393-3838. Known for its excellent dim sum. B/L/D, $$.

Cafés and Bistros

- Bistro Boris. 465 Rue McGill; 514-848-9575; www.borisbistro.com. Bistro fare on a huge, tree-shaded terrace. L/D, $$, AX/MC/V.
- Café Cherrier. 3635 Rue St-Denis; 514-843-4308; fax 514-844-3273. European-style brasserie serving Italian and Californian cuisine. B/L/D, Late, $, AX/MC/V.
- Ceramic Café Studio. 4201-B Rue St-Denis; 514-848-1119. Paint-your-own-ceramics café. S, $, MC/V.
- Holder. 407 Rue McGill; 514-849-0333. French bistro fare, lively nightlife scene. L/D, $$, AX/MC/V.
- Le Jardin Nelson. 407 Place Jacques-Cartier; 514-861-5731; e-mail jardin.nelson@videotron.ca; www.jardinnelson.com. Outdoor courtyard in summer. Musicians serenade at this crêperie. L/D, Late, $, AX/MC/V.
- Shed Café. 3515 Boul. St-Laurent; 514-842-0220. Simple classics go well with drinks at this trendy spot on The Main. L/D, $–$$, AX/MC/V.

Family Fare

- Ganges Restaurant. 6079 Rue Sherbrooke O.; 514-488-8850. Good Indian food, sometimes with live music. L/D, $, AX/MC/V.
- La Capannina. 2022 Rue Stanley; 514-845-1852. Friendly family restaurant. Specialities: fresh pastas and seafood. L/D, $, AX/MC/V.
- Maison de Cari. 1433 Rue Bishop; 514-845-0326. This hole in the wall serves up authentic, spicy Indian fare and cool British beers. L/D, $, AX/MC/V.
- Marché Mövenpick Restaurant. 1 Place Ville-Marie; 514-861-8181. A new dining experience: a dozen stands offer everything fresh, from sushi and pasta to ice-cream sundaes and fresh juices. Available on one bill. B/L/D, Late, $, AX/MC/V.
- Restaurant Daou. 519 Rue Faillon E.; 514-276-8310. Lebanese dishes made from family recipes are served in an informal dining room. L/D, $, AX/MC/V.

Fondues

- Fonduementale. 4325 Rue St-Denis; 514-499-1446. Ideal for group dining in a relaxed atmosphere. D, $–$$, AX/MC/V.
- La Fonderie. 964 Rue Rachel E.; 514-524-2100. Chinese and Swiss fondues. D, $, AX/MC/V.

Quick Eats

- Arahova Souvlaki. 256 St-Viateur O.; 514-274-7828. Serving succulent souvlaki with secret tzatziki sauce since 1972. L/D, $.
- Caribbean Curry House. 6892 Ave. Victoria; 514-733-0828. Caribbean-style jerk chicken, curried meat and potatoes and pina coladas. L/D, $, Interac only.
- Chez Claudette. 351 Laurier E.; 514-279-5173. Breakfast-all-day/late-night greasy spoon with excellent poutine and "Michigan" burger. B/L/D, $.
- Chez Lidia. 2205 Rosemont E.; 514-723-7772. For the topless breakfast experience. B/L/D, $.
- Frites Dorée. 1212 St-Laurent; 514-866-0790. Poutine with big curds in a 1950s-era setting. B/L/D, $.
- Jardin du Cari. 21 Rue St-Viateur O.; 514-495-0565. Excellent Jamaican favourites. L/D, $.
- Le Commensal McGill. 1204 Ave. McGill-College; 514-871-1480. Excellent view of Rue Ste-Catherine. Ongoing hot, cold and dessert buffet. Pay-by-weight concept. Other locations at 1720 and 5043 Rue St-Denis, 3715 Chemin Queen-Mary. L/D, $, AX/MC/V.
- Les Courtisanes. 2533 Ste-

Catherine E.; 514-523-3170. Truly retro all-day breakfast served by nude waitresses. B/L/D, $.

- The Main St. Lawrence Steak House Delicatessen. 3684 Boul. St-Laurent; 514-843-8126. Classic Montréal deli with smoked meat, applesauce, latkes and more. B/L/D, $, AX/MC/V.
- Pizza Pita. 6415 Boul. Décarie; 514-7313-7482. Natural, kosher foods with vegan options. Homemade soups, vegetarian pizza, falafel, shawarma sandwiches and spicy french fries. L/D, $.
- Rapido. 4494 Rue St-Denis; 514-284-2188. Excellent late-night poutine and all the standards. B/L/D, $.
- Schwartz's Montréal Hebrew Delicatessen. 3895 Boul. St-Laurent; 514-842-4813. Quintessential smoked meat sandwich joint. L/D, $.

FOUR-STAR DINING

- Au Tournant de la Rivière. 5070 Rue Salaberry, Carignan, QC; 450-658-7372. Call for directions (or check the dining chapter in this guide) to find this superb restaurant, located in converted barn. D, $$$$, AX/MC/V.
- The Beaver Club, Fairmont The Queen Elizabeth Hotel. 900 Boul. René-Lévesque O.; 514-861-3511; www.fairmont.com/queenelizabeth. Elegant atmosphere with open rotisserie and specialities including prime rib of beef and rack of lamb. L/D, $$$, AX/MC/V.
- Brunoise. 3807 Rue St-André; 514-523-3885; www.brunoise.ca. Upscale French market-based cuisine. Reservations recommended. D, $$$$, MC/V.
- Chez La Mère Michel. 1209 Rue Guy; 514-934-0473; fax 514-939-0709; www.chezlameremichel.com. A fine restaurant of long-standing reputation. The food is expensive but reliable. Seasonal dishes include bison and caribou. L/D, $$$, AX/MC/V.
- Le Mitoyen. 652 Rue de la Place Publique, Ste-Dorothée, QC; 514-689-2977. A short drive north out of Montréal brings you to this charming restaurant. Try the rack of Québec lamb. Hot bread and sweet butter accompany each meal. D, $$$, AX/MC/V.
- Le Muscadin. 639 Notre-Dame O.; 514-842-0588; www.lemuscadin.com. Old elegance in Old Montréal. Veal, lamb, beef and sole are all exceptional, and the wine list is arguably the best in the city. L/D, $$$, AX/MC/V.
- Les Caprices de Nicolas. 2072 Rue Drummond; 514-282-9790. Garden room with atrium, private salon. Signature dishes include caviar appetizers, foie gras, milk-fed veal loin and homemade ice cream and sherbet in basil-watermelon and vanilla-ginger flavours. L/D, $$$, AX/MC/V.
- Les Halles. 1450 Rue Crescent; 514-844-2328. A great start for those who are new to Montréal, with a trustworthy (if pricey) à la carte menu. The menu douceur at lunchtime is a bargain. L/D, $$$$, AX/MC/V.
- Med Bar & Grill. 3500 Boul. St-Laurent; 514-844-0027. Great food served with panache. Try the seared tuna or the Arctic char. The wine list suits the fare perfectly. D, $$$, AX/MC/V.
- Milos. 5357 Ave. du Parc; 514-272-3522; fax 514-272-0178. Montréal's finest Greek cuisine, with the best fish in town. L/D, $$$, AX/MC/V.
- Restaurant Cube. 355 Rue McGill; 514-876-2823; www.restaurantcube.com. The latest in sleek, urban dining. Prize-winning chef prepares unique menu, including fresh halibut served with Rose Finn Apple potatoes and duck prosciutto. L/D, $$$, AX/MC/V.
- Restaurant Le Globe. 3455 Boul. St-Laurent; 514-284-3823. Snazzy bistro with designer customers and Chef David McMillan's serious, modern cooking, which makes the best of local produce. D, $$$, AX/MC/V.
- Sofia. 3600 Boul. St-Laurent; 514-284-0092; www.sofiagrill.com. Eclectic cuisine and DJ grooves in a hip, uniquely Montréal dining spot. L/D, $$, MC/V.
- Toqué! 900 Place Jean-Riopelle; 514-499-2084; fax 514-499-0292; www.restaurant-toque.com. Sultry décor, market cuisine, organic

vegetables. Specialties include roasted leg of Québec lamb, rare yellowfin tuna tempura and, for dessert, hazelnut biscuit with lemon cream. D, $$$, AX/MC/V.

QUÉBEC CITY

REGIONAL FLAVOUR

- Auberge Baker. 8790 Ave. Royale, Château-Richer, QC; 418-824-4478 or 1-866-824-4478; www.auberge-baker.qc.ca. Game dishes served in a stone-walled room with a fireplace. Brunch/L/D, $$, AX/MC/V.
- Aux Anciens Canadiens. 34 Rue St-Louis; 418-692-1627; fax 418-692-5419; www.auxancienscanadiens.qc.ca. A menu including ham simmered in maple syrup, baked beans and blueberry pie is served in this 17th-century restaurant with five themed dining rooms. L/D, $$, AX/MC/V.
- Chez Ashton. 830 Boul. Charest E.; 418-694-0891. Québécois favourites, like poutine. L/D, $, AX/MC/V.

NON-WESTERN CUISINE

- Aviatic Club. 104–450 Rue de la Gare-du-Palais; 418-522-3555. Enjoyable French, Asian and Tex-Mex food in a classy atmosphere. L/D, $$, AX/MC/V.
- Le Carthage. 399 Rue St-Jean; 418-529-0576. North-African food, with bellydancing some evenings. D, $$, AX/MC/V.
- Le Tokyo. 415 Rue St-Jean; 418-522-7571. Québec's oldest Japanese restaurant, still serving excellent food. BYOB, non-smoking, D, $$, AX/MC/V.
- Nek8arre. 575 Rue Stanislas-Kosca, Village-des-Hurons (Wendake); 418-842-4308; www.huron-wendat.qc.ca. Interesting Huron food: buffalo, caribou, deer and clay-baked fish are served with corn and lentils. D, $$, MC/V.
- Yuzu Sushi Bar. 438 Rue de l'Église; 418-521-7253. Chic, expensive and recently nominated for having the nicest restrooms in Canada.

ITALIAN

- Au Parmesan. 38 Rue St-Louis; 418-692-0341. One of the few restaurants along the touristy stretch of Rue St-Louis that provides excellent food. Extensive wine list. L/D, $$, AX/MC/V.
- Ciccio Café. 875 Rue de Claire-Fontaine; 418-525-6161. Excellent pasta and fish. L/D, $$, AX/MC/V.
- Le Graffiti. 1191 Rue Cartier; 418-529-4949. Italian and French dishes, and a wine list with over 400 bottles. L/D, $$, AX/MC/V.
- Le Michelangelo. 3111 Rue St-Louis; 418-651-6262. An exceptional place in Québec City for Italian food. L/D, $$$, AC/MC/V.
- Les Frères de La Côté. 1190 Rue St-Jean; 418-692-5445. A Mediterranean restaurant specializing in wood-fired pizzas. Run by two boisterous brothers from the south of France. L/D/Brunch Sundays, $–$$, AX/MC/V.

CAFÉS AND BISTROS

- Bistro Sous le Fort. 48 Rue Sous-le-Fort; 418-694-0852. Good and plentiful dishes with market-fresh produce. Non-smoking, L/D, $, AX/MC/V.
- Café de la Terrasse. 1 Rue des Carrières; 418-691-3763. Standard continental fare and afternoon tea. L/D, $, AX/MC/V.
- Le Café du Monde. 84 Rue Dalhousie; 418-692-4455. Quiches, moules-frites and pâtés. Parisian brasserie atmosphere. L/D/Brunch on weekends, $, AX/MC/V.
- Le Cochon Dingue. 46 Boul. Champlain; 418-684-2013; www.cochondingue.com. The name means "crazy pig" and the bistro fare includes steak and fries, burgers and mussels. B/L/D, $, AX/MC/V.
- Le Hobbit. 700 Rue St-Jean; 418-647-2677. Great little neighborhood café. B/L/D, $, MC/V.
- Le Petit Coin Latin. 8 1/2 Rue Ste-Ursule; 418-692-2022. The specialty here is Swiss raclette: cheese and meats grilled on a small portable oven. L/D, $, MC/V.
- Pub Saint-Alexandre. 1087 Rue St-Jean; 418-694-0015. Excellent British pub grub in an authentic atmosphere. Good selection of sausages, the best Guinness in town. L/D, $, AX/MC/V.

FAMILY FARE

- L'Astral (Hôtel Loews Le Concorde). 1225 Place Montcalm; 418-647-2222 or 1-800-463-5256; www.loewshotels.com. Great view in this revolving restaurant. International cuisine and Saturday night buffets. Brunch from 10 A.M. on Sundays. L/D, $, AX/MC/V.
- La Bastille Chez Bahüaud. 47 Ave. Ste-Geneviève; 418-692-2544. Great food at tables set in tree-filled garden. L/D, $$, AX/MC/V.
- Le Parlementaire: Restaurant de l'Assemblée Nationale. 418-643-6640. The dining room of the Québec government is decorated in Beaux-Arts splendour. Reservations are recommended, as opening hours may vary according to the schedule of National Assembly business. Regional cuisine. B/L/D, $, AX/MC/V.
- Manoir Montmorency. 2490 Ave. Royale, Beauport, QC; 418-663-2877; fax 418-663-1666; www.chutemontmorency.qc.ca. Most romantic restaurant in Québec City area. Overlooks falls from a rambling wooden building. Brunch/L/D, $$, AX/MC/V.

FOUR-STAR DINING

- Aspara. 71 Rue d'Auteuil; 418-694-0232. First-prize winner at the Gala de la Restauration de Québec for exotic cuisine. Chef Beng an Khuong offers the best of Vietnamese, Thai and Cambodian cooking. L/D, $$$–$$$$, AX/MC/V.
- La Closerie. 1210 Place George-V O.; 418-523-9975. First-rate cuisine and intimate dining room. L/D, $$$, AX/MC/V.
- La Tanière. 2115 Rang Ste-Ange, Ste-Foy, QC; 418-872-4386; www.restaurantlataniere.com. A game restaurant with eight-course menu progressif; caribou, ostrich, venison and rabbit are all at home here. D, $$$$, AX/MC/V.
- Laurie Raphaël. 117 Rue Dalhousie; 418-692-4555; fax 418-692-4175; www.laurieraphael.com. Delicacies from scallops to ostrich. L/D, $$$, AX/MC/V.
- Le Café du Clocher Penché. 203 Rue St-Joseph E.; 418-640-0597. Québécois haute cuisine at affordable prices. B/L/D, $, AX/MC/V.
- Le Champlain (Château Frontenac). 1 Rue des Carrières; 418-691-3763; www.fairmont.com/frontenac. Chef Jean Soulard, the first Canadian chef to receive the Master Chef of France award, serves classic French cuisine in a lavish dining room. B/L/D, $$$, AX/MC/V.
- Le Continental. 26 Rue St-Louis; 418-694-9995. Classic menu, service and 1950s-era uptown New York setting make this long-standing restaurant one of the best in the city. Try the rack of lamb, steak tartar or Dover sole; superb wine list. L/D, $$$, AX/MC/V.
- Le Saint-Amour. 48 Rue Ste-Ursule; 418-694-0667; www.saint-amour.com. Excellent food and romantic surroundings with glassed-in terrace. L/D, $$$, AX/MC/V.
- Michelangelo. 3111 Chemin St-Louis, Ste-Foy, QC; 418-651-6262; www.restomichelangelo.com. Salmon tartar or carpaccio with basil are hits at this new, expansive restaurant with a fabulous wine list. L/D, $$$, AX/MC/V.

TOP ATTRACTIONS

MONTRÉAL

- Basilique Notre-Dame-de-Montréal. 110 Rue Notre-Dame O., 514-842-2925 or 1-866-842-2925; fax 514-842-8275; www.basiliquenddm.org. Most celebrated church in Canada.
- Biodôme. 4777 Ave. Pierre-de-Courbertin; 514-868-3000; fax 514-868-3065; e-mail biodome@ville.montreal.qc.ca; www.biodome.gc.ca. Once the site of the 1976 Olympic track-cycling races, the building has been transformed into a re-creation of four natural habitats, including a rain forest, a polar landscape and the St. Lawrence marine ecosystem. A short walk from the Insectarium and the Jardin Botanique. Open daily 9–5, summer hours 9–6.
- Biosphère. 160 Chemin Tour-de-l'Île, Parc des Îles; 514-283-5000; www.biosphere.ec.gc.ca. An eco-museum inaugurated in 1995 as the

first Ecowatch Centre in Canada. June to Sept. daily 10–6. Off-season closed Tues., open Mon., Wed. to Sat. 12–5, Sun. 10–5.
- Casino Montréal. 1 Ave. du Casino, Île Notre-Dame; 514-392-2746 or 1-800-665-2274. Cabaret du Casino. 514-790-1245 or 1-800-361-4595; www.casino-de-montreal.com. Open 24 hours.
- Jardin Botanique de Montréal. 4101 Rue Sherbrooke E.; 514-872-1400; www2.ville.montreal.qc.ca/jardin. 150 acres of gardens, greenhouses and an insectarium. Open year-round 9–5, summer hours 9–6, Sept. 10 to Oct. 31 9–9.
- La Ronde. 22 Chemin Macdonald, Île Ste-Hélène; 514-397-2000; e-mail info@laronde.com; www.laronde.com. Amusement-park rides and live entertainment all summer.
- Olympic Stadium. 4141 Ave. Pierre-de-Coubertin; 514-252-8687.
- Oratoire Saint-Joseph du Mont-Royal. 3800 Chemin Queen-Mary; 514-733-8211 or 1-877-672-8647; www.saint-joseph.org. Thousands make pilgrimages to this site each year.

QUÉBEC CITY

- Anglican Cathedral of the Holy Trinity. 31 Rue des Jardins; 418-692-2193; fax 418-692-3876; www.netministries.org/see/churches.exe/ch15988. Modelled after London's Saint-Martin-in-the-Fields, the cathedral contains precious objects donated by King George III.
- Château Frontenac. 1 Rue des Carrières; 418-692-3861; www.fairmont.com/frontenac. Historic hotel built in 1893.
- Église Notre-Dame-des-Victoires. 12 Place Royale; 418-692-1650. Oldest church in North America.
- Hôtel du Parlement. 1045 Rue des Parlementaires; 418-643-7239 or 1-866-337-8837; www.assnat.qc.ca. Built between 1877 and 1886, the parliament is used today by the provincial government.
- Monastère des Ursulines. 12 Rue Donnacona; 418-694-0694. Oldest North-American teaching institution for girls, with adjacent museum.
- Basilique Notre-Dame-de-Québec. 16 Rue Buade; 418-692-2533; fax 418-692-4382. Richly decorated with gifts from Louis XIV. Oldest parish north of Mexico.
- Place Royale. Information Centre: 27 Rue Notre-Dame; 418-646-3167; fax 418-646-9705. Among North America's oldest districts, with 400 years of Québec history.
- The Citadel. Guided tours in numerous languages. Côte de la Citadelle; 418-694-2815; fax 418-694-2853; www.lacitadelle.qc.ca. Star-shaped fortification built by the British, also known as the Gibraltar of America and still used by the military.
- Tours with the Compagnie des Six Associés. 21 Rue Ste-Angèle; 418-692-3033. Walking tours with broad themes, from medical practices in the 19th century to the evolution of crime and punishment.

FESTIVALS & EVENTS

MONTRÉAL

January–February
- Fête des Neiges. 514-872-6120; www.fetedesneiges.com. Month-long festival of outdoor activities, including skating, slides, snow sculpture and more on Île Ste-Hélène.
- Festival Montréal en Lumière. 514-288-9955 or 1-888-447-9955; www.montrealenlumiere.com. More than a week of concerts and outdoor activities at illuminated sites downtown towards the end of February.

March
- Montréal International Children's Film Festival. 514-848-0300. Presenting the finest film productions for young audiences, this competitive festival was a huge success during its debut season. Daily screenings at the historic Imperial Theatre.

April–May
- Jewish Film Festival. 514-448-5610, 514-283-4826 or 514-987-9795; www.mjff.qc.ca. For

information, check listings in local newspapers.

- Vues d'Afriques. 514-284-3322; www.vuesdafrique.org. A multi disciplinary festival to showcase African and Caribbean cultural activities. Held at various locations.

June

- Grand Prix Air Canada. Gilles Villeneuve Circuit, Parc des Îles; www.grandprix.ca. The only Formula One race in North America.
- Le Mondial de la Bière. 514-722-9640; fax 514-722-8467; www.festivalmondialbiere.qc.ca. Montréal's annual five-day outdoor beer festival. Held at Gare Windsor.
- Le Tour de l'Île de Montréal. 514-521-8356; e-mail tour@velo.qc.ca. Annual 66-kilometre urban bicycle tour.
- Montréal Chamber Music Festival. 514-489-7711; www.festival montreal.org. Ten days of outdoor concerts on Mont Royal by international musicians. Held at the Chalet de la Montagne and other locations.
- Montréal First Peoples' Festival. 514-278-4040; www.nativelynx.qc.ca. The visual arts, including screenings of films and videos, music and dance, highlight this celebration of the region's indigenous First Nations, Amerindians and Inuit.

June–July

- Montréal International Fireworks Competition. 514-397-2000; e-mail info@lemondialsaq.com; www.montrealfeux.com. Shows on Wednesdays and Saturdays, mid-June to late July. The Jacques Cartier Bridge is closed to cars during shows and offers excellent views. Seats also available for a charge at La Ronde, Île Ste-Hélène.
- Carifiesta. 514-735-2232. Annual Caribbean parade with costumes, food, music and dance held late June/early July annually. Downtown.

July

- FanTasia International Festival of Fantasy and Action Cinema. e-mail info@fantasiafestival.com; www.fantasiafest.com. The best Asian horror, sci-fi and fantasy films. Check the Web site for screening schedules and locations.
- Festival International de Jazz de Montréal. 514-871-1881 or 1-888-515-0515; www.montrealjazzfest.com. Ten days of concerts at outdoor and indoor venues downtown. Many free events.
- Festival International Nuits d'Afrique. 514-499-9239. www.festivalnuitsdafrique.com. A celebration of African and Creole film, dance and music. Various locations.
- Just for Laughs Comedy Festival. 514-845-3155 or 1-888-244-3155; www.hahaha.com. Two weeks of more than 1,300 shows indoors and out downtown.
- Les Francofolies de Montréal. 514-876-8989 or 1-888-444-9114; www.francofolies.com. A week of music at the Place des Arts complex involving 1,000 performers from the entire contemporary-music spectrum.
- Montréal Fringe Festival. 514-849-3378; www.montrealfringe.ca. Montréal's annual theatre festival celebrates art without limits. Various locations.

August

- Festival de la Gibelotte. 450-746-0283 or 1-877-746-0283; www.festivalgibelotte.qc.ca. Participating venues serve up a robust stew made from catfish with locally-brewed beer at a giant street festival. Downtown Sorel (90 minutes downriver from Montréal).
- Festival des Montgolfières. 450-347-9555; www.montgolfieres.com. About 150 hot-air balloons participate in the event. St-Jean-du-Richelieu (30 minutes south of Montréal).
- Tennis Masters Canada. 514-790-1245 or 1-800-361-4595; www.tenniscanada.com. Canada's International Tennis Championships. The tournament, held at Uniprix Stadium, alternates bewteen the male and female pros each year.

August–September

- World Film Festival. 514-848-3883; www.ffm-montreal.org. Various theatres.

Fall

- Montréal International Festival of Cinema and New Media. 514-847-9272; e-mail montrealfest@fcmm.com;

www.fcmm.com. Unusual films at interesting venues.

September

- Veillées du Plateau. 514-273-0880; e-mail info@spdtq.qc.ca. Some of Québec's finest folk musicians and callers perform traditional country hoedowns. Held on select Saturday nights between September and April.

October

- Black & Blue Festival. 514-875-7026; www.bbcm.org. Among the world's most popular gay weekend-long parties to benefit AIDS research.
- The Holocaust Education Series. 514-345-2605; www.mhmc.ca. Lectures, films, survivor testimonies and art exhibits.

November

- Cinemania. 514-878-0082; e-mail info@cinemaniafilmfestival.com; www.cinemaniafilmfestival.com. A festival of French films with English subtitles, founded by an English-speaking fan of French cinema. Musée des Beaux-Arts de Montréal.

QUÉBEC CITY

January–February

- Carnaval de Québec. 418-626-3716 or 1-866-422-7628; www.carnaval.qc.ca. The century-old annual carnival is known as the Mardi Gras of the north. Indoor and outdoor activities for the two weeks before Lent. Various locations.

June–July

- Expo-Québec. 418-691-7110 or 1-888-866-3976; www.expocite.com. The province's biggest agricultural fair, with highlights including the Carrefour Agro-Alimentaire, where culinary specialties of the region are showcased. Near Colisée de Québec.

July

- Festival d'Été de Québec. 418-523-4540 or 1-888-992-5200; www.infofestival.com. Largest North-American French-language festival of performing arts and street theatre. Various venues.
- St. Anne's Feast Day. 418-827-3781. On July 26, an annual pilgrimage attracts First Nations peoples, Gypsies and many others to the shrine of Sainte-Anne-de-Beaupré for a religious ceremony and festival.

July–August

- Grands Feux Loto-Québec. 418-523-3389 or 1-888-934-3473; www.lesgrandsfeux.com. Fireworks displays at Montmorency Falls.

August

- Fêtes de la Nouvelle France. 418-694-3311 or 1-866-391-3383; www.nouvellefrance.qc.ca. Military displays, parades and historical re-enactments, plus a 10-day crafts exhibition. Various sites.
- Plein Art. 418-694-0260; www.salonpleinart.com. An outdoor sales exhibit for crafts of all kinds. Parc de la Francophonie, rue St-Amable.
- Festival International de Musiques Militaires de Québec. 418-694-4747; www.fimmq.com. A celebration of tradition in the earliest home of military music in Canada.

August–September

- Festival International du Film de Québec. 418-523-3456; www.fifq.org. A week-long event with screenings of Canadian and foreign films.

September

- Festival des Couleurs. 418-827-4561; www.mont-sainte-anne.com. Outdoor activities and cultural events mark the beginning of the fall and winter seasons. Mont Ste-Anne.
- Festival des Journées d'Afrique. 418-640-4213; www.festivaljourneedafrique.com. Traditional and modern music showcasing emerging musicians and renowned international performers.

October

- Concours Hippique de Québec. Expo Cité grounds. 418-659-2224, x. 222; www.hippiquequebec.com. Equestrian World Cup preliminary competition.
- Festival de l'Oie des Neiges de Saint-Joachim. 418-827-5914; www.festivaldeloiedesneiges.com. This celebration of snow geese consists of watching thousands of birds fly off each morning and return each night, with activities

and craft displays in between. Côte-de-Beaupré area.

MUSEUMS & GALLERIES

MONTRÉAL

MUSEUMS

- Centre Canadien d'Architecture. 1920 Rue Baile; Wed. to Sun. 10–5, Thurs. 10–9 (free admission after 5:30 on Thurs.); 514-939-7026; www.cca.qc.ca
- Centre d'Histoire de Montréal. 335 Place d'Youville; Tues. to Sun. May to Sept. 10–5; off-season Wed. to Sun. 10–5; 514-872-3207; www.ville.montreal.qc.ca/chm
- Lieu Historique National du Commerce-de-la-Fourrure-à-Lachine. 1255 Blvd. St-Joseph; 514-637-7433 or 514-283-6054 (winter); fax 514-637-5325 or 514-496-1263 (winter); e-mail lachine_cfl@pc.qc.ca.
- Musée Juste Pour Rire. 2111 Boul. St-Laurent; call for hours (exhibits are seasonal and sometimes require a group reservation); 514-845-4000; www.hahaha.com.
- Centre de l'Interpretation du Canal de Lachine. Corner 7th Ave. and Boul. St-Joseph, Lachine; 514-637-7433. Permanent exhibit illustrates the main phases of the canal's construction and its history.
- Le Monde de Maurice (Rocket) Richard. 2800 Rue Viau; Tues. to Sun. 12–6; 514-872-6666.
- Maison Saint-Gabriel. 2146 Place Dublin, Pointe-Saint-Charles; closed Mon. (call for hours); 514-935-8136; www.maisonsaint-gabriel.qc.ca
- Lieu Historique National de Maison Sir George-Étienne Cartier. 458 Rue Notre-Dame E.; seasonal, 10–12 and 1–5; 514-283-2282.
- Musée McCord of Canadian History. 690 Rue Sherbrooke O.; Tues. to Fri. 10–6, Sat. and Sun. 10–5, Mon. in the summer months 10–5; 514-398-7100; www.mccord-museum.qc.ca.
- Musée d'Archéologie Pointe-à-Callière. 350 Place Royale; Mon. to Fri. 10–6, Sat. to Sun. 11–6, off-season Tues. to Fri. 10–5, Sat. and Sun, 11–5; 514-872-9150; www.pacmusee.qc.ca.
- Musée d'Art Contemporain de Montréal. 185 Rue Ste-Catherine O.; Tues. to Sun. 11–5, Wed. 11–9, closed Mon.; 514-847-6226; www.macm.org
- Musée des Beaux-Arts de Montréal. 1379–80 Rue Sherbrooke O.; Tues. to Sun. 11–6, Wed. 11–9; 514-285-1600; www.mbam.qc.ca
- Musée du Bienheureux Frère André, Oratoire Saint-Joseph du Mont-Royal. 3800 Chemin Queen-Mary; daily May to Sept. 7–9, off-season 7–5:30; 514-733-8211.
- Musée du Château Ramezay. 280 Rue Notre-Dame E.; daily June 1 to Sept. 30 10–6, off-season Tues. to Sun. 10–4:30; 514-861-3708; www.chateauramezay.qc.ca
- Musée de Lachine.110 Chemin LaSalle; Wed. to Sun. 11:30–4:30; (call for hours in off-season); 514-634-3471.
- Musée des Hospitalières. 201 Ave. des Pins O.; Mon. to Fri. 9–5; 514-849-2919; www.museedeshospitalieres.qc.ca
- Musée Marc-Aurèle Fortin. 118 Rue St-Pierre; Tues. to Sun. 11–5; 514-845-6108; www.museemafortin.org
- Musée Stewart. 20 Chemin Tour-de-l'Îsle, Île Ste-Hélène; daily May to Oct. 10–6, off-season Wed. to Mon. 10–5; 514-861-6701; www.stewart-museum.org

GALLERIES

- Dare-Dare Gallery. 460 Rue Ste-Catherine O.; 514-878-1088.
- Dominion Gallery. 1438 Rue Sherbrooke O.; Mon. to Fri. June to Sept. 10–5, off-season Tues. to Sat. 10–5; 514-845-7471.
- Edifice Belgo. 372 Rue Ste-Catherine O.; call for hours at the following galleries (most are open Tues. to Sat.): Galerie 303, Suite 305, 514-393-3771; Galerie René Blouin, Suite 501, 514-393-9969; Galerie Trois Pointes, Suite 520, 514-866-8008; Optica, Suite 508, 514-874-1666.
- Galerie de Bellefeuille. 1367 Ave. Greene; Mon. to Sat. 10–6, Sun. 12–5:30; 514-933-4406; www.debellefeuille.com
- Galerie Le Chariot. 446 Place

Jacques-Cartier; closed Jan., open Mon. to Sat. 10–6, Sun. 10–3, off-season Mon. to Sat. 10–4, Sun. 10–3; 514-875-4994.
- Gallery VOX. 1211 Boul. St-Laurent; Tues. to Sat. 11–5; 514-390-0382; e-mail vox@voxphoto.com.
- La Centrale. 4296 Boul. St-Laurent; Wed. 12–6, Thurs. and Fri. 12–9, Sat. and Sun. 12–5; 514-871-0268; e-mail galerie@lacentral.org.
- Leonard and Bina Ellen Gallery, Concordia University. 1400 Boul. de Maisonneuve O.; Tues. to Sat. 12–6; 514-848-2424, x. 4750; www.ellengallery.concordia.ca.
- Liane and Danny Taran Gallery, Saidye Bronfman Centre for the Arts. 5170 Côte-Ste-Catherine; Mon. to Thurs. 9–7, Fri. 9–4, closed Sat., Sun. 10–5, off-season Mon. to Thurs. 9–9, Fri. 9–2, closed Sat., Sun. 10–5; 514-734-2301.
- Quartier Éphémere, Darling Foundry. 745 Rue Ottawa; Wed. to Sun. 12–8; 514-392-1554; www.quartierephemere.org.
- Walter Klinkhoff Gallery. 1200 Rue Sherbrooke O.; Mon. to Fri. June to Aug. 9–5, off-season Mon. to Fri. 9:30–5:30, Sat. 9:30–5; 514-288-7306.
- Zeke's Gallery. 3955 Blvd. St-Laurent; 514-288-2233.

QUÉBEC CITY

Museums

- Centre d'Interprétation de Place Royale. 27 Rue Notre-Dame; 418-646-3167.
- Centre d'Interprétation du Vieux-Port. 100 Quai St-André; May to Oct.; 418-648-3000 (call for schedule and rates). Information about Québec's maritime history.
- Choco-Musée Érico. 634 Rue St-Jean; Mon. to Sat. 10–6, Sun. 11–5:30; 418-524-2122; www.chocomusee.com. A chocolate factory and free museum about the origins of cocoa.
- Citadel, Royal 22nd Regiment Museum. Open daily April 10–4, May and June 9–5, July to the first weekend in Sept. 9–6, Oct. 10–3, Nov. to April 1:30 P.M. bilingual tour (groups on reservation only); 418-694-2815; www.lacitadelle.qc.ca. Fortress built by the English and still an active military post. Guided tours of interior.
- François-Xavier Garneau House. 14 Rue St-Flavien; open Sun. for tours at 1, 2, 3 and 4 P.M.; 418-692-2240.
- Hôpital Générale. 260 Boul. Langelier; 418-529-0931. With advance notice, sisters from the Augustine order, which has run the hospital for 300 years, give guided tours of the grounds and the chapel.
- Literary and Historical Society of Québec. Morrin Centre, 44 Chaussée des Écossais; 418-694-9147. Costumed interpreters showcase the cultural contribution and present-day faces of English-speaking communities in the Québec City region.
- Maison Chevalier. 50 Rue du Marché-Champlain; Tues. to Sun. 9:30–5 (call for hours in off-season); 418-643-2158. Changing exhibits on Québec history and civilization.
- Musée de l'Amerique Française. 92 Côte de la Fabrique; daily late June to Sept., 10–5, off-season Tues. to Sun. 10–5, closed Mon.; 418-692-2843; www.mcq.org. Four seminary buildings contain religious artifacts, trompe l'oeil ceilings and 18th- and 19th-century objects from England, France and Québec.
- Musée des Augustines. 32 Rue Charlevoix; Tues. to Sat. 9:30–12 and 1:30–5, Sun. 1:30–5; 418-692-2492. Located inside the Hôtel Dieu hospital, this tiny museum contains 17th-century Louis XIII furniture and medical equipment from several centuries.
- Musée Bon-Pasteur. 14 Rue Couillard; 418-694-0243 or 1-888-710-8031 (call for schedule). Once a home for unwed mothers, nuns now run a guided tour of the grounds. Groups must reserve.
- Musée de la Civilisation. 85 Rue Dalhousie; daily June 24 to Sept. 7 9:30–6:30, Tues. to Sun. Sept. to June 10–5; 418-643-2158; www.mcq.org. Designed by Moshe Safdie, the museum contains three historic buildings and offers 10 theme-oriented exhibitions.
- Musée du Fort. 10 Rue Ste-Anne;

daily April to Oct. 10–5, Dec. 26 to Jan. 4 12–4, Thurs. to Sun. Feb. to Mar. 11–4, rest of year by reservation only; 418-692-1759; www.museedufort.com. Chronicles Québec's military battles.
- Musée National des Beaux-Arts du Québec. Parc des Champs-de-Bataille; daily June 1 to Labour Day 10–6, Wed. 10–9, off-season Tues. to Sun. 10–5; 418-643-2150 or 1-866-220-2150; www.mnba.qc.ca. Three buildings showing major Québec art from 17th-century to present.
- Musée des Ursulines. 12 Rue Donnacona; May to Sept. Tues. to Sat. 10–12 and 1–5, Sun. 1–5, off-season Tues. to Sat. 1–4:30; 418-694-0694. Treasures include a parchment signed by Louis XIII, altar cloths and porcupine-quill baskets.
- Naval Museum of Québec. 170 Rue Dalhousie; 418-694-5387 (call for schedule); www.mnq-nmq.org.
- Québec Expérience. 8 Rue du Trésor; daily May 15 to Oct. 15 10–10, off-season daily 10–5; 418-694-4000; www.quebecexperience.com. Special-effects exhibition details life in Québec from the first explorers onward.

GALLERIES

- Complexe Méduse. #582—541 Rue de St-Vallier E.; www.meduse.org. New architectural explorations and gallery space in Vieux-Québec.
- Galerie d'Art du Petit-Champlain. 88 Rue du Petit-Champlain; daily (summer) 9–10, off-season 10–5:30; 418-692-5647; www.gald.ca/gapc. Inuit art, lithographs and a vast selection of ducks.
- Galerie d'Art Le Portal-Artour. 53 Rue du Petit-Champlain; daily 10–6; 418-692-0354. Artists from Québec and abroad.
- Galerie Linda Verge. 1049 Ave. des Érables; Wed. to Fri. 11:30–5:30, Sat. and Sun. 1–5; 418-525-8393; www.galerielindaverge.ca. Contemporary art.
- Galerie Madeleine Lacerte. 1 Côte Dinan; Mon. to Fri. 9–5, Sat. and Sun. 1–5; 418-692-1566; www.galerielacerte.com. Contemporary art.
- L'Héritage Contemporain. 634 Grande Allée E.; daily June to Sept. 11:30–10, Mon. to Fri. Oct. to May 11:30–5:30, Sat. and Sun. 12–5; 418-523-7337. Works of great Canadian painters.
- Studio d'Art Georgette Pihay. 53 Rue du Petit-Champlain; daily June 24 to Sept. 30 10–9, off-season 9–5; 418-692-0297; www.studiopihay.com. The late painter-sculptor's workshop, with permanent exhibitions.

NATURE & NATURAL HISTORY

- Biodôme. (see listing p. 188)
- Biosphère. (see listing p. 189)
- Jardin Botanique de Montréal.(see listing p. 189)
- Montreal Insectarium. Located on Jardin Botanique grounds, 4581 Rue Sherbrooke E.; daily year-round 9–5, summer 9–6, Sept. 10 to Oct. 31 9–9; 514-872-1400; www.ville.montreal.qc.ca/insectarium. Butterfly house and other exhibits. Annual bug-eating festival.
- Redpath Museum of Natural History. 859 Rue Sherbrooke O.; year-round Mon. to Fri. 9–5, Sun. 1–5, closed Fri. during summer months; 514-398-4086; www.mcgill.ca/redpath. Free admission to one of Canada's oldest museums.

NIGHT LIFE

MONTRÉAL

This list will help guide you through Montréal after dark. Refer to the Night Life section for more details. For up-to-date listings, consult the most recent edition of *The Mirror* or *Hour* weekly newspapers. Or try the French weekly, *Voir*. All are available free of charge at many bars, shops and restaurants throughout Montréal.

- Aria. 1280 Rue St-Denis; 514-987-6712. Weekend after-hours with top DJs.
- Ballatu. 4372 Boul. St-Laurent; 514-845-5447. World music, mainly from Africa and the

Caribbean.
- Bifteck. 3702 Boul. St-Laurent; 514-844-6211. A raucous bar with free popcorn.
- Blizzarts. 3956A Boul. St-Laurent; 514-843-4860. Sit in a booth, check out the art, listen to electronic beats.
- Blue Dog. 3958 Boul. St-Laurent; 514-848-7006. Dark, loud, raw, this bar attracts a younger crowd.
- Bourbon Complex. 1474 Rue Ste-Catherine E.; 514-529-6969. Houses favourite gay hangouts Le Drugstore, Clubß Mississippi, La Track and Bar Cajun and late-night restaurant Club Sandwich.
- Brutopia. 1215 Rue Crescent; 514-393-9277.
- Charlie's American Pub. 1204 Rue Bishop; 514-871-1709. Kick back and listen to some American Pie tunes.
- Chez Mado. 10181 Boul. Pie-IX; 514-325-0940. Best drag-show cabaret in town.
- Dominion Pub. 1243 Rue Metcalfe; 514-878-6354.
- Edgar Hypertaverne. 1562 Ave. du Mont-Royal E.; 514-521-4661. Many different beers and an excellent cheese platter.
- Frappé. 3900 Boul. St-Laurent; 514-289-9462. Known for its happy hour, its terrace and pool tables.
- Go-Go Lounge. 3682 Boul. St-Laurent; 514-286-0882. Psychedelic colours, kitschy-cool décor and over 25 martinis.
- Grumpy's. 1242 Rue Bishop; 514-866-9010.
- Hard Rock Café. 1458 Rue Crescent; 514-987-1420. Rub elbows with the regulars and some surprise superstars while enjoying drinks, food and rock 'n' roll.
- House of Jazz (formerly Biddles). 2060 Rue Aylmer; 514-842-8656. A great place for live jazz and light eats.
- Hurley's Irish Pub. 1225 Rue Crescent; 514-861-4111; www.hurleysirishpub.com. Celtic ambience with rowdy bar upstairs and mellow sitting room downstairs. Live music is almost always Irish.
- L'Escogriffe. 4467A Rue St-Denis; 514-842-7244. Live shows some nights.
- Le Parking. 1296 Rue Amherst; 514-282-1199. Popular gay dance club.
- Le Pistol. 3723 Boul. St-Laurent; 514-847-2222. Drinks, tasty salads and unusual sandwiches.
- McKibbin's Irish Pub. 1426 Rue Bishop; 514-288-1580. Cozy traditional pub on three levels.
- Millennium. 7500 Viau; 514-721-4949. Massive after-hours dance club.
- O'Reagan's. 1224 Rue Bishop; 514-866-8464. Pub with frequent live music.
- Peel Pub. 1107 Rue Ste-Catherine O.; 514-844-6769; www.peelpub.com. A landmark drinking and eating hangout for regulars and college crowds with cheap beer and food. Open until midnight.
- Sir Winston Churchill Pub (Winnie's). 1455 Rue Crescent; 514-288-0623. Be seen on the terrace of this bar and dance hall.
- Stereo. 858 Rue Ste-Catherine E.; 514-282-3307. After-hours club with amazing sound system.
- St-Sulpice. 1680 Rue St-Denis; 514-844-9458. Huge old house with bars from the basement to the upstairs library. Large outdoor terrace in summer.
- Thursday's. 1449 Rue Crescent; 514-288-5656. Neighbourhood restaurant and bar with dancing.
- Vocalz. 1421 Rue Crescent; 514-288-9119. Popular karaoke bar.
- Quai des Brûmes. 4481 Rue St-Denis; 514-499-0467. Bar often features live music.

QUÉBEC CITY

For concerts, movies, theatre and nightlife, check local newspapers, especially the weekly *Chronicle-Telegraph*, an English-language paper which is available free of charge at tourist bureaus.

SHOPPING

MONTRÉAL

Antiques

- Antiques Hubert. 3680 Boul. St-Laurent; 514-288-3804. Vintage variety.
- Galerie Tansu. 1130 Boul. de Maisonneuve O.; 514-846-1039. This museum-like shop sells Japanese antiques and furniture.

- Grand Central. 2448 Rue Notre-Dame O.; 514-935-1467. Various antiques.
- Le Village des Antiquaries. 1708 Rue Notre-Dame O.; 514-931-5121. Several dealers under one roof.
- Milord. 1870 Rue Notre-Dame O., showroom at 1434 Rue Sherbrooke O.; 514-933-2433; www.milordantiques.com. Elegant European furniture and mirrors.
- Salvation Army. 1620 Rue Notre-Dame O.; 514-935-7425. Check out "As Is" section in thrift shop.
- Spazio. 8405 Boul. St-Laurent; 514-384-4343. Timeless collection of architectural antiques.

Art

- Born-Neo Art Gallery. 404 Rue St-Sulpice; 514-840-1135. African carvings and textiles.
- Boutique du Musée des Beaux-Arts. 1390 Rue Sherbrooke O.; 514-285-1600. Shop reflects current exhibitions and offers posters, art books and more.
- Galerie Claude Lafitte. 2162 Rue Crescent; 514-842-1270; www.lafitte.com. Paintings by Canadian, European and American masters.
- Galerie d'Art Yves Laroche. 4 Rue St-Paul E.; 514-393-1999; www.yveslaroche.com. Canvasses and prints of established artists.
- Galerie Elena Lee Verre. 1460 Rue Sherbrooke O., Suite A; 514-844-6009; www.galerieelenalee.com. Unique glass art pieces.
- Galerie le Chariot. 446 Place Jacques-Cartier; 514-875-4994; www.galerielechariot.com. Gift shop sells Inuit art pieces.
- Galerie Parchemine. 40 Rue St-Paul O.; 514-845-3368. Canvasses and prints for sale.
- Galerie Walter Klinkhoff. 1200 Rue Sherbrooke O.; 514-288-7306; www.klinkhoff.com. Work by established artists.

Books

- Anthologies Café Books. 1420 Rue Stanley; 514-287-9929. Specializes in art books and used books.
- Argo Book Shop. 1915 Rue Ste-Catherine O.; 514-931-3442. A Montréal institution. Deals in new and used books.
- Bibliomania. 460 Rue Ste-Catherine O.; 514-933-8156. Known for books, antiques and collectibles.
- Bibliophile. 5519 Chemin Queen-Mary; 514-486-7369. Specializes in Judaica.
- Chapters. 1171 Rue Ste-Catherine O.; 514-849-8825. Four floors, discount section and a Starbucks coffee counter.
- Cheap Thrills. 2044 Metcalfe; 514-844-8988; www.cheapthrills.ca. Good selection of used books.
- Diocesan Book Room. 625 Rue Ste-Catherine O. (Promenades de la Cathédrale); 514-843-9387 or 1-877-387-9387.Christian books and theology.
- Double Hook. 1235A Ave. Greene; 514-932-5093; www.doublehook.com. Stocks books by Canadian authors.
- Ethnic Origins Bookstore. 3173A Rue St-Jacques; 514-938-1188. Specializing in African and African-American culture.
- Ex Libris. 2159 Rue MacKay; 514-284-0350. Good selection of second-hand and out-of-print books.
- Indigo Books. 1500 Ave. McGill-College (Place Montreal Trust); 514-281-5549. Variety of books, cards, paper items and stationery.
- Nicholas Hoare. 1366 Ave. Greene, 514-933-4201; 1307 Rue Ste-Catherine O. (Ogilvy); 514-499-2005. Extensive selection.
- Paragraphe Books. 2220 Ave. McGill-College; 514-845-5811; www.paragraphbooks.com. Near McGill University, the shop contains a wide selection of titles plus a Second Cup coffee shop.
- Ulysses Bookstore. 560 Rue Président-Kennedy, 514-843-7222; 4176 Rue St-Denis, 514-843-9447. Travel and guide books and maps.
- Vortex Books. 1855 Rue Ste-Catherine O.; 514-935-7869. Specializes in literary works.
- S.W. Welch. 3878 Boul. St-Laurent; 514-848-9358. Excellent selection of used books.
- Westcott Books. 2065 Rue Ste-Catherine O.; 514-846-4037. Shelves filled with second-hand books.
- The Word. 469 Rue Milton; 514-845-5640. A used-book haven in the McGill University ghetto.

Cameras

- Camtec Photo (Place Victoria Cameras). 495 Rue McGill; 514-842-4818; www.camtecphoto.com. Equipment, film supplies, repairs and processing.
- Image Point. 1344 Rue Ste-Catherine O.; 514-874-0824; www.imagepoint.ca. Photo and video equipment and repairs.
- Simon Cameras. 11 Rue St-Antoine O.; 514-861-5401. New and used equipment and film supplies.

Cigars

- La Casa del Habano. 1434 Rue Sherbrooke O.; 514-849-0037. Handles importation of Cuban cigars.
- Cigars Vasco. 1327 Rue Ste-Catherine O.; 514-284-0475. Vast array of cigars.

Clothing

- Addition-Elle and A/E Sport. 724 Rue Ste-Catherine O.; 514-954-0087. Fashions for women wearing size 14-plus.
- BCBG. 960 Rue Ste-Catherine O.; 514-868-9561. Also at 1300 Rue Ste-Catherine O., 514-398-9130. On top of the latest fashions.
- BEDO. 359 Rue Ste-Catherine O., 514-842-7839; 1256 Rue Ste-Catherine O., 514-866-4962; 3706 Boul. St-Laurent, 514-987-9940; 4903 Boul. St-Laurent, 514-287-9204; 4228 Rue St-Denis, 514-847-0323. Chain carries reasonably-priced basics and funkier pieces.
- Boutique Médiévale Excalibor. 4400 Rue St-Denis, 514-843-9993; 122 Rue St-Paul E., 514-393-7260. Exclusive handcrafted medieval-style clothing, jewellery, chain mail, gargoyles and banners.
- Bovet Complexe Desjardins. 150 Ste-Catherine O. 514-281-1611. Suits and sweaters for men of all sizes.
- Caban. 777 Rue Ste-Catherine O.; 514-844-9300. From pyjamas to party dresses, this store isn't just about housewares.
- Cache Cache. 1051 Rue Laurier O.; 514-273-9700. April Cornell's long, flower-print casual dresses, matching mother-child outfits (mainly dresses for girls aged 2–6), linens, accessories and housewares.
- City Styles. 1186 Rue Ste-Catherine O., 2nd floor; 514-499-9114. Urban styles by Sean John, Zoo York, Akademic, Lacoste, Timberland, G-Unit, Reebok and others.
- Club Monaco. 1455 Rue Peel; 514-282-9609. Canadian-owned company. Trendy professional and casual clothing for men and women.
- Concerto Pour Elle. 1216 Ave. Greene; 514-933-8817. Fashions and accessories for women.
- Cours Mont-Royal. 1455 Rue Peel. Many boutiques, including Space FB, DKNY, Face London, Giorgio Emporio, Harry Rosen, 3 Monkeys, American Apparel, Arithmetik.
- Diakoumakos. 415 Rue Mayor; 514-842-4846. Stylish fur coats.
- Fidel. 4340 Rue St-Denis, 514-845-6555. Stylish Montréal-based clothing line for men and women.
- FLY. 1970 Rue Ste-Catherine O.; 514-846-6888. A wide selection of urban attire from established labels and up-and-coming local designers.
- Fourreurs Maîtres. 401 Rue Mayor; 514-845-6838. Fur fashions.
- Friperie St-Laurent. 3976 Boul. St-Laurent; 514-842-3893. Cool clothes, new and used.
- Gap. 1255 Rue Ste-Catherine O.; 514-985-5311. Staples for a preppy wardrobe.
- Grand'Heur. 4131 St-Denis; 514-284-5747. For women above 5'8".
- Guess. 1229A Rue Ste-Catherine O.; 514-499-9464. Chain selling jeans, casual wear and professional styles.
- Henri-Henri. 189 Rue Ste-Catherine E.; 514-288-0109. One of the best hat shops in town. From Borsalinos to berets, it attracts stars like Donald Sutherland and Charlie Sheen.
- IMA. 24 Rue Prince-Arthur; 514-844-0303. High style from David Bitton, creator of Buffalo clothing line.
- InWear/Matinique. 1128 Rue Ste-Catherine O.; 514-866-8755. Casual and professional fashions for men and women.
- Jacob. 1220 Rue Ste-Catherine O.; 514-861-9346. Reasonably priced casual and professional fashions.
- Jeunes d'ici. 600 Rue Peel; 514-933-5513. Fashionable clothes for children.
- Le Château. 1310 Rue Ste-

Catherine O. and other locations; 514-866-2481. Reasonably priced stylish clothes for youth and adults.
- Lululemon. 1394 Ave. Greene; 514-937-5151. Stylish Vancouver-based yoga clothing line for an active, stress-free life.
- Mexx. 1125 Rue Ste-Catherine O.; 514-288-6399. Chain store with casual wear and professional styles.
- Montréal Fripe. 371 Ave du Mont-Royal E.; 514-842-7801. An enticing array of vintage and pre-worn clothing.
- Off the Hook. 1021A Rue Ste-Catherine O.; 514-499-1021. Hip hop–influenced urban fashion.
- Oink Oink. 1343 Greene Ave.; 514-939-2634; www.oinkoink.com. Cool newborn and children's clothes and some pricey designer wear, plus piles of games, toys and gadgets in this kid-friendly shop.
- Olam. 4339 Rue St-Denis; 514-282-9994. Stylish, colourful women's fashion.
- Old River. 1115 Rue Ste-Catherine O.; 514-843-7828. Men's casual and formal wear.
- Parasuco. 1414 Rue Crescent; 514-284-2288. Centre for jeans.
- Pierre, Jean, Jacques. 150 Rue Laurier O.; 514-270-8392. Men's fashions.
- Requin Chagrin. 4430 Rue St-Denis; 514-286-4321. A renowned Montréal frippery full of vintage fashion finds.
- Roots. 1035 Rue Ste-Catherine O.; 514-845-7559. Sporty clothes, caps and jackets.
- Rudsak. 1400 Rue Ste-Catherine O.; 514-399-9925; www.rudsak.com. Beautiful soft-leather jackets and handbags in unexpected colours.
- Scarlett. 254 Ave. du Mont-Royal E.; 514-844-9435; www.boutiquescarlett.com. Features daring clothing lines for men and women.
- Screaming Eagle. 1424 Boul. St-Laurent; 514-849-2843. Leather world.
- SOHO Mtl. 3715 Boul. St-Laurent; 514-843-8201. Stylish clothing and shoes for the office or bar. Men's and women's styles.
- Space FB. 3632 Boul. St-Laurent, 514-282-1991; Les Cours Mont-Royal, 1455 rue Peel, 514-848-6494. Simple staples and more in jersey, wool and cotton by hip Montréal- based label.
- Tristan & America. 1001 Rue Ste-Catherine O.; 514-289-9609. Chain store with casual and formal clothes for men and women.
- U&I (Women) 3650 Blvd. St-Laurent; (Men) 3652 Boul. St-Laurent; 514-844-8788. Unique designs and upscale style.
- Urban Outfitters. 1250 Rue Ste-Catherine O.; 514-874-0063. Trendy urban wear.

Surplus Stores
- Surplus International. 1431 Boul. St-Laurent; 514-499-9920. Cargo pants emporium.
- Army Surplus Canam. 1423 Boul. St-Laurent; 514-842-3465. Stylish surplus clothes.

Collectibles
- Antiques Lucie Favreau. 1904 Rue Notre–Dame O.; 514-989-5117. Like a visit to a sports hall of fame.
- Pause Retro. 2054 Rue St-Denis; 514-848-0333. Old toys, memorabilia and sports cards specialty.
- Retro-ville. 2652 Rue Notre-Dame O.; 514-939-2007. Coca-Cola items, old magazines, toys and neon signs.

Department Stores
- The Bay. 585 Rue Ste-Catherine O.; 514-281-4422. Fashions and more for the whole family.
- Holt Renfrew. 1300 Rue Sherbrooke O.; 514-842-5111. Top-of-the-line fashions for men and women.
- Ogilvy. 1307 Rue Ste-Catherine O.; 514-842-7711. Upscale women's fashions, fine jewellery, perfume, books.
- Simons. 977 Rue Ste-Catherine O.; 514-282-1840. Trendy women's fashions and clothing for the whole family.

Electronics
- Alma Eléctronique. 1595 Boul. St-Laurent; 514-847-0366. Be prepared to haggle.
- Audiotronic. 368 Rue Ste-Catherine O. and 1622 Boul. St-Laurent; 514-861-5451. Decent prices on home items and camera equipment.
- Dumoulin La Place. 2050 Boul. St-

Laurent; 514-288-7755. Reasonable prices.
- Eléctronique Multi-Systèmes. 1593 Boul. St-Laurent; 514-845-0059. Reasonable prices, open to haggling.
- Future Shop. 460 Rue Ste-Catherine O.; 514-393-2600; www.futureshop.ca (check for other locations). Low-priced computer equipment, home electronics and CDs.

Games & Toys
- FrancJeu. 4152 Rue St-Denis; 514-849-9253. Educational toys and games for kids of all ages.
- La Grande Ourse. 129 Ave Duluth E.; 514-847-1207. Beautiful handmade wooden toys and games.
- Valet d'Coeur. 4408 Rue St-Denis; 514-499-9970. Gadgets and toys to stimulate creative exploration.
- Oink Oink. (see listing p. 198)

Housewares
- Atmosphère. 4349 Rue St-Denis; 514-527-1293. Furniture and art pieces.
- Caban. (see listing p. 197)
- Collage Tapis. 1480 Rue Sherbrooke O.; 514-933-3400. Imported Persian carpets.
- Côté Sud. 4338 Rue St-Denis; 514-289-9443. Beautiful accents for bed, bath and beyond.
- Indiport Tapis Orientaux. 100 Rue St-Paul E.; 514-871-1664. Persian carpets.
- Morphée. 4394 Rue St-Denis; 514-282-0744; www.mmorphee.com. Striking furniture and domestic accessories.
- Senteurs de Provence. 4077 Rue St-Denis, 514-845-6867; 1061 Rue Laurier O., 514-276-7474. Blue-and-yellow-printed fabrics, scents and soaps.

Jewellery
- AmberLux. 625 Rue Ste-Catherine O. (Promenades de la Cathédrale); 514-844-1357. Amber set in pieces of all shapes and sizes.
- Bijouterie Elégant. 377 Rue Ste-Catherine O.; 514-844-2770. Gold objects and jewellery.
- Bijouterie Eliko. 680 Rue Ste-Catherine O.; 514-871-8528. Specializes in watches: Rolex, Swiss Army, Swatch, Tag Heuer and more.
- Bijoux Marsan. 462 Rue Ste-Catherine O.; 514-395-6007. Primarily gold.
- Birks. 1240 Square Phillips; 514-397-2511. Wide variety of fine-quality jewellery, silverware and china.

Music
- Archambault. 5005 Rue Ste-Catherine E.; 514-849-6201; 677 Rue Ste-Catherine O. (Complexe Les Ailes), 514-875-5975; www.archambault.ca. Large selection of CDs, sheet music and songbooks.
- HMV. 1020 Rue Ste-Catherine O.; 514-875-0765. A three-floor megastore with thousands of CDs and DVDs.
- Le Pop Shop. 3656 Boul. St-Laurent; 514 848-6300. New and used CDs and vinyl.
- Primitive. 3830 Rue St-Denis; 514-845-6017. Wide selection of used CDs and vinyl.

Shoes
- Boutique Courir. 4452 Rue St-Denis; 514-499-9600. An impressive selection of shoes and clothing for runners and lovers of the outdoors.
- Browns. 1191 Rue Ste-Catherine O.; 514-987-1206. Brand-name footwear for all occasions.
- La Godasse. 3686 Boul. St-Laurent, 514-286-8900; 4340 Rue St-Denis, 514-843-0909. An impressive selection of stylish, hard-to-find sneakers.
- Marie Modes. 469 Rue Ste-Catherine O.; 514-845-0497. Cowboy-boot specialists.
- Mona Moore. 1446 Rue Sherbrooke O.; 514-842-0662. Ultra-hip boutique with designer shoes for women.
- Sena. 4200 Rue St-Denis; 514-849-7243. Ecco, Birkenstock and other brands.
- Tony Shoe Shop. 1346 Ave. Greene; 514-935-2993. Stocks latest styles plus hard-to-find sizes and bargain annex.
- UN Iceland. 1378 Rue Ste-Catherine O.; 514-876-7877. A wide selection of footwear fashions.

Odds & Ends
- Au Papier Japonais. 24 Ave. Fairmount O.; 514-276-6863. Beautiful handmade paper and a delightful array of paper products,

cards and gifts.

- Bell Centre Canadiens Boutique. 1260 Rue de la Gauchetière O. (Bell Centre); 514-989-2836. Jerseys, books, photos sold exclusively for the Habs.
- Boutique Médiévale Excalibor. (see listing p. 197)
- La Capoterie. 2061 Rue St-Denis; 514-845-0027. Condoms in 21 flavours and other gag gifts.
- Dix Milles Villages. 4282 Rue St-Denis; 514-848-0538. Fair-trade handcrafted goods from around the world.
- Dressmaker Garnitures Ltée. 2186 Rue Ste-Catherine O.; 514-935-7421. Open since the 1950s, this shop has an endless array of beads, feathers and ribbons.
- L'Echoppe du Dragon Rouge. 3804 Rue St-Denis; 514-840-9030. Medieval outfits, swords, jewellery and household items.
- Essence du Papier. 4160 Rue St-Denis; 514-288-9152; www.essencedupapier.com. Stationery, journals and writing implements.
- Grand Central. 2448 Rue Notre-Dame O.; 514-935-1467. Antiques.
- Jet-Setter. 66 Rue Laurier O.; 514-271-5058. Luggage plus loads of travel gadgets.
- Kamikaze Curiosités. 4156 Rue St-Denis; 514-848-0728. This store sells scarves, socks and accessories by day, but by night the space is transformed into a bar.
- Marché Almizan. 1695 Boul. de Maisonneuve O.; 514-938-4142. Sells imported spices and such Middle-Eastern specialties as fig marmalade and halvah.
- Mediaphile. 1901 Rue Ste-Catherine O.; 514-939-3676. Hundreds of magazines on display, with order forms for 10,000 more, plus top-notch inexpensive cigars from Cuba and Jamaica.
- Mélange Magique. 1928 Rue Ste-Catherine O.; 514-938-1458. New-Age and Pagan books, tarot decks and other items.
- Montréal Museum of Archaeology and History Pointe-à-Callière. 350 Place Royale; 514-872-9150. Stocks unique reproductions, jewellery, pottery and toys.
- Rubans, Boutons. 4818 Rue St-Denis; 514-847-3535. A store dedicated to ribbons and buttons.
- Tilley Endurables. 1050 Rue Laurier O.; 514-272-7791. Travel wear, well-known for hats.

QUÉBEC CITY

Antiques

- Antiquités du Matelot. 137 Rue St-Paul; 418-694-9585. Specialties include engravings, old Canadian and Québec prints and white ironstone.
- Décenie. 117 Rue St-Paul; 418-694-0403. Reupholstered vinyl furniture from the 1960s.
- Gérard Bourguet Antiquaire. 97 Rue St-Paul; 418-694-0896. Known for 18th- and 19th-century pine furniture.

Art

- Canadeau. 1124 Rue St-Jean; 418-692-4850. Reupholstered vinyl furniture and other finds from the 1960s.
- Lambert & Co. 1 Rue des Carrières; 418-694-0048. Features regional arts and crafts.
- Rue du Trésor, an open-air market near Notre-Dame Basilica showcasing locally produced prints and paintings. www.ruedutresor.qc.ca
- Sculpteur Flamand. 49 Rue du Petit-Champlain; 418-692-2813. Wood carvings.

Books

- Librairie du Nouveau Monde. 103 Rue St-Pierre; 418-694-9475. Features books by Québec authors and publishers.
- Librairie Historia. 155 Rue St-Joseph E.; 418-525-9712. Volumes of used books.
- Librairie Pantoute. 1100 Rue St-Jean; 418-694-9748. Selection of English-language guidebooks for the region.

Clothes

- Autrefois Saïgon. 55 Boul. René-Lévesque; 418-649-1227. Québec-made women's clothing with an Eastern touch.
- Bibi & Co. 40 Rue Garneau; 418-694-0045. Hats galore.
- Boutique Paris Cartier. 1180 Ave. Cartier; 418-529-6083. Fine women's fashions.
- La Corriveau. 24 Côte de la Fabrique; 418-694-0048.

Handmade sweaters and moccasins.

- Laliberté. 595 Rue St-Joseph; 418-525-4841. Workshop and store famous for furs.
- Lambert & Co. 1 Rue des Carrières; 418-694-2151. Colourful wool socks.
- Logo Sport. 1047 Rue St-Jean; 418-692-1351. Sports gear.
- Magasin Latulippe. 637 Rue St-Vallier O.; 418-529-0024. Large selection of work wear and outdoor wear, including great warm hats.
- Mountain Equipment Co-op. 405 St-Joseph E.; 418-522-8884. New to Québec City, this is the ultimate destination for outerwear and camping gear.
- Oclan. (Women) 52 Boul. Champlain; (Men) 67 1/2 Rue du Petit-Champlain; 418-692-1214; www.oclan.net. Designer clothes from Québec and beyond.
- Peau sur Peau. 70 Boul. Champlain; 418-692-5132. Specializing in leather.
- Simons. 20 Côte de la Fabrique; 418-692-3630. Small branch of department store known for its own brand of men's and women's clothing, especially sweaters and hats.
- La Soierie Huo. 91 Rue du Petit-Champlain; 418-692-5920. Hand-painted silk scarves.
- X20. 200 Rue St-Joseph E.; 418-529-0174. Funky line of streetwear.

Jewellery

- Pierres Vives Joaillerie. 23 1/2 Rue du Petit-Champlain; 418-692-5566. specializing in exquisite cut gems and cultivated pearls, works of Québec designers and more.
- Zimmermann. 46 Côte de la Fabrique; 418-692-2672. High-end jewellery.

Odds & Ends

- Baltazar Objets Urban. 461 Rue St-Joseph E.; 418-524-1991. Hip decorative objects.
- Boutique Médiévale Excalibor. 1055 Rue St-Jean; 418-692-5959. Medieval madness.
- Comptoir Emmaus. 915 Rue St-Vallier E.; 418-692-0385. Thrift shop heaven! Four floors of second-hand clothes, books, furniture and housewares.
- Copiste du Faubourg. 545 Rue St-Jean; 418-525-5377. Handmade paper specialists.
- J.A. Moisan. 699 Rue St-Jean; 418-522-0685. Oldest grocery store in North America; stocks large selection of fine foods.
- J.E. Giguère. 59 & 61 Rue de Buade; 418-692-2296. Québec-made pipes, Cuban cigars and other tobacco products.
- Mall Centre-Ville. Rue St-Joseph. Billed as the world's longest covered street, with dollar stores, bargain shops and restaurants.
- Paradis des Étampes Petra Werner. 603 Rue St-Jean; 418-523-6922. Huge choice of rubber stamps.
- Royaume de la Tarte. 402 Ave. des Oblats; 418-522-7605. Baked goods and decorated cupcakes.

Shopping Centres

- Halles le Petit Cartier. 1191 Ave. Cartier; 418-522-0201. A mini-mall of interest to gourmets.
- Place Québec. 900 Boul. René-Lévesque E.; 418-529-0551. Rather dreary, but useful, with post office, 40 stores and restaurants.
- Ailes de la Mode. 2450 Laurier, Ste-Foy; 418-652-4537 or 1-888-242-4537. This fashion plaza offers shuttle service to downtown hotels.
- Food & Flea Market. 936 Rue Roland Beaudin, Ste-Foy. Lively outdoor food and flea market.
- Galeries de la Capitale. 5401 Boul. des Galeries; 418-627-5800; www.galeriesdelacapitale.com. Enormous roller coaster in indoor playground amidst dozens of shops.
- Place Laurier. 2700 Boul. Laurier, Ste-Foy; 418-651-5000; www.placelaurier.com. More than 350 stores under one roof is worth the trip.
- Place Ste-Foy. 2452 Boul. Laurier, Ste-Foy; 418-653-4184. Features 130 boutiques, including department stores such as Simons.

Toys

- Boutique L'Echelle. 1039 Rue Garneau; 418-694-9133. Jam-packed with toys of all kinds.
- Club Jouet. 150–1100 Rue Bouvier; 418-624-9451. Popular and educational toys.

PHOTO CREDITS

T = top; C = centre; B = bottom.

Introduction
Théodore Lagloire: 12B, 13T, 15,16T; Julia Levine: 10, 16B; Tourisme Montréal 11B, 12T, 17, 18; Anne Whiteside: 1, 11T,13B, 14.

Montreal
Photographs by Phil Carpenter, except for those listed below.
Les Amis de la Montagne: 20B; Anton's Photo Express: 95B; Association Touristique des Laurentides: 111, 115T; Basilique Notre-Dame-de-Montréal: 29T; Beaver Club: 80T; Biodôme de Montréal: Julie d'Amour Léger: 49B, Sean O'Neill 50, 51T; Biosphère: 55; Les Caprices de Nicholas: 78B&C; Centre Canadien d'Architecture: Richard Bryant: 41T, Robert Burley: 42T, Alain LaForest: 41B; Centre d'histoire de Montréal: 38; Château Ramezay Museum: 37; Corporation de la Vieux-Port de Montréal/A.P.E.S.: 93B, 94B; Festival International de Jazz de Montréal/Caroline Guertin: 69T, 70T, Fort Chambly National Historic Site: 112; Les Francofolies de Montréal: 71; Jardin Botanique de Montréal: 25T, 52, Michel Tremblay: 25B, 26, 51, 53; Jean-François Leblanc: 69B; Julia Levine: 20T, 73B, 77, 78T, 79T, 80B; Shelley MacDonald: 43C, 47B, 59C&B, 60, 61, 62T&C, 64B, 65, 67C&B, 82C, 83, 84T, 104B; Milos Restaurant: 79B; Mont-Tremblant Resort: 114, 116T&C; Montréal Insectarium: 54, René Limoges: 54C&B; Musée d'Archéologie Pointe-à-Callière: 36B; Musée des Beaux-Arts: 44, 45, Timothy Hursley: 43T; Musée d'art contemporain de Montréal: Cöpilia: 46B, Caroline Hayeur: 47T, Richard-Max Tremblay: 47C; Musée Missisquoi: 118B; Musée McCord: 35, 36T; Musée Redpath: 56; Musée Stewart: 23B, 40C&B; Parc des Îles de Montréal/Bernard Brault: 22B; Pierre Pouliot: 115B; Parks Canada: 113, Normand Rajotte: 39; Place des Arts: 46T; Société des casinos du Québec Inc.: 23T; Le Tour de l'Île de Montréal: Robert Laberge: 72; Tourisme Cantons-de-l'Est: 117T&B, Peter Quine: 118T; Tourisme Montréal 17, 18, 19, 21, 70C,71T, 92T, 94T, 95T, Stéphane Poulin: 32T&B, 34, 73T, 86, 87T&C, 89B; Ville de Montréal: Alain Chagnon: 91B, Dennis Farley: 28T, 88B, 90B, Denis Labine: 24T; Anne Whiteside: 22T, 24B, 27, 33B, 43B, 48B, 57, 63T, 66, 75, 82T, 85, 88T, 91, 96, 97T, 89, 99T, 100B, 101, 102B, 105, 106B, 108.

Quebec City
Photographs by Théodore Lagloire, except those listed below.
Carnaval de Québec Kellogg's: 132; ExpoCité: 133; Festival d'été de Québec: 134B; Fondation Bagatelle: 163B; Laurie Raphäel: 140T; Mont Sainte-Anne: Jean Sylvain: 167B, 168B; Musée de la Civilisation: 152C; Office du tourisme et des congrès de la Communauté urbaine de Québec: 165B; François Tremblay: 131, 134T; Alain Vinet: 119; Yuzu Sushi Bar: 139T, 142T.

Maps by Andrew Cameron and Peggy McCalla.